Youth Crime and Justice

Youth Crime and Justice

Critical Issues

Edited by

Barry Goldson and
John Muncie

SAGE Publications

London • Thousand Oaks • New Delhi

First published 2006

SAGE Publications Ltd
1 Oliver's Yard
55 City Road
London EC1Y 1SP

SAGE Publications Inc.
2455 Teller Road
Thousand Oaks, California 91320

SAGE Publications India Pvt Ltd
B-42, Panchsheel Enclave
Post Box 4109
New Delhi 110 017

British Library Cataloguing in Publication data

A catalogue record for this book is available from the
British Library

ISBN 1 4129 1137 0   978 1 4129 1137 5
ISBN 1 4129 1138 9   978 1 4129 1138 2

Library of Congress Control Number 2005936297

Typeset by C&M Digitals (P) Ltd., Chennai, India
Printed on paper from sustainable resources
Printed in Great Britain by The Cromwell Press, Trowbridge, Wiltshire

Contents

List of Contributors

Tim Bateman is a Senior Policy Development Officer with Nacro, a UK-based crime reduction agency, England.

Chris Cunneen is the New South Global Professor of Criminology at the Faculty of Law, University of New South Wales, Australia.

Matthew Follett is a Lecturer in Criminology at the University of Leicester, England.

Loraine Gelsthorpe is Reader in Criminology and Criminal Justice at the Institute of Criminology, University of Cambridge, England.

Barry Goldson is a Senior Lecturer in Sociology at the University of Liverpool, England.

Kevin Haines is Head of Applied Social Sciences at the University of Swansea, Wales.

Lynn Hancock is a Lecturer in Sociology at the University of Liverpool, England.

Harry Hendrick is an Associate Professor of History at the University of Southern Denmark, Denmark.

Gordon Hughes is Professor of Criminology at the International Centre for Comparative Criminological Research at the Open University, England.

Fergus McNeill is a Senior Lecturer at the Glasgow School of Social Work, Universities of Glasgow and Strathclyde, Scotland.

Phil Mizen is a Senior Lecturer in Sociology at the University of Warwick, England.

John Muncie is Professor of Criminology and Co-Director of the International Centre for Comparative Criminological Research at the Open University, England.

David O'Mahony is a Senior Lecturer in Youth Justice at the Institute of Criminology and Criminal Justice, School of Law, Queen's University Belfast, Northern Ireland.

Gilly Sharpe is a Doctoral Research Student at the Institute of Criminology, University of Cambridge, England.

David Smith is Professor of Criminology at Lancaster University, England.

Roger Smith is a Senior Lecturer in Social Work at the University of Leicester, England.

Colin Webster is a Senior Lecturer in Criminology at Leeds Metropolitan University, England.

Rob White is Professor of Sociology and Head of the School of Sociology and Social Work at the University of Tasmania, Australia.

Editors' Introduction

This book is a companion volume to *Comparative Youth Justice: Critical Issues,* edited by John Muncie and Barry Goldson and published simultaneously by Sage. Taken together, they are designed to encourage critical reflection on contemporary juvenile/youth justice reform. Whereas *Comparative Youth Justice* identifies major international shifts in policy and practice, this volume focuses more sharply – although not exclusively – on UK jurisdictions and, in particular, England and Wales, arguably the site of the most punitive youth justice system in Europe.

In many industrialised countries, youth crime has attracted, and continues to attract, increasing levels of attention in the modern period; as the behaviour of the young is exposed to moralistic scrutiny and political concern. It follows that many (but certainly not all) contemporary youth justice jurisdictions are characterised by energetic policy formation and practice development, often providing for more heavily interventionist, wide-ranging and ultimately punitive interventions. This is especially evident in England and Wales (Goldson, 2000; Muncie, 2004; Pitts, 2001; Smith, 2003) and most of the chapters that follow engage critically with such phenomenon, particularly as they have evolved during three successive terms of New Labour government.

Indeed, within months of coming to power in 1997, the first New Labour government published a White Paper: *No More Excuses: A New Approach to Tackling Youth Crime in England and Wales*. The White Paper served to consolidate the administration's 'tough' policies and it signalled the far-reaching reforms that have since been implemented. Perhaps most significant amongst a mass of statute, the Crime and Disorder Act 1998 and the Youth Justice and Criminal Evidence Act 1999 have ushered in the most radical reform of the youth justice system in England and Wales in the post-war period.

Paradoxically, whilst distinctive and divergent in many respects, policy developments in other UK jurisdictions have recently adopted comparable priorities and elements of convergence are evident. In Scotland (McAra, 2006) and Northern

Ireland (Davey et al., 2004), for example, politically derived anxieties and the steadily developing conflation of 'crime', 'disorder' and 'anti-social behaviour' is similarly serving to legitimise expanding and diversifying modes of intervention, regulation and governance targeted especially at troublesome, or potentially troublesome, children and young people.

Notwithstanding the fact that 'official' crime surveys appear to indicate that patterns of youth crime are essentially stable across the UK and other industrialised countries – and certain data even suggest that the incidence of youth crime is actually decreasing – youth justice systems continue to extend their reach. In England and Wales, the 'front end' or 'shallow end' of the system is characterised by multiplying and increasingly interventionist powers and processes, whilst the 'back end' or 'deep end' has been marked by a substantial expansion and diversification of custodial responses. The rationales for system expansion disproportionate to the actual incidence of youth crime, and for modes of 'preventive' intervention that are just as likely to impose iatrogenic effects, are key sites of ambiguity, controversy and debate. Such contestation is especially significant given that politicians and their principal policy advisors consistently claim legitimacy for the 'new' approaches by appealing to 'evidence'; 'evidenced-based policy' has become a mantra of 'modernised' government and a legitimising principle for 'new' modes of governance.

Indeed, youth crime discourses are increasingly underpinned by the rhetoric of rationality: 'evidenced-based' responses; 'what works' priorities; 'best value' imperatives and the need to ensure that 'programmes' are routinely 'evaluated' and 'outputs' are assiduously monitored. On one level it is difficult to quarrel with any tendency that seeks to apply evidence drawn from research, evaluation and practice experience to the processes of policy formation and practice development. On another level, however, the methodological rigour of much that passes for 'evaluation', together with the means by which 'evidence' is interpreted and applied, is open to serious question (Bottoms, 2005). Conversely, contemporary policy formation and practice development pay scant regard to a wider body of criminological 'evidence' (both theoretically and empirically derived). A certain selectivity of 'evidence' is apparent, therefore, whereby politically convenient (populist) messages are profiled whilst less convenient knowledges are marginalised. In other words, the 'evidence' itself is open to challenge and in many important respects there is a conspicuous discordance between research findings, policy formation and practice development (Goldson, 2001).

Youth crime and youth justice policy developments (together with crime and disorder reduction 'targets' and community safety rationales that pervade many other policy domains either directly or indirectly), the contexts from which they are emerging and their contested sources of legitimacy, demand analysis and critical scrutiny. This volume explores such questions; it examines the intrinsic tensions – even contradictions – between 'evidence' and policy formation and it engages with some of the most pressing debates in contemporary youth justice. In order to present an integrated and coherent text, the book is organised into three inter-related parts. Moreover, each of the authors addresses comparable conceptual themes and concerns including: a critical assessment of the key sources of 'evidence' in respect of their particular subject-matter; an analysis of what the 'evidence' actually tells us and how it might be understood (historically, theoretically and/or empirically); a consideration of the extent to which 'evidence' is informing contemporary youth justice law, policy and practice; and a reflective interpretation of how any discordance between 'evidence' and policy formation might be conceived.

Part One situates youth crime and youth justice within historical and social-structural contexts. In Chapter 1, Harry Hendrick historicises youth crime and justice by tracing key policy developments and the rationales that drove them, from the early nineteenth century to the late 1980s. By profiling change, order, professional/administrative and class agendas, political priorities and inter-generational relations, Hendrick's analysis contextualises the contemporary conditions that have served to re-popularise and re-politicise youth crime and justice. In Chapter 2, Rob White and Chris Cunneen explore the relations between social class, structural marginalisation and criminalisation. They argue that a critical understanding of such relations 'has rarely been more relevant to social analysis and to any consideration of youth justice'. In Chapter 3, Colin Webster builds upon and develops some of the key themes introduced by Hendrick, White and Cunneen, and shapes his discussion around the intersections of social class, place and 'race', focusing upon the 'cumulative inter-generational crises faced by black and Asian young people'. In Chapter 4, Loraine Gelsthorpe and Gilly Sharpe engage with the question of gender and, more specifically, with girls and young women within the youth justice system. Such analyses continue to be neglected within 'malestream' criminology and Gelsthorpe and Sharpe redress some of the imbalance. They argue that traditional constructions of the 'welfari-sation' of female young offenders are becoming less salient within a context in which the processes of criminalisation, punishment – and ultimately incarceration – are being more readily applied to girls and young women within contemporary youth justice in England and Wales.

Taken together, the four chapters in Part One of the book re-establish both the importance of historical memory for understanding the present, and the primary significance of structural relations and social divisions for conceptualising: the adverse socio-economic and cultural contexts within which identifiable groups of children and young people are growing up in 'advanced' industrial societies; the complex material conditions within which youth crime is located; and the means by which disadvantaged young people are regulated, controlled and even criminalised by youth justice agencies. In short, the historical reflections demolish the myth that the nature and scope of youth crime are an aberration of 'late modernity', and the class, 'race' and gender-based analyses shift the analytical emphasis from individualised constructions of criminogenic pathology to the complex social-structural formations that give rise to social harm, adversity and the injustices of the 'justice' process.

Part Two engages explicitly with the symbolic hegemony of 'evidenced-based policy' within dominant youth justice discourse, and it subjects both the evidence and its relation to policy to critical assessment. In Chapter 5, Tim Bateman discusses the difficulties involved with reading and interpreting statistical evidence and the associated complexities of determining 'fact' and 'truth'. Notwithstanding this, Bateman argues that 'asking the right questions' of the data serves to 'generate an important body of knowledge' and this in turn raises further questions with regard to the legitimacy of 'the more interventionist and expansionist elements of contemporary youth justice'. In Chapter 6, David Smith reflects upon evaluative research and the positivist conceptions that inform 'what works' paradigms. Smith, like Bateman, considers the possibilities of applying evidence to policy formation but he warns that a slavish attachment to a positivist social science is myopic and problematic. Furthermore, by developing Bateman's critique, he observes that in many important respects youth justice has 'proved politically too sensitive an issue for the evidence to be allowed to get in the way'.

From analyses of generic 'evidence' to more narrowly focused reflective assessments, the next four chapters are directed towards specific modes of youth justice intervention. In Chapter 7, Roger Smith examines the pre-occupation with actuarialism, 'risk'-based paradigms and early intervention within contemporary youth justice policy and practice. In Chapter 8, Kevin Haines and David O'Mahony consider the meaning of restorative justice and the application of restorative approaches within youth justice practice in England and Wales and Northern Ireland. In Chapter 9, Fergus McNeill critically explores community supervision and argues that any considered reading of the research evidence indicates that 'context and relationships matter'. In many senses McNeill's analysis re-connects with Part One of the book in arguing that an explicit awareness of social-structural relations is key to the success or otherwise of community supervision. If children and young people are to 'desist' from crime, youth justice professionals need to develop nuanced and empathetic relations with them that extend beyond the claustrophobic confines of regulation, monitoring, surveillance and mechanistic 'soft policing'. In Chapter 10, Barry Goldson argues that the increasing application of penal custody – particularly in England and Wales – is rooted in forms of intolerance and punitiveness that are fundamentally irrational and conspicuously indifferent to a wealth of evidence. The unifying messages of this sequence of chapters include: youth justice interventions essentially encompass society's most distressed and disadvantaged children and young people; the politicisation of contemporary youth justice distorts and disfigures the translation of evidence to policy formation and practice development; the manifest strain between more benign and inclusionary initiatives and starkly exclusionary and punitive imperatives presents complex, perhaps even irreconcilable, tensions.

The final three chapters within Part Two serve to broaden the analytical field beyond the strictures of conventional youth justice inquiry by addressing the inter-related questions of extended system reach, the burgeoning criminalisation of social policy, and the preoccupation with questions of order and disorder in other policy domains and areas of state intervention. In Chapter 11, Gordon Hughes and Matthew Follett engage with the contested and controversial questions of 'community safety' and 'anti-social behaviour'. In particular, they argue that in both conception and application, 'anti-social behaviour' discourses privilege negative constructions of children and young people and serve to 'define deviance up'. Hughes and Follett observe, however, that the interventionist powers and responsibilities provided and imposed by legislation and guidance to 'tackle' 'anti-social behaviour', have been unevenly applied across England and Wales indicating some positive resistance to, and subversion of, crude punitive excesses. In Chapter 12, Lynn Hancock turns attention to the processes of urban regeneration. She observes that major regeneration programmes are being implemented in many towns and cities across the UK, at precisely the same time that 'inequalities are becoming more visible and proximate in urban space'. Hancock critically explores the 'relationships, connections and tensions between regeneration, crime reduction, social inclusion and social control' and she endorses a core contention that runs through the book in arguing that: 'current policies are ideologically driven rather than the product of "evidenced-based" policy-making'. Advancing some of the arguments contained within Hughes and Follett's essay, Hancock illuminates the strain between approaches 'designed to "include" children and young people in the regeneration of urban neighbourhoods, and the widespread perception that "anti-social behaviour" (often centred on young people) is a "threat" to regenerating communities'. Throughout her discussion, Hancock remains attentive to the divisive and polarising consequences of economic restructuring. This echoes some of the contentions introduced in relation to history, class, 'race' and gender in the opening four chapters of the book. Within this context young people's employment prospects and labour market opportunities are crucial. It is fitting, therefore, that Part Two of the book concludes with a critical analysis of the 'new deal' for the young unemployed. In Chapter 13, Phil Mizen observes that young people without work are now confronted with the 'toughest unemployment benefits regime the United Kingdom has ever seen'. Alongside this parsimonious benefits system, the New Deal for Young People has consolidated and is essentially a coercive 'welfare-to-work' scheme. Variously conceptualised as a social inclusion initiative, part of a broader crime and disorder reduction strategy, a reskilling programme, a means of replacing direct state support for the young working class and/or as a technique to ameliorate the excesses of structural economic adjustment, Mizen presents a critique of the 'New Deal' on the basis of hard evidence and theoretical analysis.

Part Three comprises an extended concluding chapter in which we attempt to integrate many of the themes that run through the book. We argue that 'youth justice' itself is a contested and multi-faceted construct; and that 'youth justice systems' comprise settlements of multiple, and often competing, thematic imperatives. Any analytical reading of contemporary youth justice policy in the UK, and particularly in England and Wales, has to embrace the complexities, contradictions and controversies around which it is moulded. In keeping with each of the preceding chapters, we observe that the relationship between 'evidence' and policy formation is profoundly strained. Furthermore, we argue that the tensions that are lodged between rationality and instrumental political calculations serve to distort and disfigure the wider corpus of policy with regard to children and young people. At a time when social inclusion, anti-child poverty and joined-up welfare imperatives – however limited – are evident across wide tranches of social and economic policy, key aspects of youth justice policy paradoxically serve to compound the exclusion, criminalisation and punishment of identifiable groups of disadvantaged children and young people.

From introspective critical reflection we move towards a more prospective vision of a principled youth justice. By drawing upon: international standards, treaties, rules and conventions that provide the children's human rights framework; exemplars of progressive policy and practice from the international juvenile/ youth justice community; and some of the key messages embedded within research evidence and practice experience, we sketch the contours of an alternative model of justice.

By building upon key academic disciplines including criminology, sociology, social policy, socio-legal studies, social history and psychology, alongside the knowledge bases that inform professional practice in law, social work, community justice, youth justice and youth and community work, this book aims to critically assess the relation between 'evidence' and policy as a means of understanding youth crime and justice. Moreover, alongside its companion volume – *Comparative Youth Justice: Critical Debates* – the two books are intended to advance the development of a theoretically-informed and policy-relevant interventionist *youth criminology*.

Barry Goldson and John Muncie
January 2006

References

Bottoms, A. (2005) 'Methodology matters', *Safer Society*, 25: 10–12.

Davey, C., Dwyer, C., McAlister, S., Kilkelly, U., Kilpatrick, R., Lundy, L., Moore, L. and Scraton, P. (2004) *Children's Rights in Northern Ireland*. Belfast: Northern Ireland Commissioner for Children and Young People.

Goldson, B. (ed.) (2000) *The New Youth Justice*. Lyme Regis: Russell House Publishing.

Goldson, B. (2001) 'A Rational Youth Justice? Some Critical Reflections on the Research, Policy and Practice Relation', *Probation Journal*, 48(2): 76–85.

McAra, L. (2006) 'Welfare in Crisis? Key Developments in Scottish Youth Justice', in J. Muncie and B. Goldson (eds) *Comparative Youth Justice: Critical Issues*. London: Sage.

Muncie, J. (2004) *Youth and Crime*. (2nd edn). London: Sage.

Pitts, J. (2001) *The New Politics of Youth Crime: Discipline or Solidarity*. Basingstoke: Palgrave.

Smith, R. (2003) *Youth Justice: Ideas, Policy, Practice*. Cullompton: Willan.

PART ONE

Historical and
Social-Structural Contexts

Histories of Youth Crime and Justice

Harry Hendrick

Nostalgia (upon which authoritarianism feeds) is a powerful cultural force, and nowhere is it more on display than in the public (adult) condemnation of the behaviour of young people. Whether it be the consequences of 'permissiveness', the influence of celebrity culture, an insolent attitude towards authority, the 'decline' in parental discipline, too much pocket money, or the so-called 'crisis' of childhood, children and adolescents today are said to pose more of a threat to the social order than at any time in the past. Governments, in conjunction with the media, continually devise policies to deal with this 'new' malaise in an effort to return to 'the old days' when, apparently, civil society was just that: civil, peaceable, respectful, and cohesive (Muncie, 2004; Pearson, 1994). In exposing these cruelly deceptive myths, this chapter illustrates the variability of concepts such as 'juvenile delinquency', 'anti-social behaviour', and 'youth justice'. Through brief discussions of a chronological selection of debates and policy developments from *c.*1800 to the end of the 1980s, the chapter summarises the overwhelming conclusion of historical and sociological research, namely that 'juvenile delinquency', in common with 'crime', can only be understood if the meaning of the term is considered within a broad socio-political context (Bailey, 1987; Gattrell, 1990; Gelsthorpe and Morris, 1994; Muncie, 2004; Pearson, 1983). In other words, the argument here, albeit schematically presented, is that youth crime and youth justice (an integral feature of which has, until recently, been the welfare–justice binary), should be approached historically in relation to matters that at first sight may appear to be marginal to the topic, notably: (*a*) 'change' (particularly social, political, economic and personal), (*b*) 'order' (cultural, social and political), (c) the influence of professional and administrative class agendas, (d) party political programmes for the content and management of governance and, by no means least, (e) age and generational relations. As will become evident, these contexts are not presented hierarchically; rather they are integrated within and across the narrative.

The early nineteenth century: 'The child' as delinquent

With respect to the early nineteenth century, current scholarship speaks of a 'reconception' rather than an 'invention' of 'juvenile delinquency', and argues that it was not until then 'that a specific definition of the criminal child, particular in legal discourse, really started to emerge' (King, 1998: 199; Shore, 1999: 148). Three main developments have been noted: an increase in *recorded* juvenile crime, a widespread and influential public debate, and the evolution of penal and legal strategies to cope with the growing problem (Shore, 1999: 15). Why should this have been so? First, the period c.1780s–1820s, which witnessed the early stages of the industrial revolution, was one of seminal historical *change*, including the social and political upheaval caused by the Napoleonic Wars (1793–1815), growth in population, rapid developments in urbanisation, and an increase in levels of poverty owing to the effects of industrialisation on rural and urban labour markets (Royle, 1987; Thompson, 1963). Such trends and events affected a range of politically explosive issues, not least the overriding problem of social stability, of which 'crime' is always a feature bearing in mind its variable significance in different historical epochs (Gattrell, 1990).

The second reason lies in the birth of modern childhood, which heralded an innovative stage in *age relations*. The process is usually ascribed to four sources: the influence of Rousseau through his elevation of the 'natural' child; the place of the 'child figure' in Romantic literature (notably Blake and Wordsworth); the very different kind of place of the child in the teachings of the Evangelical Revival; and the role of the child in the 'Domestic Ideal' as a cultural norm. Rousseau's claim that 'Nature wants children to be children before they are men' and the Romantics' belief in 'original innocence' collided with and in many respects were subdued by the puritanical Evangelical view that children 'are sinful polluted creatures', a prescription that was promulgated through the family form (cited in Hendrick, 1997: 36–9). As 'the child' emerged in the new post-Enlightenment industrialising society, so 'its' identification as both 'victim' and 'threat' became central to a number of socio-political and literary debates, particularly those involving child labour, 'children of the streets' and the adjustment of the 'self' to the 'social' (Andrews, 1994; Berry, 1999; Coveney, 1967; Hendrick, 1997; Hendrick, 2003: 7–11).

Given the contemporary political environment, however, it was not children *per se*, but the 'children of the poor' who were said to present the greatest threat to the precarious social order (Cunningham, 1991). No wonder, then, that among the numerous causes of delinquency identified, the most important were 'the improper conduct of parents; the want of education; the want of suitable employment; and the violation of the Sabbath; habits of gambling in the public streets' (cited in Shore, 1999: 20). Thereafter various legislative Acts, themselves in part the results of governmental and philanthropic inquiries and responses to 'public' concern, broadened the notions of 'crime' and 'criminality' to include many behaviours that had previously been regarded as 'nuisances', including public gambling and stealing apples from orchards and gardens (May, 1973), and also encouraged the apprehension of 'all loose, idle and disorderly persons not giving good account of themselves' (quoted in Muncie, 2004: 58–59). This was a significant widening of the net, for the legislation reflected a growing unwillingness to overlook the 'crimes' of children and, therefore, expressed a policy of consciously drawing 'children into the criminal justice system' (Shore, 1999: 150).

The reconception of juvenile delinquency can be explained if the inclusion of children into the increasingly complex and heterogeneous justice system is seen in terms of a search for order, as the old 'moral economy' was declining under the impact of an evolving and completely new urban industrial capitalism, for example: the years of political 'crisis and repression' (1815–21); the pros and cons of working-class education; arguments for and against child labour; agitation and riots preceding the Great Reform Act (1832); and the intensely controversial New Poor Law Act (1834) (Royle, 1987; Thompson, 1963). The rubric of political stability demanded that young people, who were perceived as a conspicuous 'threat' to the urban equilibrium, not least owing to their growing numbers, be brought under the control of civil society. Clearly, with respect to juvenile delinquency (which was a feature of generational tension), 'crime' was becoming 'a vehicle for articulating mounting anxieties about issues which really had nothing to do with crime at all: social change and the stability of social hierarchy. These issues invested crime with new meanings, justified vastly accelerated action against it, and have determined attitudes to it ever since' (Gattrell, 1990: 249). The importance of this observation can hardly be exaggerated.

The early to mid-Victorian years: Creating 'willing obedience' through the justice/welfare imperative

The social unrest of the early nineteenth century, which seemed to have been successfully quelled by the 1830s, made a new and dramatic reappearance through Chartism – the first mass working-class movement, especially the 'uprising' of 1842 and the subsequent show trial of 59 leaders (Royle, 1987). In response, Lord Ashley, England's 'greatest' social reformer, called for the compulsory education of the children of the 'dangerous classes', and warned of the 'fearful multitude of untutored savages' (a recurring image, along with 'children of the streets'), which represented a problem 'so prodigiously vast, and so unspeakably important' (cited in Pearson, 1985: 159; Cunningham, 1991: 97–134). Reformers were fearful that '[the delinquent] ... is a little stunted man already – he knows much and a great deal too much of what is called life ... he has to be turned again into a child ...' (cited in May, 1973: 7). Here was one of the first unambiguous expressions of a hierarchical age relationship. That 'age' mattered in a number of ways, as we have seen, had been known since the end of the eighteenth century. However, from the 1830s onwards there was a growing need to theorise social-penal issues in relation to the specificity of 'childhood' and 'youth' (in certain respects following the example set by the Factory Act, 1833) in order to better understand delinquent acts and to create policy. Although in 1838 Parkhurst was opened as the first juvenile penal institution, the exact nature of the appropriate response within what would become a 'penal-welfare complex' (Garland, 1985) was still undecided. Central to the question was how to conceptualise the child: as a *victim* or as a *threat* (Hendrick, 2003: 7–10)?

Besides Lord Ashley, the other influential Evangelical reformer was Mary Carpenter who did so much to define the matter in terms of the 'dangerous' and the 'perishing' classes, and who, in common with other commentators, attributed the plight of outcast children to a personal and virtuous deficit on the part of parents, rather than to poverty (Pearson, 1983: 175; Radzinowicz and Hood, 1986: 161–78). This moralistic conception of 'need' was significant since it framed the solution in terms of moral reclamation. According to Carpenter, existing methods of dealing with delinquents (and neglected children) did nothing to rehabilitate them – they were merely punished. Prisons, she said, had failed to reform because they could not obtain a '*willing* obedience' since there was no 'softening power of love' to subdue the delinquent: 'It is utterly vain to look for any real reformation where the heart is not touched' (cited in Pearson, 1983: 180). While the concept of 'welfare' was implicit rather than explicit, the notion of a 'willing' obedience was critical for the mid-Victorian debate on social stability and working-class compliance, for it expressed a growing political view that respectable working men should be brought within the Constitution through enfranchisement, to which they would then give their consent. In other words, the debate on anti-social behaviour more than mirrored political anxieties regarding the governance of a society known as 'the workshop of the world'.

In response, for the first time Parliament legislatively recognised juvenile delinquency 'as a distinct social phenomenon' in passing the Youthful Offenders Act, 1854 (which established Reformatories for convicted delinquents – *threats*), and the Industrial Schools Act, 1857 (which provided Schools for 'neglected' children – *victims*) (Goldson, 2004: 87–92; May, 1973: 7–29). The legislation (and subsequent Acts in the 1860s), consolidated the importance of 'age' as a distinguishing feature of penal policy. In this way imprisonment, whipping, and transportation slowly began to yield to a structure of institutional surveillance and control, with a combined inmate population (in Industrial Schools and Reformatories) of more than 30,000 young persons by the end of the century (Radzinowicz and Hood, 1986: 181).

The late Victorian and Edwardian years: 'Child saving' in the 'modern' social services state

In place of the child 'savage', the period c.1880–1914 had a new spectre: 'Hooliganism', a term used to describe the 'loutish' behaviour of working-class youth, and portrayed by the press as a particularly virulent form of urban unrest (Pearson, 1985: 74–5). Statistically, apprehension about the perceived rise in delinquency had some validity, for while rates of recorded adult crime were declining, there was a decided upward trend in recorded juvenile crime (Gillis, 1975: 99). But the 'increase' in 'convictions' begged at least two important questions: why and how. First, the 'crimes' were largely of the non-indictable variety such as drunkenness, malicious mischief, loitering, begging and dangerous play. Second, the conviction rate owed more to the aggressive attitude of the police and courts in prosecuting 'traditional' working-class youthful leisure activities than to either a greater propensity among juveniles to break the law or new forms of delinquent behaviour (Gillis, 1975; Springhall, 1986). This is a clear example of juvenile delinquency being *created* through structural and administrative procedures which, as is shown below, were reactions to social and political change.

During the period there were important developments in both class and age relations that help to explain middle-class sensitivity towards 'youth culture'. Although the matter of participatory democracy for adult men had more or less been settled by the end of the century, the female franchise remained a contentious subject. Where class antagonism was concerned, there were serious issues surrounding the 'rediscovery' of poverty, the 'new' trades unionism, industrial unrest, socialism, and the spectre of physical degeneration. Furthermore, imperialism presented a number of economic, political and military anxieties, while the muddle of the Boer War (1899–1902) unleashed an elitist movement calling for 'National Efficiency', not least to counter the relative decline in the strength of the economy. This is not to say that everything was doom and woe but as the new century opened Britain's position in the world and the social and physical health of the society were by no means secure (Freeden, 1978; Harris, 1993). Historical understanding of adult attitudes and policies towards juvenile delinquency requires consideration of these larger political contexts for it is they that determine how 'social constructions' of young people (and 'crime') are 'put together' (Hendrick, 1997: 34–5).

The early 1900s are famous for the Liberal Reform Programme (1906–11), which created a 'social services state' (Fraser, 1973). The overriding objective of the government was to increase the stability of institutions by giving the male working class an interest in maintaining them (an example of 'willing obedience') (Harris, 1993). In addition to the innovative pensions and national insurance schemes, the Programme included a number of 'child-saving' measures: infant welfare, protection against cruelty, school meals, school medical inspection and treatment, and the care and education of the physically and mentally disabled (Hendrick, 1994 and 2003). Aside from the Youthful Offenders Act 1901 and the Probation Act 1907, both of which extended the use of alternatives to prison, the major policy response to juvenile delinquency and neglected children was the Children Act 1908. This Act was notable for its attempt to reconcile welfare and justice imperatives through the establishment of the 'juvenile court' with both civil jurisdiction over the 'needy' child and criminal jurisdiction over the offending child. In effect, the Act enshrined the principle of *rehabilitation,* articulated through positivist psycho-medicine with its emphasis on *treatment* (Garland, 1985: 231–63; Muncie, 2004: 77). However, as the court was to be an agency 'for the rescue *as well as* the punishment of juveniles', so 'conflict and ambivalence were embedded' in the very concept of its existence (Gelsthorpe and Morris, 1994: 951).

With reference to the significance of age relations, there were three important developments peculiar to these years. First, the evolving science of psychology promoted the emergence of 'adolescence' (primarily related to boys) as a psychological and social 'fact' – a stage of life with, it was claimed, precise and potentially threatening characteristics if not made subject to good guidance, discipline and physical exercise. Second, there was a 'panic' of sorts by social and economic commentators with regard to the juvenile labour market – 'the boy labour problem' – which, although a complex matter involving the nature of skill and differential labour demands, was often portrayed as a situation whereby boys were lured into 'blind alley' employment with relatively high wages. Third, there occurred a rapid growth of youth clubs and uniformed youth organisations, which in turn was part of the wider 'child-saving' movement (Hendrick, 1990; 1994; Springhall, 1986). Considered together, the new concept of adolescence, the problem of 'boy labour', and the middle-class attempt to provide 'rational recreation' may be seen as indices of social change.

It is sometimes claimed that during the Edwardian years 'a stage of life, adolescence, replaced station in life, class, as the perceived cause of misbehaviour' (Gillis, 1975: 97). The psychology of adolescence was certainly influential, but it was combined with, rather than replaced, social class as the principal anxiety of penal reformers and youth workers (Hendrick, 1990: 101–6, 120). Where 'juvenile delinquency' is concerned, 'social class' has never been far from the thoughts of governments. And the reason is simple: 'the poor' in particular, as opposed to the children of the 'respectable' working class, are always regarded as liable to disrupt social stability, if only through low-level anti-social behaviour. Thus delinquents (embodied in a fused image of both class and age), are a convenient 'Other', who are presented to us as a constant reminder of how precarious and fragile *our* apparently civilised values are and, therefore, of the need for constant surveillance, discipline and punishment (Garland, 1985: 231-63).

The inter-war years: Rationalizing the welfare-justice model

The foregrounding of 'welfare' as a legitimate feature of juvenile justice continued in the inter-war period through a growing acceptance of 'the social conception of delinquency', which understood offending as 'merely a symptom of a delinquent's social and personal condition' and saw juvenile crime as 'but one inseparable portion of the larger enterprise of child welfare' (Bailey, 1987: 62; Burt, 1927: 610; Davis, 1990: 72-3; Hendrick, 2003: 113-24). This view was associated with a broader psycho-social movement represented by newly established child guidance clinics, 'progressive' elementary education, and the propagation of liberal child-rearing methods via psychodynamic principles (Hendrick, 1994; 2003; Wooldridge, 1995). The impact of the subtle inter-play between this movement and the theory and practice of juvenile justice was historically significant for it not only sought to delineate new understandings of 'welfare' and 'justice', but also implicitly to establish the contours for more nuanced age relations in general. Its role (together with that of Home Office officials who were under its influence) is evident in the Children and Young Person Act 1933, which provided for juvenile courts to act *in loco parentis* as a closer link was forged between delinquent and neglected children in the belief that: 'there is little or no difference in character and needs between the delinquent and the neglected child' (cited in Hendrick, 1994: 182). The Act expressed the prevailing 'hegemony of child welfare', with the wider use of probation, approved schools, and boarding out (Bailey, 1987: Part 2), as well as a wider use of varieties of 'knowledge' (from parents, teachers, doctors, and others) about the young person before the court (Garland, 1985; Rose, 1985). The approach, however, remained controversial with the police and magistrates, particularly as the welfare measures resulted in an increased rate of recorded delinquencies (Bailey, 1987: 165).

Juvenile justice in the welfare state: 1948-1970s

In order to understand conceptions of juvenile delinquency and resulting legislation in the decades prior to 'Thatcherism' we have to appreciate the political significance of the post-1945 Welfare State, which was governed through a broad consensus informed by Keynesian economic theory, and providing full employment and a significant rise in the average standard of living. It is within this context that the period is often described in terms of 'the cult of youth', 'the youth spectacle', 'the teenage revolution' and similar phrases (Davis, 1990; Osgerby, 1998; Pearson, 1985). Certainly a major characteristic of those years was the promotion of a 'succession of spectacular fringe delinquent working-class youth subcultures': Teddy Boys (1950s), Mods (early 1960s), Skinheads (1960s–1970s), together with a number of middle-class youth movements associated with the expansion of higher education and political protest (Davis, 1990: 142). In general, the post-war period up to the 1970s was unquestionably that of 'youth' (not so much of children) and this cultural 'moment', with all its unforeseen tensions, together with the consensual, if limited, acceptance of 'welfare' as a political principle, profoundly influenced all manner of attitudes and policies. Not for the first time, the 'youth question' served to provide a means of discussing the multiplicity of social, economic, political and cultural issues that arise at a time of fundamental social change. Put another way, the 'state of the nation' was viewed through the perceived condition of its youth (Davis, 1990; Gelsthorpe and Morris, 1994; Osgerby, 1998).

From the late 1940s, the subject of juvenile delinquency began to feature in various academic and professional discourses, largely within the welfarist framework of the 1948 Children Act, which established a local authority child-care service (Gelsthorpe and Morris, 1994: 953–7; Hendrick, 2003: 133–40). Throughout the 1950s there was much talk about the effects of the war on young people and of the impact of 'Americanisation', which was thought to be threatening the 'British way of life' (Pearson, 1985: 20). By the early 1960s the dominant mood was one of introspection as to why the 'welfare state' was failing to eradicate crime altogether, combined with a growing realisation that youth was representative of 'new' (and worrying) cultural forces (Davis, 1990; Osgerby, 1998: 5–49; Springhall, 1986: 190–2). Delinquent youth, argued the liberal intelligentsia, was the product of 'deeper structural conflicts within British society', brought about by the consequences of affluence, the dissolution of the Empire, the erosion of economic and political supremacy, the advance of science and technology; and new sexual and familial (and gendered) patterns of behaviour, many of which weakened 'the family' and undermined 'traditional' moral values (Davis, 1990: 148–9, 151–7; Marwick, 1990; Springhall, 1986: 192–9). Despite these anxieties, the fact that 'youth' was also viewed sympathetically reflected a continuing belief in the future. Alongside this, however, there remained major concerns with wider issues relating to generational conflict and the governance of an affluent mass democracy.

When it came to policies, the culminating legislation of the 1960s, the product of a decade of debate, was the Children and Young Persons Act 1969 (Bottoms, 2002: 216–27). The decade opened, however, with the Ingleby Report (1960), which identified a major weakness in the juvenile court system, namely the confusion between the expectation of 'just deserts' raised by 'the forms of a *criminal* trial' and the direction that when considering treatment the court had a duty to have regard 'for the welfare of the child or young person' (cited in Bottoms, 2002: 218). This highlighted one of the central problems in conceptualising juvenile delinquency within a 'criminal' jurisdiction: in the early stages of apprehension, the delinquent tends to be treated as a rational being by the police and the court, but in the later stages, there is more of an emphasis on pathology, psychic disturbance, or 'welfare' (Bottoms, 2002: 218–19; Hendrick, 2003: 142–4). Much of the 1960s debate was about how this contradiction should be resolved.

The subsequent Children and Young Persons Act 1963 raised the age of criminal responsibility to 10, and gave local authorities powers to do preventive social work, thereby confirming the view that 'it is the situation and the relationships within the family which seem to be responsible for many children being in trouble, whether the trouble is called delinquency or anything else' (cited in Hendrick, 2003: 143). In effect, the 1963 Act maintained the perception of young people as a 'threat' while simultaneously attempting to reconcile it with a notion of 'neglect' (victim). Using the framework of the local authority childcare service, it sought to do this through a broadening of the therapeutic complex involving social workers, teachers, psychologists, doctors, and probation officers (Hendrick, 2003, 140–7; Rose, 1990). However, despite the apparent rise in the number of juvenile offenders (Hendrick, 2003: 147), the debate continued to be shaped by largely welfarist sentiments.

These sentiments were most radically expressed in the controversial Children and Young Persons Act 1969, which sought: to raise the age of criminal responsibility from 10 to 14; to substitute non-criminal care proceedings in place of criminal procedures for the 10–14 age group; to encourage a more liberal use of non-criminalised care proceedings for those aged 14–17; and to involve parents with social workers in deciding on a course of 'treatment' in order to avoid court appearance. The Act, which was the result largely of a conjunction of social work and civil servant interests and Labour Party ideology (Bottoms, 2002: 225–6), represented 'the high point of therapeutic familialism as a strategy for government through the family' since the court was to become 'a place of last resort' (Hendrick, 2003: 149–53; Rose, 1990: 175). The weight of authority and discretion moved from the police, magistrates and the prison department towards local authorities and the Department of Health and Social Security: it seemed that 'the hour of the "child-savers" had finally arrived' (Thorpe et al., 1980: 6). The newly elected Conservative government (1970), however, which was sympathetic to the police and magistracy, both of whom strongly opposed the 'welfare' orientation of the Act, ensured that it was never fully implemented. On reflection, the significance of the decade's debate is that it was 'a political metaphor' for a legislative programme 'geared to the development of … a more just society' and, therefore, in certain respects the Act was the last gasp of post-war Labour Party liberalism in criminal affairs (Gelsthorpe and Morris, 1994: 958; Muncie, 2004: 253).

The failure of Liberalism to protect welfarism in juvenile penal policy was caused by a complex set of factors, perhaps the immediate one being the technical and inherent difficulty in trying to match the punishment and welfare approaches into a single piece of legislation that would reassure all political interests. But there was another influential factor: the issue of governance among an electorate that was increasingly disillusioned with the promise and the vision of the post-war welfare state. The new mood was aptly captured in the Conservative general election manifesto, which referred to law and order 'peculiar to the age of demonstration and disruption'. This link between law-breaking and defiance of authority would prove to be significant in the future, not least because it was the beginning of the effective Conservative reaction to the 'permissiveness' of the 1960s, a decade when Britain had become the most liberal nation in Europe (Downes and Morgan, 1994: 183–4, 187–8; Pugh, 1999: 297–310). In the subsequent 'retreat from welfare' that proceeded throughout the 1970s, a key feature was a 'widespread shift in the techniques for governing the family and its troublesome offspring' (Gelsthorpe and Morris, 1994: 963–71; Rose, 1990: 29). This was due mainly to the break-up of the alliance of progressives within politics, social work, and medicine which, in underlining the important role of professional interests, since the 1950s had projected the family as a 'therapeutic agent' in a programme of rehabilitative interventionism. The social changes of the 1960s, in particular, feminism, anti-psychiatry, 'radical' social work, mounting critiques of the 'failures' of the welfare state and, perhaps most importantly, economic difficulties, all led to a loss of direction by the Liberal Left, and enthused the New Right with confidence to advance neo-liberalism with its free markets and economic libertarianism.

The 1980s: Neo-liberal reaction and contradiction

By the mid-1970s, the image of Britain was of a society in 'national decline': economic problems, racial tensions, discontent with the health and social services, violent political struggles between Left and far-Right demonstrators, trade union militancy, the emergence of a so-called 'underclass', and criminality and juvenile 'delinquency' – all of which culminated in the 'winter of discontent' of 1978–79. The media deemed Britain to be 'ungovernable', and Labour lost the general election (Downes and Morgan, 1994, 189–90). Soon 'crime' was being associated with 1960s permissiveness, which was said to have undermined traditional values, encouraged the spread of pornography and glamourised violence, especially political violence. The Conservatives, with a significant and innovatory agenda regarding governance, argued that this 'decline' in public morality was not simply a matter for the police, but should be the concern of parents, teachers, and the community, and in so doing introduced a new emphasis on the role of 'active citizenship' and 'community' action (Downes and Morgan, 1994: 191–2, 225; Gelsthorpe and Morris, 1994: 971). Thus juvenile justice was yet again incorporated into a larger debate about the nature of social and political order.

Despite the tough talking of the Conservative government, while it was politically secure at the polls, the years between 1982 and 1992 present an intricate picture. Policy responses were relatively liberal and the period has been described as a 'time of optimism', albeit limited optimism, in youth justice. The use of custody declined; there was a fall in recorded juvenile delinquency; and the 'youth justice system' itself seemed to be in decline (Gelsthorpe and Morris, 1994, 971–80; Newburn, 1996: 74). In fact there emerged a somewhat paradoxical coalescence between a number of disparate factors including academic research, social work with juvenile offenders, certain policy objectives of Thatcherism, and the interests of the police and the courts to reduce all forms of delinquency (Goldson, 1997: 124). Consequently, a 'fragile consensus' developed, hinging as it did on three principles: 'diversion, decriminalisation and decarceration', which produced a remarkably progressive period in the treatment of juvenile delinquents (Goldson, 1999: 4). In terms of policy responses, these principles were 'minimum necessary intervention, systems management, effective monitoring, intra-agency strategies, systematic diversionary approaches, community supervision and alternatives to custody' (Goldson, 1999: 4). Not only did the Conservatives echo academic researchers in proclaiming that juveniles 'grow out of crime' (quoted in Newburn, 1996: 67), but the courts were also reminded that they had to have regard for the welfare of those young persons brought before them. Of course, the 1980s did not witness an ideological conversion to welfarism. The efficiency of the police and the courts in reducing 'criminal' activity was being questioned and keeping young people out of penal custody was one means of meeting a key objective of Thatcherism, namely reducing overall expenditure. Given the onset of neo-liberal styles of governing, increasing attention was being given to 'unofficial' forms of discipline and control (Gelsthorpe and Morris, 1994: 980; Muncie and Hughes, 2002: 1–16).

All in all, the nature and the existence of the consensus illustrate the contradictions of juvenile justice in contemporary society. The post-war 'moment' of political and cultural optimism finally collapsed with the failure of liberalism to provide solutions to a problematic economy, muddled moral codes, labour market restructuring and uncertain class relations. And after the killing of the toddler Jamie Bulger by two ten-year-old boys in 1993 a media-induced 'crisis in childhood' was confirmed (Jenks, 1996). This offered government and adult authority the opportunity to self-righteously express their anger and disappointment while seeming to be 'doing something', thereby relieving their sense of frustration and impotence. Thus it was ultimately disillusionment that gave way to 'authoritarian populism' (Newburn, 1996: 98) which, in accelerating the 'adulteration' of juvenile justice, has severely undermined the historical principle of child and youth 'welfare' in favour of 'self-responsibility and obligation' (Muncie and Hughes, 2002: 4–5).

Conclusion

This historical overview has been concerned with *change, order, party political agendas, professional* and *administrative influence*, and *age relations*. It has sought to show that there is nothing new about debates concerning young people's behaviour. Nor until the end of the 1980s was there much in the way of policy innovation for, as we have seen, from the early nineteenth century the central theme in policy discourse was how to reconcile 'welfare' with 'justice' in a variety of circumstances, within the context of the evolving relationships between individual and society on the one hand and family and state on the other. The reconciliation took different forms during the period, but essentially it always dealt with the control, rehabilitation and punishment of young people who found themselves somewhere along the spectrum of victim/threat/neglected/delinquent. Only since the end of the 1980s has the welfare/justice model been significantly restructured in line with a form of neo-liberalism.

In seeking to grasp the essence of debates (past and present) on juvenile delinquency and juvenile justice, two themes are worth reiterating. First, 'juvenile justice' is not simply a response to variations in apparent crime rates since it fundamentally reflects strategies for coping with social and political change and the related search for stability. This was obviously so throughout the nineteenth century in response to the urgent demands of a developing democracy, industrial relations, population growth and urban discipline. Similarly, in the war-torn twentieth century in relation to Britain's much disputed world economic and political position, the development of a liberal democracy, the emergence of the affluent society and the rise of neo-liberalism. In other words, how society *creates* and reacts to juvenile misbehaviour 'ultimately tells us more about social order, the state and political decision making than it does about the nature of young offending and the most effective ways to respond to it' (Muncie, 2004: 303).

Second, it should now be clear that 'juvenile delinquency' in all its forms and ambiguities is fundamentally a matter of *both* class *and* age relations, which are usually intertwined in subtle and complex notions of troubled and troubling young people (victims and threats). This matter of 'age', which is culturally embedded, often goes unquestioned as 'natural' and, therefore, is downplayed in preference either to 'class' or 'the state'. But, as has been shown, the nineteenth-century reformers had no doubt as to the importance of age *vis-à-vis* what is known as 'the child figure' in political and fictional writing. From Rousseau onwards, 'age' became a critical conceptual tool in understanding both the 'self' and the 'social', and without it a notion of juvenile delinquency could hardly have evolved. In the late Victorian-Edwardian period, the 'invention' of adolescence added a critical psycho-biological dimension to what had hitherto been simply a class perspective of delinquency, and throughout the 1920s and 1930s the 'New Psychology' (Child Guidance clinics) gained increasing significance in explaining 'maladjustment' as a sociological function of varieties of modernity. In the post-war period up to the 1970s, age relations took on an importance hitherto unknown, as 'youth' was positioned in classic figurative form: between past, present and future; a visible expression of cultural evolution, with all the ambivalence and ambiguity such a status entails. So, as has been shown here, 'age', like 'social change', is a permanent feature of all histories of youth crime and justice.

References

Andrews, M. (1994) *Dickens and the Grown-Up Child*. Basingstoke: Macmillan.

Bailey, V. (1987) *Delinquency and Citizenship. Reclaiming the Young Offender, 1914–1948*. Oxford: Clarendon Press.

Berry, L. C. (1999) *The Child, the State and the Novel*. Charlottesville, PA: University of Pennsylvania Press.

Bottoms, A. (2002) 'On the Decriminalisation of English Juvenile Courts', in John Muncie, Gordon Hughes, and Eugene McLaughlin (eds) *Youth Justice: Critical Readings*. London: Sage. pp. 216–27.

Burt, C. (1927) *The Young Delinquent*. London: University of London Press.

Coveney, P. (1967) *The Child Figure in Literature*. Harmondsworth: Pelican.

Cunningham, H. (1991) *Children of the Poor*. Oxford: Blackwell.

Davis, J. (1990) *Youth and the Condition of Britain*. London: Athlone.

Downes, D. and Morgan, R. (1994) '"Hostages to Fortune?" The politics of law and order in post-war Britain', in M. Maguire, R. Morgan and R. Reiner (eds) *The Oxford Handbook of Criminology*. Oxford: Oxford University Press.

Fraser, D. (1973) *The Evolution of the British Welfare State*. Basingstoke: Macmillan.

Freeden, M. (1978) *The New Liberalism*. Oxford: Clarendon Press.

Garland, D. (1985) *Punishment and Welfare*. Aldershot: Gower.

Gattrell, V. (1990) 'Crime, Authority and the Policeman-State', in F. M. L. Thompson (ed.) *Cambridge Social History of Britain 1750–1950,* Vol. 3. Cambridge: Cambridge University Press.

Gelsthorpe, L. and Morris, A. (1994) 'Juvenile Justice, 1945–1992', in M. Maguire, R. Morgan and R. Reiner (eds) *The Oxford Handbook of Criminology*. Oxford: Oxford University Press.

Gillis, J. R. (1975) 'The Evolution of Juvenile Delinquency in England 1890–1914', *Past and Present*, 67: 96–126.

Goldson, B. (1997) 'Children in trouble: State Responses to Juvenile Crime', in P. Scraton (ed.) *'Childhood' in 'Crisis'?* London: UCL Press.

Goldson, B. (1999) 'Youth (In)Justice: Contemporary Developments in Policy and Practice', in B. Goldson (ed.) *Youth Justice: Contemporary Policy and Practice*. Aldershot: Ashgate.

Goldson, B. (2004) 'Victims or Threats? Children, Care and Control', in J. Fink (ed.) *Care: Personal Lives and Social Policy*. Bristol: The Policy Press in association with The Open University.

Harris, J. (1993) *Private Lives, Public Spirit: Britain, 1870–1914*. London: Penguin.

Hendrick, H. (1990) *Images of Youth. Age, Class and the Making of the Male Youth Problem, 1880–1920*. Oxford: Clarendon Press.

Hendrick, H. (1994) *Child Welfare: England 1872–1989*. London: Routledge.

Hendrick, H. (1997) 'Constructions and Reconstructions of British Childhood: an Interpretative Survey, 1800 to the Present', in A. James and A. Prout (eds) *Constructing and Reconstructing Childhood*. (2nd edn) Basingstoke: Falmer.

Hendrick, H. (2003) *Child Welfare: Historical Dimensions, Contemporary Debate*. Bristol: The Policy Press.

Jenks, C. (1996) *Childhood*. London: Routledge.

King, P. (1998) 'The Rise of Juvenile Delinquency in England 1780–1840: Changing Patterns of Perception and Prosecution', *Past and Present*, 160: 116–66.

Marwick, A. (1990) *British Society since 1945*. London: Penguin.

May, M. (1973) 'Innocence and Experience: the Evolution of the Concept of Juvenile Delinquency in the Mid Nineteenth-Century', *Victorian Studies*, 17(1): 7–29.

Muncie, J. (2004) *Youth and Crime*. (2nd edn) London: Sage.

Muncie, J. and Hughes, G. (2002) 'Modes of Youth Governance: Political Rationalities, Criminalization and Resistance', in J. Muncie, G. Hughes and E. McLaughlin (eds) *Youth Justice: Critical Readings*, London: Sage.

Newburn, T. (1996) 'Back to the future? Youth Crime, Youth Justice and the Rediscovery of "Authoritarian Populism"', in J. Pilcher and S. Waggs (eds) *Thatcher's Children*. London: Falmer.

Newman, J. (2001) *Modernising Governance*. London: Sage.

Osgerby, B. (1998) *Youth in Britain since 1945*. Oxford: Blackwell.

Pearson, G. (1983) *Hooligan: A History of Respectable Fears*. London: Macmillan.

Pearson, G. (1994) 'Youth, crime and society', in M. Magure, R. Morgan and R. Reiner (eds) *The Oxford Handbook of Criminology*. Oxford: Oxford University Press.

Pugh, M. (1999) *State and Society, 1870–1997*. London: Arnold.

Radzinowicz, L. and Hood, A. (1986) *A History of English Criminal Law*, Vol. 5. London: Stevens and Sons.

Rose, N. (1985) *The Psychological Complex: Psychology, Politics and Society in England, 1869–1939*. London: RKP.

Rose, N. (1990) *Governing the Soul: The Shaping of the Private Self*. London: Routledge.

Royle, E. (1987) *Modern Britain: A Social History, 1750–1985*. London: Edward Arnold.

Shore, H. (1999) *Artful Dodgers: Youth and Crime in Early Nineteenth Century*. London: Boydell Press.

Shore, H. (2002) 'Reforming the Juvenile: Gender, Justice and the Child Criminal in Nineteenth Century England', in J. Muncie, G. Hughes and E. McLaughlin (eds) *Youth Justice: Critical Readings*. London: Sage.

Springhall, J. (1986) *Coming of Age: Adolescence in Britain 1860–1960*. London: Gill and Macmillan.

Thompson, E. P. (1963) *The Making of the English Working Class*. London: Gollancz.

Thorpe, D., Smith, D., Green, C. and Paley, J. (1980) *Out of Care*. London: George Allen and Unwin.

Wooldridge, A. (1995) *Measuring the Mind*. Cambridge: Cambridge University Press.

Social Class, Youth Crime and Justice

Rob White and Chris Cunneen

This chapter discusses the central place of social class in understanding the reasons for the marginalisation and criminalisation of substantial sections of the youth population in 'advanced' industrialised countries. Given the prevalence of neo-liberal ideologies, the huge changes taking place in basic class relationships due to globalisation, and the impoverishment of growing numbers of young people associated with these changes, it is important to understand the structural impacts of social inequality. A substantial part of this chapter, therefore, considers the making of a new layer of socially disadvantaged young people and the response of the state to the growth in what are seen as problematic populations. The youth justice system has a major role to play in these social processes.

Class, criminalisation and crime

Class has rarely been more relevant to social analysis and to any consideration of youth justice in particular. Class, as defined here, is basically a *social relation*. It is directly associated with economic, social and political power, and it is evident in how laws are framed, institutions are organised and societal resources are distributed (White and van der Velden, 1995). Class is also a lived experience. People act in the world in accordance with their relationships with other people around them and the communal resources available to them (see for examples, Chatterton and Hollands, 2003; McDonald, 1999; White and Wyn, 2004). Such resources are both material and cultural in nature. The class situation of young people is contingent, therefore, it very much depends upon family and community resources and it changes over time. Typically, young people's class situation is defined and distinguished on the basis of: the type and geographical location of their housing; the capacity of their parent/s to provide material support; the nature of their education – state school or private school; the age at which their formal education terminates; the nature of qualifications (if any) they receive on completion of education; their age at entry into the labour market and the nature of their employment (if any); and the type of leisure activities that they pursue (Jamrozik, 2001). Community resources are distributed via the market, the state, and informal community and family networks. For young people, what happens in each of these spheres has a huge bearing on their class situation. The phenomenon of unemployment is the biggest single factor in the transformation of young people, their families and their communities. In a wage-based economy, subsistence is largely contingent upon securing paid employment. If this is not available, then a number of social problems are often invoked, including and especially crime.

The context within which concern about juvenile offending is occurring, and is perceived to be a growing problem, is defined by the reconfiguration of economic and political relations, one consequence of which is the increasing polarisation of rich and poor, both between countries and within countries. Wealth and power are increasingly concentrated into fewer and fewer hands. Simultaneously, there is the impoverishment of many communities, neighbourhoods and families around the globe, and the escalation of unemployment (and underemployment) worldwide. For young people in particular, the collapse of the full-time labour market has been devastating. The decline in manufacturing industries, the use of new labour-saving technology, the movement and flight of capital away from inner-cities and regional centres, changing workplace organisation based on casualised labour, massive retrenchments by private and public sector employing bodies, and competition from older (especially female) workers, have all served to severely diminish the employment opportunities and conditions of young people in Western countries (White and Wyn, 2004). This is the context within which youth crime routinely occurs.

Why is it that the social profiles of 'young offenders' tend to look basically the same throughout youth justice systems in 'advanced' industrial countries? Predominantly young men with an over-representation of youth drawn from minority ethnic communities, low income, low educational achievement, poorly paid and/or casualised employment (if any) and strained familial relations, are the standard defining characteristics of children and young people most frequently found in juvenile detention centres and custodial institutions, whether this be in Australia (Cunneen and White, 2002), England and Wales (Goldson, 2002; Muncie, 2004), Canada (Schissel, 2002) or the USA (Krisberg, 2005). The processes whereby identifiable groups of young people are criminalised tend to follow a distinctive social pattern. In effect, the youth justice system has a series of filters which screen young people on the basis of both offence categories (serious/non-serious; first time/repeat offending) and social characteristics (gender, ethnic status, cultural background, family circumstances, education, employment, income). It is the most disadvantaged and structurally vulnerable young people who tend to receive the most attention from youth justice officials at all points of the system.

The propensity for some young people to engage in criminal activity is mirrored in, and an outcome of, the prevalent divisions and social inequalities characteristic of wider social and economic structural forms. It is also very much influenced by the processes of criminalisation in themselves. Entrenched economic adversity has been accompanied by state attempts to intervene in the lives of marginalised groups, usually by coercive measures, which is itself a reflection of a broader shift in the role of the state, from concerns with 'social welfare' to renewed emphasis on the 'repressive' (Goldson, 2005; White, 1996). The intrusiveness of the state is, in turn, biased toward some groups of young people more than others. This is indicated in the extreme over-representation of indigenous young people in the criminal justice system in Australia (Cunneen, 2001), New Zealand (Ministry of Justice and the Ministry of Social Development, 2002) and Canada (Department of Justice, 2004). It is demonstrated in the massive over-representation of African Americans in gaol, prison, or on probation or parole in the United States (Krisberg, 2005), and the ways in which black young people are disproportionately negatively treated in England and Wales (Goldson and Chigwada-Bailey, 1999). The history and dynamics of state intervention in particular communities vary considerably. There can be no doubt, however, that institutionalised racism, including that which is evident in the ways in which societal resources are allocated to different communities, has been, and will continue to be, extremely damaging to these groups.

The labelling of some communities and identifiable groups of young people as 'no hopers', an 'underclass', 'dangerous' and/or 'criminal', feeds back into the very problems of marginalisation and unemployment which lie at the heart of much youthful criminality (see Inniss and Feagin, 1989; Schissel, 2002). That is, the structural transformations in global political economy are refracted socially in ways that reinforce negative images of, and the repressive law enforcement practices directed at, the most vulnerable sections of the community. These processes serve to entrench further the unemployability, alienation and social outsider status of members of these communities. The core picture of neo-liberal ideology and practice includes permanent structural unemployment and underemployment, privatisation of state services and withdrawal of income support, a shrinking of capital's contribution to the tax base as well as reducing overall state revenue as a proportion of gross domestic product, and the internationalisation of the economy. The social impact of capitalist restructuring is manifest in the immiseration of large numbers of people and the polarisation of income. One aspect of this is the expansion of the truly disadvantaged, invariably youthful in appearance and social construction.

Many young people in 'modern' and 'advanced' industrialised societies are not simply marginal to the labour market, they are literally excluded from it – by virtue of family history, structural restrictions on education and job choices, geographical location, racial and ethnic segregation, stigmatised individual and community reputation, and so on. Put simply, economic restructuring on a global plane has sharpened the disjuncture between viable reserve labour and non-viable reserve labour, and it is the long-term unemployed who are slipping into the most marginalised situation as skills and knowledge become redundant. In addition to absolute unemployment, marginality is also constituted through permanent part-time work; through seasonal or irregular employment combined with unemployment; through minimum or sub-standard conditions at, near or even below the poverty line; through short-term contract employment; and through accelerated reductions in the social wage (for example, education and health) through the privatisation of services and the introduction of 'user-pays' services. This comprises a condition of existence for a substantial proportion of working-class young people. The class situation of young people is ultimately defined by the contours of unemployment and the general status of wage-labour in the economy (see for example, Senate Community Affairs References Committee, 2004).

The social ecology of poverty and unemployment

Analyses of the social ecology of poverty and unemployment are crucial to understanding the precise nature and extent of juvenile offending in any particular locale. While in many respects school exclusion and/or youth unemployment is the principal foundation underpinning offending (witness the social background of most juveniles in detention), it is within conditions of multiple and intersecting modes of social adversity that it has its most profound impact. In other words, examining the extent of inequality in specific community resources, of which unemployment is but one indicator, is essential in order to begin to account for youthful offending.

More particularly, to understand existing patterns of juvenile offending, we must appreciate the prime influence of local community conditions on youth behaviour and life experiences. The concentration of large numbers of unemployed young people in particular geographical locations increases the difficulties of gaining paid work for specific individuals (Hunter, 1998; Wilson, 1996). Such demographic concentration simultaneously fosters the shared identification and physical congregation of unemployed young people with each other. It thus can act both to preclude young people from attaining jobs and to make them more visible in the public domain as an 'outsider' group. In essence, the young poor are being locked into areas characterised by concentrations of poverty, scarce employment prospects and overall declining economic fortunes. Poverty is being entrenched at a spatial level and this has major ramifications in terms of local community infrastructure. Poor people often live in areas with deteriorating housing, they suffer more profoundly any cutbacks in public amenities, and they are more likely to experience declining quality in their health, educational and welfare services. In addition, the neighbourhoods become heavily stigmatised as 'crime prone', giving rise to a policy of containment and attracting the more repressive interventions from state agencies.

The most structurally vulnerable, the most dispossessed, the poorest and the most deprived people are funnelled into ghettoised neighbourhoods. As indicated in British research, unemployment, disability and sole parenthood are particularly prevalent in certain geographically defined residential locations. The composition of these areas and housing estates (for example, disproportionately high numbers of those suffering from mental illness) is such that 'nuisance neighbours' are more numerous than might otherwise be the case in more socially heterogeneous neighbourhoods (Burney, 2000). The recent history of public housing has, in essence, been witness to consolidating forms of residualisation. As demonstrated in British research, it is the most vulnerable of the vulnerable who are located within the least attractive accommodation (Goodchild and Cole, 2001). These kinds of trends have obvious implications for the employment and educational opportunities of young people, and how they perceive themselves and their future prospects.

The social status and crime rate of specific neighbourhoods impact upon the likelihood of young people becoming involved in offending behaviour independent of their specific socio-economic status (Reiss, 1986). For example, a young person from a low income background living in a high crime rate area is far more likely to engage in offending behaviour than the same person living in a low crime neighbourhood. Community context is, therefore, an integral part of why some unemployed young people have a greater propensity to commit crime, and to be criminalised, than other young people in a similar social position (see also Weatherburn and Lind, 2001). The level and extent of welfare provision and services at a local level also have a big impact on youth lifestyle and life chances, as indicated in Canadian research into 'street-present' young people (Hagan and McCarthy, 1997).

Blaming the victims: Individualisation, responsibilisation and coercion

Where large numbers of young working-class people congregate in particular areas, they constitute visible evidence of failing social and economic conditions within which poverty and inequality are rife, and the threats to social order posed by such structural failure. Such analyses are increasingly peripheralised within dominant discourses that tend to privilege individual agency, underpinned by notions of marginalised young people constituting a particular type of *moral category*. In this way, members of the so-called 'underclass' are perceived and portrayed as morally corrupt and as needing to be disciplined and reformed (see especially Herrnstein and Murray, 1994; Murray, 1990). The dominant political offensive in periods of high unemployment and low levels of collective labour mobilisation is to place even greater pressure on 'losers' to either 'cope' with their situation, or to face the coercive penalties of state intervention. One way in which the social cost of inequality and disadvantage is neutralised within state ideology, is through 'official' constructions that serve to reinforce the individualised nature of complex social problems. A related response is through coercive action, generally involving some form of criminalisation of the poor, and containment of social and economic difference via geographical segregation.

In effect, welfare and law enforcement policies serve to reinforce the distinction between 'the virtuous poor' (who are thought to exhibit positive attitudes toward self-improvement, healthy lifestyle and ready submission to state criteria for welfare assistance) and the 'vicious poor' (who are conceptualised as lacking industry and the work ethic, and who are seen as idle, wanderers and generally unrespectable). It is the 'deserving' poor who are the object of state welfare, while the 'undeserving' poor are subject to unrelenting intervention by the more repressive and coercive arms of the state, including criminal/youth justice systems. The new 'dangerous classes' are framed within discourses of contempt and fear – a social attitude that pervades the popular media and political elites.

The ideological representation of the young poor and deprived as an irresponsible, feral 'underclass' is built into the policy apparatus of the state in relation to both welfare and criminal justice. Unemployment is reduced to 'bad attitudes' and 'bad families'. The response, therefore, is to impose varying forms of mutual obligation on the poor – below poverty line benefits and inadequate services in return for work search obligations and imposition of training and employment programmes. For those who do not 'play the game', there is withdrawal of state support. For those who 'ignore the game' and make a living through alternative means, there is state coercion in the form of increased policing, harsher sentencing and greater use of imprisonment.

The dilemma facing the most marginalised has been expressed as follows:

> ... the hypercasualization of the labour market, and fall in opportunities and incentives for formal employment of less skilled workers, [have] led to an increase in informal activities of many kinds, including crime. It has also generated informal clubs of various sorts, based on the acquisition, consumption and exchange of semi-legal or illegally acquired goods, the sharing of information about informal activities, and the pooling of risks associated with illegality. In this way, poor and excluded people have sought to compensate themselves for the inequities of market-based outcomes, to 'tax' the better-off of the unjustified gains they have made, and to gain revenge on the various authorities that oppress them, as well as on the mainstream population who despise and exclude them. (Jordan, 1996: 218)

The response in many places to this phenomenon has been to introduce expanded law enforcement measures (including a wide range of legislation intended to deal with 'anti-social behaviour', including youth curfews) and more intensive and extensive regulation of welfare provision (including 'workfare'-type schemes and systematic penalisation of any breaches in welfare provision rules). The crux of state intervention is how best to manage the problem of disadvantaged groups (their presence and activities), rather than to eradicate disadvantage, poverty, inequality and consolidating modes of social and economic polarisation.

Social exclusion, public space and social identity

The systematic marginalisation of young people (and their communities) is marked by the disintegration of connections with mainstream social institutions (such as school and work), and a tenuous search for meaning in an uncaring and unforgiving world. The quality and quantity of youth crime are heavily overlaid by geographical location in that local economic resources, social networks and the spatial organisation of (un)employment shape the options and opportunities available to young people. Making ends meet, therefore, is contingent upon local contacts and local alternative economic structures.

For those without adequate economic resources to buy consumer goods, there are strong pressures to engage in alternative consumptive activity, and to compensate for the lack of consumer purchasing power by taking the possessions of others (Adamson, 1998; Miles, Cliff and Burr, 1998). Exclusion from the legitimate spheres of production (paid employment), and thus exclusion from other forms of legitimate identity formation (as workers), also force attention to alternative sites where social identity can be forged. In particular, if social identity and social belonging are made problematic due to institutional exclusion from paid work and commodity consumption, then the appeal of 'street culture' and the 'street scene' becomes more appealing.

The phenomenon of groups of young people 'hanging out' in the public domains of the streets, shopping centres and malls is one manifestation of the search for social connection. The precise character and composition of these groups vary enormously depending upon national and local context (see Duffy and Gillig, 2004). There is a diversity of youth subcultural forms, as well as youth gangs, although youth formations of these types have long been a source of consternation among sections of the adult population (Cohen, 1973; Pearson, 1983). The social status of young people in groups today has also been influenced by broader changes in the nature of public space itself. This is evident in research that has examined the rise of consumerism, the mass privatisation of public space and intensified regulation of this space (Davis, 1990). The use of public space by low income, marginal groups of young people has been accompanied by concerted efforts to make them invisible in the urban landscape. The response of state police and private security companies to their presence in the 'commercial' spaces of shopping centres, for example, has been to move them on, to exclude them from community life and participation (see White and Alder, 1994). Thus the very use of space itself is increasingly constructed around the notion of space as a commodity – those with the resources have access; those without are denied. This process of imposed social exclusion, and criminalisation, is not class neutral. It is primarily directed at the most marginalised sections of the youth population. Ultimately, what is at issue is the containment of the most dispossessed and structurally vulnerable sections of the working class (often compounded by processes of racialisation) living in the more disadvantaged areas of towns and cities (Collins et al., 2000).

Hollowed-out communities and social control

The concentration of poor people in poor areas carries with it a range of implications for social policy and state intervention. In the Australian context, for instance, the reality for many such neighbourhoods is that even when economic growth and employment fortunes are generally on the rise, these areas tend not to benefit. Poverty is thus spatially entrenched, and this entrenchment persists over time. In describing these kinds of social processes in the United States, Wilson makes the point that:

> The consequences of high neighborhood joblessness are more devastating than those of high neighborhood poverty. A neighborhood in which people are poor but employed is different from a neighborhood in which people are poor and jobless. Many of today's problems in the inner-city ghetto neighbourhoods – crime, family dissolution, welfare, low levels of social organization, and so on – are fundamentally a consequence of the disappearance of work. (1996: xiii)

As economic formations 'modernise' and global economic restructuring leads to diminishing employment opportunities (particularly in manufacturing industries) in many Western countries, whole communities are negatively affected. Significantly, however, when these jobs are lost, it is particular ethnic minority migrant groups who are most affected (Moss, 1993; see also Wilson, 1996). As the number of jobs in specific geographical areas decline, so too do amenities within the neighbourhood. In other words, economic transformations (involving the demise of manufacturing) and economic recession (characterised by high levels of unemployment) compound the physical deterioration of particular locales and hasten the social and economic homogenisation – characterised by impoverishment – of specific neighbourhoods. The flight of capital, including small businesses, from these areas, combined with the inability of residents to afford to either travel or live outside the area, cements such processes. The net result is ghettoisation, as middle-class people retreat to different suburbs, governments disinvest in public infrastructure (such as schools and hospitals) and neighbourhoods become marked with negative reputations and known as 'no go' zones.

For young people in these circumstances life is hard and legitimate opportunities for social advancement are seriously circumscribed. Doing it 'tough' can translate into the creation of alternative social and economic structures at the local level. For example, if no paid work is available in the formal waged sectors of the economy, the alternative economy may comprise the only viable option. Here we may see the emergence of what could be called 'lumpen capitalists' and 'outlaw proletarians': people who subsist through illegal market activity. Davis (1990) illustrated this in discussing how cocaine, once the preserve of the rich, was transformed into a 'fast food' drug known as 'crack cocaine', thereby opening up both extensive new markets, and entrepreneurial activity at street level. The emergence of 'gangs' is likewise linked to both economic necessity (if activity is centred around illegal means of accessing money and goods) and social imperative (methods of acquiring a sense of meaning, purpose and belonging).

New social structures at the local neighbourhood level, based upon networks of friends, families and peers, can serve to collectively reconstitute the 'social' at a time when the welfare state is in retreat. The 'Family' or the 'Gang' may represent a turn to subterranean sources of income, emotional support, and sharing and distribution of goods and services when formal market mechanisms and state supports are of negligible assistance. Furthermore, communal networks of this kind can consolidate around shared social markers, such as geography, ethnicity and local history. Coming from a certain area may thus be transposed as a badge of communal membership and internal territorial identity, to counter the external stigma pertaining to the area due to its low economic status and negative reputation. In other cases, identity can be constructed within the crucible of conflict. For instance, there may over time be continuous cultural and physical resistance to aggressive (racist) policing, and this may be manifest in the language of the streets, in its music and dance, in police–citizen confrontations including, at the extremes, uprisings and urban riots.

The response of the state to social disadvantage and alternative cultural formations can take several different forms typically comprising the criminalisation of specific 'types' of young people and activities via anti-social behaviour legislation, imposition of curfews, electronic monitoring and surveillance technologies, aggressive prosecution of family members and the application of sanctions on parents. Alternatively, the petty bourgeois layers of particular populations may be called upon to play a mollifying and pacifying role (see Davis, 1990; Headley, 1989). More specifically, there is an instrumental role for 'community leaders' (often with regard to ethnic minorities) in assisting with the implementation of containment strategies *vis-à-vis* the most marginalised sections of the young working class. In return for public kudos within the symbolic politics of 'community', and the possibility of investment and financial gain, 'community leaders' pledge to 'clean up the streets' as vociferously as the most repressive state agencies.

The intersection of class and 'race' is illuminated by Wilson's analysis of the over-representation of African Americans within the unemployed in the United States. A crucial factor is the location of many black Americans in segregated ghettos, a process exacerbated by specific government policies and programmes

(Wilson, 1996). Similar concentrations of ethnic minority groups in heavily disadvantaged areas is apparent in Sydney, Australia (Collins et al., 2000). So too, in Germany, segregation based upon class and 'race' is a major problem:

> Not surprisingly, when the traditional forms of social recognition through work and mainstream social institutions become increasingly inaccessible, new forms of recognition are sought. Ethnic encapsulation provides a problematic solution to social recognition because it frequently involves cultures of violence. (Heitmeyer, 2002: 106)

Resurgent interest in street gangs, youth and violence in North America (Gordon, 2000), Europe (Klein et al., 2001) and Australia (White, 2002) provides increasingly important insights into the consequences of such complex social phenomena.

From a class perspective, mention also has to be made of the particular and peculiar role of local elites and civic/community 'leaders' in the regulation of specific populations. As described earlier, such people may be recruited or implicated in 'community' attempts to 'clamp down' on undesirable behaviour. This specific political role of local elites, however, is bolstered by the general vulnerabilities experienced by local small businesses that lend support particularly on matters of law and order:

> ... their deep and pervasive perception – supported somewhat by practical experience – is that their businesses, personal property, and physical integrity are front-line targets for street crime (e.g., armed robbery, breaking and entering, shoplifting, mugging, etc.). For them, the visibility of working-class street culture, particularly that of various 'underclass' strata, is a source of anxiety for their own persons, their property, their customers, and trade. (White and van der Velden, 1995: 69)

This anxiety translates into perpetual 'moral panics' over 'street-present' working-class young people in particular. Congregations of young people, especially if they are not spending money as consumers, may constitute both symbolic and material barriers to commerce; conceptualised as representing disorder and decline. Young people often congregate and 'hang out' in and around *commercial spaces* and their very visibility, perceived lack of financial power, and behaviour (hanging around in groups, making noise) can render them an unwelcome presence – regardless of whether or not they actually transgress the law or actively engage in offensive activity (White and Alder, 1994).

Conclusion

The principal aim of this chapter has been to briefly survey changes in the class situation of young people (especially in relation to the most marginalised sections of the working class), and the responses of the state to the existence and activities of the disadvantaged (primarily through mobilisation of the forces of law and order). Fundamentally, the dearth of paid employment in 'advanced' industrial economies is the key reason for heightened social dislocation and disorganisation. When accompanied by neo-liberal policies that place great emphasis on moral agency and individual responsibility within a material context defined by the retreat of state welfare support, this becomes a recipe for compounded structural disadvantage.

The consequence of class inequality and transformations in the class structure that deepen this inequality, is a sharpening of social tension and antagonism. A big issue for young people is that they are increasingly made to feel as if they are 'outsiders'. This is confirmed daily in the form of exclusionary policies, and coercive security and policing measures which are designed precisely to remove them from the public domain. For young people, this is often seen as unfair and unwarranted. It can certainly breed resentment and various forms of social resistance (see for example, Hayward, 2002; White and Wyn, 2004).

In responding to youth crime and the images of youth deviance, many countries employ a combination of coercive measures (such as youth curfews, aggressive street policing, anti-gang interventions) and developmental measures (such as sports programmes, parent classes, educational retention programmes). While the specific approach to youth justice varies considerably from jurisdiction to jurisdiction (see Muncie, 2002; Muncie and Goldson, 2006), a common element is the essential construction of the problem and those young people who are held to be responsible. Most justice systems deal predominantly with offenders from working-class backgrounds (including indigenous and ethnic minority people), and thereby reflect the class biases in definitions of social harm and crime, as well as basing responses on these biases. In so doing, they reinforce the ideological role of law and order discourse in forging a conservative cross-class consensus about the nature of social problems. The reinforcement of this discourse also unwittingly enhances the legitimacy of coercive state intervention in the lives of working-class young people, even if under the rationale of 'repairing harm' as in the case of restorative justice. At a social-structural level, such processes confirm the role of 'crime' as the central problem (rather than poverty, unemployment, racism), neglecting or avoiding entirely the roles of class division and social inequality.

References

Adamson, C. (1998) 'Tribute, Turf, Honor and the American Street Gang: Patterns of Continuity and Change since 1920', *Theoretical Criminology*, 2(1): 57–84.

Burney, E. (2000) 'Ruling Out Trouble: Anti-Social Behaviour and Housing Management', *The Journal of Forensic Psychiatry*, 11(2): 268–73.

Chatterton, P. and Hollands, R. (2003) *Urban Nightscapes: Youth Cultures, Pleasure Spaces and Corporate Power*. London: Routledge.

Cohen, S. (1973) *Folk Devils and Moral Panics*. London: Paladin.

Collins, J., Noble, G., Poynting, S. and Tabar, P. (2000) *Kebabs, Kids, Cops and Crime: Youth, Ethnicity and Crime*. Sydney: Pluto Press.

Cunneen, C. (2001) *Conflict, Politics and Crime: Aboriginal Communities and the Police*. Sydney: Allen and Unwin.

Cunneen, C. and White, R. (2002) *Juvenile Justice: Youth and Crime in Australia*. Melbourne: Oxford University Press.

Davis, M. (1990) *City of Quartz: Excavating the Future in Los Angeles*. London: Vintage.

Department of Justice, Canada (2004) 'A One-Day Snapshot of Aboriginal Youth in Custody Across Canada: Phase II' at: http://canada.justice.gc.ca./en/ps/rs/rep/snap2/3html#_Toc599941402 – 7 accessed March 2005.

Duffy, M. and Gillig, S. (eds) (2004) *Teen Gangs: A Global View*. Westport, Connecticut: Greenwood Press.

Goldson, B. (2002) 'New Punitiveness: the Politics of Child Incarceration', in J. Muncie, G. Hughes and E. McLaughlin (eds) *Youth Justice: Critical Readings*. London: Sage.

Goldson, B. (2005) 'Taking Liberties: Policy and the Punitive Turn', in H. Hendrick (ed.) *Child Welfare and Social Policy*. Bristol: Policy Press.

Goldson, B. and Chigwada-Bailey, R. (1999) '(What) Justice for Black Children and Young People?', in B. Goldson (ed.) *Youth Justice: Contemporary Policy and Practice*. Aldershot: Ashgate.

Goodchild, B. and Cole, I. (2001) 'Social Balance and Mixed Neighbourhoods in Britain since 1979: a Review of Discourse and Practice in Social Housing', *Environment and Planning D: Society and Space*, 19: 103–21.

Gordon, R. (2000) 'Criminal Business Organizations, Street Gangs and "Wanna-Be" Groups: a Vancouver perspective', *Canadian Journal of Criminology*, January: 39–60.

Hagan, J. and McCarthy, B. (1997) *Mean Streets: Youth Crime and Homelessness*. Cambridge: Cambridge University Press.

Hayward, K. (2002) 'The Vilification and Pleasures of Youthful Transgression', in J. Muncie, G. Hughes and E. McLaughlin (eds) *Youth Justice: Critical Readings*. London: Sage.

Headley, B. (1989) 'Killings That Became "Tragedy": a Different View of What Happened in Atlanta, Georgia', *Social Justice*, 16(4): 55–74.

Heitmeyer, W. (2002) 'Have Cities Ceased to Function as "Integration Machines" for Young People?', in M. Tienda and W. J. Wilson (eds) *Youth in Cities: A Cross-National Perspective*. Cambridge: Cambridge University Press.

Herrnstein, R. and Murray, C. (1994) *The Bell Curve*. New York: Basic Books.

Hunter, B. (1998) 'Addressing Youth Unemployment: Re-Examining Social and Locational Disadvantage within Australian cities', *Urban Policy and Research*, 16(1): 47–58.

Inniss, L. and Feagin, J. (1989) 'The Black "Underclass" Ideology in Race Relations Analysis', *Social Justice*, 16(4): 13–34.

Jamrozik, A. (2001) *Social Policy in the Post-Welfare State: Australians on the Threshold of the 21st Century*. Frenchs Forest, NSW: Pearson Education Australia.

Jordan, B. (1996) *A Theory of Poverty and Social Exclusion*. Cambridge: Polity Press.

Klein, M., Kerner, H-J., Maxson, C. and Weitekamp, E. (2001) *The Eurogang Paradox: Street Gangs and Youth Groups in the U.S. and Europe*. Dordrecht: Kluwer Academic Publishers.

Krisberg, B. (2005) *Juvenile Justice: Redeeming Our Children*. Thousand Oaks, CA: Sage.

McDonald, K. (1999) *Struggles for Subjectivity: Identity, Action and Youth Experience*. Cambridge: Cambridge University Press.

Miles, S., Cliff, D. and Burr, V. (1998) '"Fitting in and Sticking Out": Consumption, Consumer Meanings and the Construction of Young People's Identities', *Journal of Youth Studies*, 1(1): 81–96.

Ministry of Justice and the Ministry of Social Development (2002) 'Te Haonga Youth Offending Strategy: Preventing and Reducing Offending and Re-Offending by Children and Young People' at http://www.justice.govt.nz/pubs/reports/2002/youth-offending-strategy/youth-strategy/part-2.html#6 – accessed 7 March 2005.

Moss, I. (1993) *State of the Nation: A Report on People of Non-English-Speaking Backgrounds* (Human Rights and Equal Opportunity Commission). Canberra: Australian Government Publishing Service.

Muncie, J. (2002) 'Policy Transfers and What Works: Some Reflections on Comparative Youth Justice', *Youth Justice*, 1(3): 27–35.

Muncie, J. (2004) *Youth and Crime*. (2nd edn) London: Sage.

Muncie, J. and Goldson, B. (eds) (2006) *Comparative Youth Justice*. London: Sage.

Murray, C. (1990) *The Emerging Underclass*, London: Institute of Economic Affairs.

Pearson, G. (1983) *Hooligan: A History of Respectable Fears*. London: Macmillan Education.

Reiss, A. (1986) 'Why Are Communities Important in Understanding Crime?', in A. Reiss and M. Tonry (eds) *Communities and Crime*. Chicago: University of Chicago Press.

Schissel, B. (2002) 'Youth Crime, Youth Justice, and the Politics of Marginalization', in B. Schissel and C. Brooks (eds) *Marginality and Condemnation: An Introduction to Critical Criminology*. Halifax: Fernwood Publishing.

Senate Community Affairs References Committee (2004) *A Hand Up Not a Hand Out: Renewing the Fight Against Poverty*, Report on poverty and financial hardship. Canberra: Senate Printing Unit, Parliament House.

Weatherburn, D. and Lind, B. (2001) *Delinquent-Prone Communities*. Cambridge: Cambridge University Press.

White, R. (1996) 'The Poverty of the Welfare State: Managing an Underclass', in P. James (ed.) *The State in Question: Transformations of the Australian State*. Sydney: Allen and Unwin.

White, R. (2002) 'Understanding Youth Gangs', *Trends and Issues in Criminal Justice*, No. 237. Canberra: Australian Institute of Criminology.

White, R. and Alder, C. (eds) (1994) *The Police and Young People in Australia*. Melbourne: Cambridge University Press.

White, R. and van der Velden, J. (1995) 'Class and Criminality', *Social Justice*, 22(1): 51–74.

White, R. and Wyn, R. (2004) *Youth and Society: Exploring the Social Dynamics of Youth Experience*. Melbourne: Oxford University Press.

Wilson, W. J. (1996) *When Work Disappears*. New York: Knopf.

'Race', Youth Crime and Justice

Colin Webster

Introduction

Perhaps more than any other study, Stuart Hall et al.'s (1978) seminal *Policing the Crisis* captured the mood and the means by which a post-colonial Britain criminalised many of its young black citizens. Reflecting back on the visceral street conflict between the new generation of British black youth and the police during the late 1970s and 1980s, Hall later stated his belief that at the time this new generation would have 'committed a kind of collective social suicide' without the birth of a new black British identity, rooted in defiance of racism and marginality at school, in employment and in the ways black young people were policed (Phillips and Phillips, 1998). Hall's imagery evokes the felt isolation and precariousness of being black in British society during the 1970s and 1980s. This chapter outlines the cumulative, intergenerational crises faced by black and Asian young people as they attempt to form new identities and adapt to economic and social change from the 1970s to the present. Changes in schooling and youth training, in eligibility and entitlement to welfare benefits, in youth labour markets and drug markets, and changes to their neighbourhoods, marginalised and polarised their experiences. Minority ethnic young people's offending and their victimisation, their complaints about, and conflict with, the police, and their treatment by the youth justice system cannot be understood outside the context of these changes. Minority ethnic young people's transitions to adulthood often take place in inner city neighbourhoods and peripheral estates characterised by de-industrialisation, destabilisation, deprivation and high levels of crime and violence. These social experiences are captured here in historical context, enumerated by survey evidence, and are pursued in terms of theoretical implications for analysing 'race', youth crime and justice.

To talk about 'race' and ethnicity in the same breath as talking about crime invites a number of pitfalls, including the belief that such a thing as 'black or Asian crime' exists. To be sure, some white, black and Asian young people commit crime, possibly for very similar reasons. What is at issue here is whether they are treated differently because of their supposed racial background or ethnicity. Feilzer and Hood (2004: 30) warn that: 'the research carried out on this issue over several years has failed to reveal any findings that conclusively prove whether these different outcomes for minority ethnic people have been due to discrimination – either direct or indirect – or the result of other factors.' After all, ethnicity is just one of a complex of socially constructed experiences, which may or may not take on significance in particular circumstances or situations. Some visible minority ethnic groups of young people are decidedly under-represented in self-reported crime and in the youth justice system compared to their numbers in the population.

This chapter first argues that black and Asian young people's experiences of the police and youth justice system are explained by changes in their social conditions through the interaction of social class, place and 'race'. Second, a consistent – but unexplained – finding of statistical studies of the influence of 'race' on crime rates, policing and youth justice is that different or discriminatory outcomes vary by area. This geography of 'race', crime, policing and youth justice has often remained unexplained because studies have lacked local contextual data, whether of a particular neighbourhood, court, or a local history of police racism. Third, sources of racism and racial discrimination are found in changing social relations between subordinate working-class majority and minority ethnic groups, in relations between social control professionals and their minority ethnic clients, as well as between employers and employees. In consequence, the ways in which white ethnicity is formed becomes important to understanding discrimination. Fourth, not only is it the case that 'race' and ethnicity on their own do not tell the whole story, their meaning changes. Although social class, gender, 'race' and ethnicity continue to have salience in reproducing disadvantage and identity, it is recognised that young people in particular, subjectively experience these social relationships differently from the past. As class and ethnic identities become both differentiated *and* polarised, they give way to more individualised and heterogeneous experiences of disadvantage. As the disorders in Bradford, Burnley and Oldham in 2001 demonstrate, for some Asian young people, the inverse may be true, as their collective sense of identity is strengthened by an embattled and growing sense of threat and hostility (Webster, 2003). By the same token, ways of talking about and acting on class, ethnic identity and disadvantage have become more 'coded' – racial connotation has become less explicit in public discourse and social practices. Offending is talked about by reference to group and individual deficits and 'risks' rather than by reference to 'race' and class, although the former may simply substitute for the latter (see Feeley and Simon, 1994).

History: Change and continuity in the lives of black and Asian young people

There are few institutions that can be said to have had such a consistently significant impact on the lives of Britain's minority ethnic population than the criminal justice process, and the police in particular (Kalra, 2003). However, to construct police–black relations through a sole focus on crime obscures wider experiences of black young people. Policing, as we shall see, plays a key role in 'recruiting' black and Asian young people to the youth justice system. It also racialises different groups through marking out, creating and maintaining distinct bounded ethnicities. Beginning with policing, this section sketches some of the changes that occurred in the lives of minority ethnic young people resulting from the sustained economic depressions of the post-1973 years. If the 1970s were the years of crisis, the 1980s brought the 'solutions' to this crisis – a series of cumulatively repressive measures against working-class young people in general and black young people in particular.

Whitfield (2004) has noted how deterioration in relations between the police and London's Caribbean community went unnoticed during the crucial early years of immigration. Although the new generation inherited their parents' experience of racial exclusion and isolation, they faced very different conditions and problems (Phillips and Phillips, 1998). In the early to mid 1970s black youth unemployment began to rise, but it was their experience of school that marked the new generation. ESN ('educationally subnormal') Special Schools and Approved Schools contained disproportionate numbers of black children because of the influence of teachers' prejudice and low expectations of black children's abilities and performance (Cashmore and Troyna, 1982; Coard, 1971). Beginning in 1975 the police made a series of highly public statements claiming disproportionate black criminality. Collusion between the police and the media served to produce and reproduce this 'story' over the next decade. Thus in 1983 the *Sun* ran the headline BLACK CRIME SHOCK and carried the statement: 'Blacks carried out twice as many muggings as whites in London last year' (cited in Lea and Young, 1993: 105). Some authors argued that in effect, the police consciously conspired to criminalise young black people – exaggerate and construct them as a serious threat to law and order – so as to enhance their own powers and resources as the 'thin blue line' holding back a tide of alleged black criminality (Bridges, 1983; Cashmore and McLaughlin, 1991; Gilroy, 1987; Gutzmore, 1983). Others (Lea and Young, 1993) wrote of an interaction effect between disproportionate black crime, disadvantage and police harassment. Whatever the truth of these claims, the police routinely used their discretionary powers to stop and search, harass and criminalise large numbers of young black men thought to be 'suspicious'.

The means by which some black youth attempted to 'redress' police powers are now well known (Benyon and Solomos, 1987; Gilroy, 1987; Hall et al., 1978; Rowe, 1998; Solomos, 2003). The 'riots' in Bristol (St Pauls), London (Brixton and Southall), Liverpool (Toxteth), Manchester (Moss Side) and Birmingham (Handsworth) in 1980 and 1981 were mostly triggered by the local arrest and police detention of young black men. But Cashmore and Troyna (1982) argued that alleged harassment, although heightening black collective identity and hostility to the police, hid what was of pivotal importance in the production of crisis – the funnelling of black youth into unemployment or unproductive and uncreative work at the bottom of the labour market (Hall et al., 1978). In 1982, 60 per cent of 16–20-year-old black young people available for work were without a job (Muncie, 2004). The 1970s' and 1980s' generation of black young people – the parents and grandparents of today's children – were marginalised by age, school experience, space, place, and employment. It is hardly surprising the police marginalised them too. The 1970s and 1980s were marked by repression. Black youth constituted over a third of detention centre and borstal populations in the south of England. The numbers of 14-16-year-old males – whites and black – sent to custody more than doubled between 1971 and 1981. Periods of intense politicisation of youth crime – 1970, 1979–83 and 1992–98 – were punitive and intensely racialised (Goodey, 2001; Pitts, 2001; Solomos, 2003; Webster, 1997). It is difficult not to agree with Keith's (1993: 232) conclusion that: 'in the 1980s the variables of "race", crime and public order did not just interact, they came in part to define each other.'

The 1990s followed a similar pattern but took a different turn. Again, collusion between the police and the media constructed 'Asian' ethnicity in the language of criminality, alleging the widespread involvement of Asian young men in street rebellion, gang violence, crime and drugs (Goodey, 2001; Webster, 1997). Parlous deprivation, high levels of imposed residential segregation, school failure, increasing conflict with the police and high levels of local racism all conspired to racialise and criminalise young British Pakistanis and Bangladeshis (Goodey, 2001; The Bradford Congress, 1996; Webster, 1996; 2003; 2004). This complex of factors eventually resulted in widespread disorders in Bradford in 1995 and in Bradford, Burnley and Oldham in 2001. These events marked the abrupt end of the 'multicultural settlement' that had governed race relations in the 1980s and 1990s (Kalra, 2003; Webster, 2003).

Overview of survey evidence about 'race', youth crime and justice

Survey evidence about ethnic minorities in relation to policing and in the criminal justice system has been comprehensively summarised elsewhere (Bowling and Phillips, 2002). This section will therefore limit itself to the main outline of findings presented by Bowling and Phillips, a focus on young people and youth justice, bring some of the arguments and findings up to date, and introduce some critical observations about these studies.

Over-representation

Dozens of studies over 25 years have shown that black people, both men and women, have been over-represented at every stage in the criminal justice process and whites have been under-represented relative to their numbers in the population. However, Asian people were not over-represented. These ethnic differences have not significantly changed, and are as marked among young people as they are among the adult population (Bowling and Phillips, 2002; Home Office, 2004). In 2001, black people aged 10–17 made up 3 per cent of the population in England and Wales, but accounted for 9 per cent of 14–17-year-olds arrested, 6 per cent cautioned and 15 per cent of young people aged 15–17 serving a custodial sentence. On the other hand, Asian young people aged 10–17 were substantially under-represented in arrests, cautions and youth custody (Feilzer and Hood, 2004). Nationally, black and mixed parentage young people are very substantially over-represented in decisions to remand them in custody and to receive detention and training orders compared to other groups (Feilzer and Hood, 2004). More locally focused studies of youth justice have found that black young men and women were very considerably over-represented, and white and Asian young men and women were under-represented relative to their numbers in the relevant local population, although the extent that this was the case varied by area (Feilzer and Hood, 2004).

Perceptions of fairness and equality

Black people in particular have displayed a lack of trust and confidence in the police and the criminal justice system for some considerable period of time. However, the 2002/3 British Crime Survey found that, except in relation to the police, Asian and especially black people gave significantly higher ratings of confidence in different aspects of the effectiveness of the criminal justice system than whites, including the youth courts, although those of mixed origin showed the lowest police rating of all groups (Home Office, 2004; Nicholas and Walker, 2004). Hood et al.'s (2003) qualitative study of ethnic minority perceptions of fairness and equality of treatment in the criminal courts (even after they received custodial sentences) lends support to the thesis that black people's experiences of treatment in the courts have improved. However, this somewhat encouraging picture is contradicted by evidence from the Home Office *Citizenship Survey* which shows that black respondents, especially younger people, rated their trust in the police and the courts less favourably than all other ethnic groups, and were more likely than white people to expect discriminatory treatment. Overall, the police and prisons continue to be agencies distrusted and believed to be unfair among black, especially young black, people (Home Office, 2004).

Racist policing?

Studies of the policing of minority ethnic young people, and their processing through the youth justice system, have found that Asian young people's experiences have been different to those of black young people, being similar to, or more favourable than whites at each stage of the police and youth justice processes, from stop and search through to court decisions (Webster, 2004). Whether different treatment of Asians is as significant as it is for African-Caribbeans, will become clearer as studies emerge that disaggregate 'Asians', particularly Pakistanis and Bangladeshis living in poor neighbourhoods (see Clancy and Hough, 2001). However, studies appear to show that some police officers hold hostile, stereotypical and prejudiced attitudes towards Asian and black young people. As a consequence they are more likely to be selected and stopped on 'speculative' grounds for some types of offences, especially robbery and drug offences, than white young people. Recent evidence continues to show that black young people are disproportionately stopped and searched on foot and in a car (Clancy and Hough, 2001; FitzGerald et al., 2002). Black people are six times as likely, and Asian people are twice as likely, to be stopped and searched than white people. The search rate for black and Asian people under the Terrorism Act 2000 was four and five times that for white people (Dodd and Travis (2005) in *The Guardian*). Indeed, throughout the 1990s police discretionary and legal powers to stop children and young people in the street were significantly extended, and predictably, these powers were much more likely to be used against Asians and African-Caribbeans (Muncie, 2004).

Drawing on earlier Institute of Race Relations Reports (1979, 1987), Bowling and Phillips amply illustrate the sources of black–police hostility in more intensive surveillance, higher rates of stops and arrests and harassment:

> ... pervasive, ongoing targeting of black areas involving stopping vehicles 'often on a flimsy pretext', persistent stop and search on the streets, commonplace rude and hostile questioning accompanied by racial abuse, arbitrary arrest, violence on arrest, the arrest of witnesses and bystanders, punitive and indiscriminate attacks, victimisation on reporting crime, acting on false information, forced entry and violence, provocative and unnecessary armed raids, and repeated harassment and trawling for suspects. (2002: 129)

Some studies have challenged this view of pervasive police racism on grounds that there is a disjuncture between the attitudes and behaviour of police officers – between their private attitudes and their professional behaviour – noting that the prevalence of racism and stereotyping has little impact in terms of the way in which officers go about their duties (Waddington, 1999). Alternatively, because black and Asian young people feel that they are subject to excessive police surveillance, it might be – as claimed by Macpherson (1999) – that the police organisation is 'institutionally racist' and police officers are unwittingly racist (see the critical discussion in Marlow and Loveday, 2000; Lea, 2000; Rowe, 2004). Waddington et al.'s (2004) rare observation study argues that the 'available population' – those who use public space on a regular basis – does not have the same demographic or ethnic characteristics as the resident population against whom disproportionate stops are usually compared. Taking this into account they conclude that compared to the 'available population', those stopped and searched are not disproportionately drawn from minority groups. In general, the disproportionality in stop and search experiences by young men of *all* racial and ethnic groups may simply attest to their greater availability for being stopped and searched, rather than any particular selectivity on the part of the police. Factors such as the visibility of police targets, elderly vehicles, available population at different times of day and night and variation between police force areas, were more important factors in police decisions to stop and search than ethnicity *per se* (see Hallsworth and Maguire, 2004). Whether the findings of this important study are replicated in areas other than the ones they studied is open to question.

Turning to wider police processes, Bowling and Phillips' (2002) summary of the evidence concludes that when black young people come into contact with the police whether as victims or witnesses, when they report crime, seek information, or as suspects, their position in terms of the treatment they receive and their perceptions and experiences of the police tends to be worse than comparable Asian and white young people. Blacks and Asians are more likely to seek legal advice and less likely to admit the offence for which they have been arrested compared to whites. There is some evidence of a more punitive police response towards black and Asian juveniles for certain offences including public order and violence against the person offences. Blacks and Asians are less likely to be cautioned than whites, and both black and Asian suspects are more likely to be refused bail compared with white suspects. It follows that black suspects are significantly more likely to be remanded – held at the police station and/or custodial institution prior to court – than either white or Asian suspects.

Writers have for some time argued that working-class young people – white, Asian and black – are treated as 'police property', as Muncie (2004: 232) notes, 'histories of police–youth relations are replete with examples of the proactive policing of young people's use of public space'. Reiner (1985: 132) was able to conclude that 'the disproportionate black arrest rate is the product of black deprivation, police stereotyping and the process by which each of these factors amplifies the other'. It is unlikely that we have entered a more benign 'post-Macpherson' policing era. A report by the Commission for Racial Equality (2005) suggested that lessons had still not been learnt and had not percolated down the police ranks (also see Marlow and Loveday, 2000). What *is* certain is that police processes are important triggers that can 'recruit' and propel young people into the youth justice system.

Disproportionality in the youth justice system: Difference or discrimination?

Studies of minority ethnic young people in the youth justice system are relatively scarce and/or are so dated that social and demographic change may have invalidated their findings. Mhlanga's (1997) was the first systematic study of youth justice prosecution and court decisions among 10–17-year-old Asian, black and white children, living in the London Borough of Brent between 1982 and 1987. The study found that there were racial differences in the treatment of young offenders that could not be explained by a myriad of other factors, both social and legal, such as significant racial differences in the nature of, and involvement in criminality. For example, the police seemed more ready to presume guilt and prosecute black young people on insufficient evidence and were more lenient towards white and Asian young people, with whom the police were more likely to have taken no further action or to have cautioned. Black young people were more likely to receive a custodial sentence than their Asian and white counterparts.

Hood's (1992) study of Crown Courts in the West Midlands included people under the age of 21, but age did not affect a disproportionate use of custody against black defendants. After taking into account all legitimate factors, Hood concluded that black defendants had a 5 per cent greater probability of being sentenced to custody than their white counterparts. Regardless of whether they pleaded guilty or not guilty, black and Asian defendants received longer sentences than whites. Hood concluded that 7 per cent of the over-representation of black males in prison was the result of the use of custody in ways which could not be explained by legitimate factors. Crucially, the proportions of ethnic minorities sentenced to custody at the different Crown Courts studied were even larger. The proportion of blacks sentenced to custody was 17 per cent higher than for whites at the Dudley courts, but racial differences at Birmingham Crown Court disappeared when legal and social factors were taken into account. This implies that judges at Dudley were influenced by 'race' when sentencing, with easily foreseen consequences of rises in the black prison rate.

Feilzer and Hood's (2004) recent study of minority ethnic young people in the youth justice system examined 17,054 cases of 12–17-year-old white, Asian, black and mixed-parentage young people, male and female, in eight Youth Offending Team areas in England. This, the first study to systematically explore decisions relating to minority ethnic groups at all the various stages of the youth justice process, used multivariate analysis to examine decisions by the police, the Crown Prosecution Service and the courts. The study collected information on a wide range of relevant legal and social variables such as education, school exclusion, employment status, family structure and other 'risk factors', which might singularly or together influence decision-making. It was found that among those prosecuted, convicted and sentenced, a higher proportion of black and mixed-parentage males had been remanded in secure conditions and a higher proportion had been committed for sentence at the Crown Court. Although this would predict a higher likelihood of a custodial sentence, no evidence was found that either black or mixed-parentage males were more likely to receive a custodial sentence than white males, once the characteristics of their cases had been taken into account. However, youth court magistrates were more ready to commit marginal cases involving black young people to the Crown Court than they were white young people. An unexpected finding was that Asian young people were more likely to be sentenced to custody than expected from their case characteristics (but the proportions sentenced to custody were the same as whites). Asians and mixed-parentage – but not black – young males were more likely to be sentenced to a more restrictive community sentence than whites. Young females, including those of black ethnicity were treated more leniently than their male counterparts, and black females appear not to have been treated differently from their white counterparts. The study found overall, though, that there were at different stages of youth justice processes, different outcomes that were consistent with discriminatory treatment of Asian and black males, and especially mixed-parentage males and females, in respect of prosecution, remand, conviction, the use of more restrictive community penalties and longer custodial sentences. The key finding was that large differences or discrimina-tory treatment of minority ethnic young people were found between Youth Offending Team areas. This was tantamount to youth justice by 'race' and geog-raphy. The study raises important issues in respect of discriminatory treatment against mixed-parentage young people.

Youth crime, victimisation and ethnicity

Despite the disproportionate presence of some minority ethnic groups in the youth justice system, self-report studies suggest that there is little overall dif-ference between minority ethnic and white groups in offending rates (Feilzer and Hood, 2004; Graham and Bowling, 1995; Home Office, 2004), although Jefferson (1988) argues that we cannot know the *real* black (Asian or white) crime rate. Young people, particularly from minority ethnic groups, are dispro-portionately victimised compared to the general adult population. As a conse-quence, they experience a heightened fear of becoming a victim of crime while their victimisation is ignored or not taken seriously by the police and other adults. Young Asians, particularly Pakistanis and Bangladeshis, suffer greater risks of victimisation than any other group, particularly from repeated racist violence (FitzGerald and Hale, 1996; Kershaw et al., 2000; Muncie, 2004; Percy, 1998; Webster, 1995; 2003; 2004).

Young people's experience of crime is dominated by street crime and the majority of offenders and victims of street crime are typically aged between 14 and 19 (Hallsworth, 2005). Street crime or street robbery – often evoked by ele-ments in the mass media, as 'mugging' so as to racialise it – is the type of acquis-itive crime most often associated with young black men (see Bowling and Phillips, 2002; Burney, 1990; Webster, 2001). Across the UK, black young men account for a significantly higher proportion of offenders being supervised by Youth Offending Teams for robbery than would be expected from their repre-sentation in the general population. Although in more ethnically homogeneous areas the population of offenders is almost universally white, in ethnically mixed areas black young men are still represented in the population of offenders more than would be expected from their numbers in the local resident black population (FitzGerald and Hale, 2002; FitzGerald et al., 2002; Hallsworth, 2005; Smith, 2003). FitzGerald et al. (2002) found a correlation between high levels of unemployment and a concentration of youth poverty, and high recorded street crime rates in London boroughs. Hallsworth (2005) argues that the reason some areas have disproportionately higher levels of street robbery than others is because of new patterns of economic development in high crime areas that attract suitable victims to these areas.

Evidence about known offenders suggests that different ethnic groups are apparently over-represented in different crimes, including street robbery – whites mostly commit offences such as burglary and motoring offences. Some of these differences might be explained through the police selectively stopping and searching, arresting and prosecuting black young men for street robbery. Whether or not minority ethnic young people offend differently or for different or the same reasons as white young people, the cardinal sin is to assume that the ethnic or class profile of the offender population is representative of that ethnicity or class, rather than of the offender group and their particular circumstances, opportunities and constrained choices – in which class and ethnicity play a part.

Context, theory and implications: Criminalisation and racialisation of British black and Asian youth

For our purposes here 'criminalisation' refers to the process whereby some groups receive more attention from, and are more likely to come into contact with, the police and the criminal justice system by virtue of some imputed or ascribed characteristic of criminality. 'Racialisation' is taken to refer to those instances where social relations between people have been structured by attributing meaning to biological and/or cultural characteristics, as a result of which individuals may be assigned to a social group – a general category of persons – which is said to reproduce itself biologically and/or culturally (see Miles and Brown, 2003). This process defines and constructs different groups, usually through assigning negative attributes such as 'inferiority' or 'criminality'. When criminalistion and racialisation are conjoined, for example 'the couplet *Black youth* can be employed in racist discourse to signify *criminality*' (Keith, 1993: 234), then terms like 'crime' and 'riot' become racially loaded. This section traces the context and theory whereby 'race', youth and criminality become connected, with considerable implications for discussion of the youth justice system.

Context

Despite a large body of literature documenting changed modes of childhood–youth–adult transitions, it is often forgotten and can remain hidden, that during the economic restructuring of the 1980s and 1990s the social conditions of working-class young people substantially worsened. Incomes, benefit entitlements, job availability and security were reduced or withdrawn first from 16–17-year-olds, and later from 18–25-year-olds also. As a consequence, transitions have become increasingly extended, precarious and sometimes chaotic for working-class white, Asian and black young people (Banks et al., 1992; Barry, 2005; Fergusson, 2002; Fergusson et al., 2000; Furlong and Cartmel, 1997; Garrett, 2002; Hollands, 1990; Kalra et al., 2001; MacDonald, 1997; Mizen, 2004; Muncie, 2004; Osgerby, 1998; Percy-Smith and Weil, 2002; Pitts, 2001; Roberts, 1995; Webster et al., 2004).

Offender populations are disproportionately drawn from young people not engaged in education, employment or training (NEET), and from those who have lived in the care system (Bentley and Gurumurthy, 1999; Britton et al., 2002; Goldson, 2002; Graham, 1988; Graham and Bowling, 1995; Graham and Utting, 1996; Johnston et al., 2000; Pearce and Hillman, 1998; SEU, 1998). Estimates suggest that up to 20 per cent of 16- and 17-year-olds are NEET and at least 9 per cent of the NEET population appears to be from minority ethnic groups. Young people who are NEET are concentrated in deprived areas and African-Caribbean, Bangladeshi and Pakistani young people are especially at risk of NEET (Britton et al., 2002; Coles et al., 1998; SEU, 1999; Stone et al., 2000; Williamson, 1996). There is some correlation between early truancy and school exclusions, which disproportionately affect young African-Caribbean men and children in care (SEU, 1998), and later NEET (and offending) status. Often, studies have simply causally related truancy and school exclusions to offending without explaining why truancy occurs. Britton et al.'s (2002) qualitative study of white, black, Bangladeshi and Pakistani 16–17-year-olds' intermittent routes into NEET found that disaffection and boredom at school were linked to troubles and traumas outside of school, so that early school disaffection, truancy, troubled early and later lives and negative experiences of being in state 'care' were linked. For minority ethnic young people the disadvantages of 'care' interact with their experience of racism in 'care'.

Although the increased precariousness of youth transitions and disengagement from education, employment and training disproportionately affects some minority ethnic young people, for other groups this has not been the case. Growing polarisation between and within different minority ethnic groups complicates processes of social exclusion and disadvantage in respect of these groups. There is evidence of both upward and downward inter-generational and intra-generational educational and occupational mobility (Kalra, 2000; Mason, 2003; Pilkington, 2003). Although for most ethnic minority groups, the second and third generation have made significant educational progress (especially girls and young women), Caribbean, Pakistani and Bangladeshi boys have made least progress. When social class background is taken into account, Caribbean boys in particular, continue to do less well than their white counterparts. Pakistani and Bangladeshi young people are geographically concentrated and segregated in de-industrialised urban areas, where they disproportionately suffer joblessness and belong to the poorest ethnic groups in British society (Mason, 2003; Modood, 2003; Owen, 2003;

Pilkington, 2003; Webster, 2003). Here, vital class processes interpenetrate with ethnicity to compound enduring structural disadvantage.

Theoretical implications and conclusions

Understanding 'race', youth crime and justice cannot rely on surveys alone. Although important in providing 'statistical context', multivariate analysis cannot provide understanding of the 'community context' in which racism may or may not flourish. Surveys that attempt to measure racism are hampered by their inability to properly 'model' complex processes and contexts of decision-making that exist in the real world because '... social life consists not of events but experience, and thus the same happening can carry totally different meanings for people in different social contexts' (Pawson, 1989: 13; Pawson and Tilley, 1997). Qualitative research into 'race', crime and justice faces a different set of problems in the reluctance of teachers, police officers and court officials to reveal their attitudes or the underlying reasons they deploy in making decisions (see Hood et al., 2003). Neighbourhood-based ethnographic studies of minority ethnic youth transitions in Britain and the United States can offer insight, extend understanding and add considerable nuance to the picture painted thus far (Alexander, 2000; Anderson, 1990; Bourgois, 1995; Desai, 1999; Foster, 1999; Harrison, 1985; Hercules, 1999; Keith, 1993; Nightingale, 1993; Taylor, 1996; Wardak, 2000; Webster, 1996; 1997).

Among other things, these studies show how police and youth justice responses to youth crime, in effect, criminalise the poor, furthering their disadvantage (Hope, 2001; Pitts, 2001; Webster, 2003; 2004). Contrary to popular belief, offender populations living in de-industrialised neighbourhoods, strongly share the mainstream aspirations and values of the wider society. If anything, they over-identify with consumerist values around them. At the same time, these aspirations are difficult to realise because of racial and social segregation, and poverty. It is their 'normality' – whether they are involved in criminality or not – which is most striking. Rooted for their survival in local social networks, they associate with people like themselves and have few bridges or connections, formally or informally, to wider support in accessing educational opportunities, jobs or other resources. What many seem to share are negative experiences of schooling. In respect of social exclusion at school, Muslim, black and white working-class boys in particular can be particularly susceptible to peer-based antagonism and resistance to teachers and schooling (Archer, 2003; Ball et al., 2000; Gillborn and Youdell, 2000; Mac an Ghaill, 1988; O'Donnell and Sharpe, 2000; Sewell, 1997). A racialised 'exaggerated masculinity' grows by way of compensation against humiliation and anticipated school 'failure' – an expectation reinforced by teachers and school structures – the outcome of which is permanent school exclusion or self-exclusion, especially among black boys (Parsons et al., 2004). The principal source of this disaffection is the way in which school racism becomes coded and individualised by 'the new IQism' and 'the rationing of education in the A-to-C economy' (Gillborn and Youdell, 2000: 212).

As this review demonstrates, there are striking similarities of marginalisation across different domains of transition – from schooling, care, policing, youth justice to employment – for many white, black, Pakistani and Bangladeshi working-class young people growing up in Britain. Young black men in particular, disproportionately find themselves under the supervision of a continuum of social control agencies. For these groups, three decades of de-industrialisation and economic restructuring have worsened their social conditions, destabilised their families and neighbourhoods, subjected them to harassment and discrimination by the police, the youth justice, care and schooling systems, and offered them a precarious future at the bottom of a casualised youth labour market. The politicisation and racialisation of youth crime have lent legitimacy to the measures of social control that economic restructuring requires and also to the fact that the reproduction of racial divisions in society is a part of these linked processes (Keith, 1993; Pitts, 2001; Solomos, 2003; Wacquant, 2005). Unless issues of discrimination and reform in schooling, policing, youth justice and the casualised labour market are addressed, rather than concerns about individualised and ethnicised 'deficits', then the social and economic processes identified will continue to racialise and criminalise working-class black, Asian *and* white young men.

References

Alexander, C. (2000) *The Asian Gang: Ethnicity, Identity, Masculinity*. Oxford: Berg.

Anderson, E. (1990) *Streetwise: Race, Class and Change in an Urban Community*. Chicago: University of Chicago Press.

Anderson, E. (1999) *Code of the Street: Decency, Violence, and Moral Life of the Inner City*. New York: W.W. Norton.

Archer, L. (2003) *Race, Masculinity and Schooling: Muslim Boys and Education*. Maidenhead: Open University Press.

Attwood, C., Singh, G., Prime, D. and Creasey, R. (2003) *The 2001 Home Office Citizenship Survey*. Home Office Research Study No. 209. London: Home Office.

Ball, S.J., Maguire, M. and Macrae, S. (2000) *Choice, Pathways and Transitions Post 16: New Youth, New Economics in the Global City*. London: Routledge.

Banks, M., Bates, I., Breakwell, G., Bynner, J., Emler, N., Jamieson, L. and Roberts, K. (1992) *Careers and Identities*. Buckingham: Open University Press.

Barry, M. (ed.) (2005) *Youth Policy and Social Inclusion*. London: Routledge.

Bentley, T. and Gurumurthy, R. (1999) *Destination Unknown: Engaging with the Problems of Marginalized Youth*. London: DEMOS.

Benyon, J. and Solomos, J. (1987) *The Roots of Urban Unrest*. Oxford: Pergamon.

Bourgois, P. (1995) *In Search of Respect: Selling Crack in El Barrio*. Cambridge: Cambridge University Press.

Bourne, J., Bridges, L. and Searle, C. (1994) *Outcast England: How Schools Exclude Black Children*. London: Institute of Race Relations.

Bowling, B. and Phillips, C. (2002) *Race, Crime and Justice*. London: Longman.

Bradford Congress (1996) *The Bradford Commission Report*. London: The Stationery Office.

Bridges, L. (1983) 'Policing the Urban Wasteland', in B. Hudson (ed.) (1996) *Race, Crime and Justice*. Aldershot: Ashgate.

Britton, L., Chatrik, B., Coles, B., Craig, G., Hylton, C. and Mumtaz, S. with Bivand, P., Burrows, R. and Convery, P. (2002) *Missing Connexions: The Career Dynamics and Welfare Needs of Black and Minority Ethnic Young People at the Margins*. Bristol: The Policy Press.

Burney, E. (1990) *Putting Street Crime in its Place*. London: Centre for Inner City Studies, Goldsmiths' College, University of London.

Cabinet Office (2003) *Ethnic Minorities and the Labour Market: Final Report*. London: Cabinet Office Strategy Unit.

Cashmore, E. and McLaughlin, E. (1991) *Out of Order? Policing Black People*. London: Routledge.

Cashmore, E. E. and Troyna, B. (eds) (1982) *Black Youth in Crisis*. London: Allen and Unwin.

Clancy, A. and Hough, M. (2001) *Crime, Policing and Justice: The Experience of Ethnic Minorities. Findings from the 2000 British Crime Survey*. London: Home Office.

Coard, B. (1971) *How the West Indian Child is Made Educationally Sub-Normal in the British School System*. London: New Beacon Books.

Coles, B., Rugg, J. and England, J. (1998) *Young People on Estates*. Coventry: Chartered Institute of Housing.

Commission for Racial Equality (2005) *The Police Service in England and Wales*. London: CRE.

Desai, P. (1999) 'Spaces of Identity, Cultures of Conflict: The Development of New British Asian masculinities', PhD thesis, Goldsmiths College, University of London.

Dodd, V. and Travis, A. (2005) 'Muslims Face Increased Stop and Search', *The Guardian*, 2 March.

Feeley, M. and Simon, J. (1994) 'Actuarial Justice: the Emerging New Criminal Law', in D. Nelken (ed.) *The Futures of Criminology*, London: Sage.

Feilzer, M. and Hood, R. (2004) *Differences or Discrimination? Minority Ethnic People in the Youth Justice System*. London: Youth Justice Board.

Fergusson, R. (2002) 'Rethinking Youth Transitions: Policy Transfer and New Exclusions in New Labour's New Deal', *Policy Studies*, 23(3/4): 173–90.

Fergusson, R., Pye, D., Esland, G., McLaughlin, E. and Muncie, J. (2000) 'Normalised Dislocation and New Subjectivities in Post-16 Markets for Education and Work', *Critical Social Policy*, 20(3): 283–306.

FitzGerald, M. and Hale, C. (1996) *Ethnic Minorities: Victimisation and Racial Harassment: Findings from the 1988 and 1992 British Crime Surveys*. Home Office Research Study 154, London: Home Office.

Fitzgerald, M. and Hale, C. (2002) *Young People and Street Crime*. London: Youth Justice Board.

FitzGerald, M., Hough, M., Joseph, I. and Qureshi, T. (2002) *Policing for London*. Cullompton: Willan.

Foster, J. (1990) *Villains: Crime and Community in the Inner City*. London: Routledge.

Foster, J. (1999) *Docklands: Cultures in Conflict, Worlds in Collision*. London: UCL Press.

Furlong, A. and Cartmel, F. (1997) *Young People and Social Change: Individualization and Risk in Late modernity*. Buckingham: Open University Press.

Garrett, P. M. (2002) '"Encounters in the New Welfare Domains of the Third Way": Social Work, the Connexions Agency and Personal Advisors', *Critical Social Policy*, 22(4): 596–618.

Gillborn, D. and Youdell, D. (2000) *Rationing Education*. Buckingham: Open University Press.

Gilroy, P. (1987) *There Ain't No Black in the Union Jack: The Cultural Politics of Race and Nation*. London: Hutchinson.

Goldson, B. (1998) 'Re-visiting the "Bulger Case": the Governance of Juvenile Crime and the Politics of Punishment – Enduring Consequences for Children in England and Wales', *Juvenile Justice Worldwide*, 1(1): 21–22, Geneva: UNESCO Defence for Children International.

Goldson, B. (2000) *The New Youth Justice*. Lyme Regis: Russell House.

Goldson, B. (2002) *Vulnerable Inside: Children in Secure and Penal Settings*. London: The Children's Society.

Goodey, J. (2001) 'The criminalization of British Asian youth', *Journal of Youth Studies*, 4(4): 129–50.

Graham, J. (1988) *Schools, Disruptive Behaviour and Delinquency*. Home Office Research Study No. 96. London: HMSO.

Graham, J. and Bowling, B. (1995) *Young People and Crime*. London: Home Office.

Graham, J. and Utting, D. (1996) 'Families, Schools and Criminality Prevention', in T. Bennett (ed.) *Preventing Crime and Disorder: Targeting Strategies and Responsibilities*. Cambridge Cropwood Series. Cambridge: Institute of Criminology.

Gutzmore, C. (1983) 'Capital, "Black Youth", and Crime', *Race and Class*, XXV(2): 13–30.

Hall, S., Critcher, C., Jefferson, T., Clarke, J. and Roberts, B. (1978) *Policing the Crisis: Mugging, the State, and Law and Order*. London: Macmillan.

Hallsworth, S. (2005) *Street Crime*, Cullompton: Willan.

Hallsworth, S. and Maguire, M. (2004) *Profiling the City of London Exercise of Stop and Search*. London: Report for the City of London Police.

Harrison, P. (1985) *Inside the Inner City*. Harmondsworth: Penguin

Hercules, T. (1999) *Labelled a Black Villain*. London: Fourth Estate.

Hollands, R. (1990) *The Long Transition: Class, Culture and Youth Training*. Basinstoke: Macmillan.

Home Office (2004) *Race and the Criminal Justice System: An Overview to the Complete Statistics 2002–2003*. London: Home Office.

Hood, R. (1992) *Race and Sentencing*. Oxford: Clarendon Press.

Hood, R., Shute, S. and Seemungal, F. (2003) *Ethnic Minorities in the Criminal Court: Perceptions of Fairness and Equality of Treatment*, Research Series No. 2/03, London: Lord Chancellor's Department.

Hope, T. (2001) 'Crime victimisation and inequality in risk society', in R. Matthews and J. Pitts (eds) *Crime, Disorder and Community Safety*. New York: Routledge.

Institute of Race Relations (1987a) *Policing Against Black People*. London: Institute of Race Relations.

Institute of Race Relations (1987b) *Deadly Silence: Black Deaths in Custody*. London: Institute of Race Relations.

Jefferson, T. (1988) 'Race, Crime and Policing: Empirical, Theoretical and Methodological Issues', *International Journal of the Sociology of Law*, 16: 521–39.

Johnston, L., MacDonald, R., Mason, P., Ridley, L. and Webster, C. (2000) *Snakes and Ladders: Young People, Transitions and Social Exclusion*. Bristol: The Policy Press.

Kalra, V. S. (2000) *From Textile Mills to Taxi Ranks: Experiences of Migration, Labour and Social Change*. Aldershot: Ashgate.

Kalra, V. S. (2003) 'Police Lore and Community Disorder: Diversity in the Criminal Justice System', in D. Mason (ed.) *Explaining Ethnic Differences: Changing Patterns of Disadvantage in Britain*. Bristol: The Policy Press.

Kalra, V. S., Fieldhouse, E. and Alam, S. (2001) 'Avoiding the New Deal', *Youth and Policy*, 72: 63–79.

Keith, M. (1993) *Race, Riots and Policing: Lore and Disorder in a Multi-racist Society*. London: UCL Press.

Kershaw, C., Budd, T., Kinshott, G., Mattinson, J., Mayhew, P. and Myhill, A. (2000) *The 2000 British Crime Survey*. London: Home Office.

Lea, J. (2000) 'The Macpherson Report and the Question of Institutional Racism', *The Howard Journal*, 39(3): 219–33.

Lea, J. and Young, J. (1993) *What Is to be Done about Law and Order?* Revised edition. London: Pluto.

Mac an Ghaill, M. (1988) *Young, Gifted and Black: Student-Teacher Relations in the Schooling of Black Youth*. Milton Keynes: Open University Press.

MacDonald, R. (ed.) (1997) *Youth, the 'Underclass' and Social Exclusion*. London: Routledge.

Macpherson, W. (1999) *The Stephen Lawrence Inquiry: Report of an Inquiry by Sir William Macpherson*. London: HMSO.

Marlow, A. and Loveday, B. (2000) *After McPherson: Policing after the Stephen Lawrence Inquiry*. Lyme Regis: Russell House.

Mason, D. (ed.) (2003) *Explaining Ethnic Differences: Changing Patterns of Disadvantage in Britain*. Bristol: The Policy Press.

Mhlanga, B. (1997) *The Colour of English Justice: A Multivariate Analysis*. Aldershot: Avebury.

Miles, R. and Brown, M. (2003) *Racism*. London: Routledge.

Mizen, P. (2004) *The Changing State of Youth*. Basingstoke: Palgrave.

Modood, T. (2003) 'Ethnic differentials in educational performance', in D. Mason (ed.) *Explaining Ethnic Differences: Changing Patterns of Disadvantage in Britain*. Bristol: The Policy Press.

Muncie, J. (2004) *Youth and Crime*. (2nd edn), London: Sage.

Nicholas, S. and Walker, A. (eds.) (2004) *Crime in England and Wales 2002/2003: Supplementary Volume 2: Crime, Disorder and the Criminal Justice System – Public Attitudes and Perceptions*. Home Office Statistical Bulletin 2/04, London: Home Office.

Nightingale, C. (1993) *On the Edge*. New York: Basic Books.

O'Donnell, M. and Sharpe, S. (2000) *Uncertain Masculinities: Youth, Ethnicity and Class in contemporary Britain*. London: Routledge.

Osgerby, B. (1998) *Youth in Britain since 1945*. Oxford: Blackwell.

Owen, D. (2003) 'The Demographic Characteristics of People from Minority Ethnic Groups in Britain', in D. Mason (ed.) *Explaining Ethnic Differences: Changing Patterns of Disadvantage in Britain*. Bristol: The Policy Press.

Parsons, C., Godfrey, R., Annan, G., Cornwall, J., Dussart, M., Hepburn, S., Howlett, K. and Wennerstrom, V. (2004) *Minority Ethnic Exclusions and the Race Relations (Amendment) Act 2000*. London: Department for Education and Skills.

Pawson, N. and Tilley, N. (1997) *Realistic Evaluation*. London: Sage.

Pawson, R. (1989) *A Measure for Measures*. London: Routledge.

Pearce, N. and Hillman, J. (1998) *Wasted Youth: Raising Achievement and Tackling Social Exclusion*. London: IPPR.

Percy, A. (1998) 'Ethnicity and Victimisation: Findings from the 1996 British Crime Survey', Home Office Statistical Bulletin, 6/98, 3 April, London: Home Office.

Percy-Smith, B. and Weil, S. (2002) 'New Deal or raw Deal? Dilemmas and Paradoxes of State Interventions into the Labour Market', in M. Cieslik and G. Pollock (eds) *Young People in Risk Society*. Aldershot: Ashgate.

Phillips, M. and Phillips, T. (1998) *Windrush: The Irresistible Rise of Multi-Racial Britain*. London: HarperCollins.

Pilkington, A. (2003) *Racial Disadvantage and Ethnic Diversity in Britain*. Basingstoke: Palgrave Macmillan.

Pitts, J. (2001) *The New Politics of Youth Crime: Discipline or Solidarity?* Basingstoke: Palgrave.

Reiner, R. (1985) *The Politics of the Police*. Brighton: Wheatsheaf.

Roberts, K. (1995) *Youth and Employment in Modern Britain*. Oxford: Oxford University Press.

Robins, D. (1992) *Tarnished Vision: Crime and Conflict in the Inner City*. Oxford: Oxford University Press.

Rowe, M. (1998) *The Racialisation of Disorder in Twentieth Century Britain*. Aldershot: Ashgate.

Rowe, M. (2004) *Policing, Race and Racism*. Cullompton: Willan.

(SEU) Social Exclusion Unit (1998) *Truancy and Social Exclusion*. Cm 3947, London: SEU/The Stationary Office.

(SEU) Social Exclusion Unit (1999) *Bridging the Gap*. Cm 4405, London: SEU/The Stationery Office.

Sewell, T. (1997) *Black Masculinities and Schooling: How Black Boys Survive Modern Schooling*. London: Trentham Books.

Smith, H.O.J. (2003) *The Nature of Personal Robbery*. Home Office Research Study 254, London: Home Office.

Solomos, J. (2003) *Race and Racism in Britain*. (3rd edn) Basingstoke: Palgrave Macmillan.

Stone, V., Cotton, D. and Thomas, A. (2000) *Mapping Troubled Lives: Young People Not in Education, Employment or Training*. London: Department for Education and Employment.

Taylor, I. (1996) *A Tale of Two Cities: Global Change, Local Feeling and Everyday Life in the North of England. A Study of Manchester and Sheffield*. London: Routledge.

Wacquant, L. (2005) 'The Great Penal Leap Backward: Incarceration in America from Nixon to Clinton', in J. Pratt (ed.) *Punitiveness: Current Trends, Theories, Perspectives*. Cullompton: Willan.

Waddington, P. A. J. (1999) *Policing Citizens*. London: UCL.

Waddington, P. A. J., Stenson, K. and Don, D. (2004) 'In Proportion: Race, and Police Stop and Search', *British Journal of Criminology*, 44: 1–26.

Wardak, A. (2000) *Social Control and Deviance: A South Asian Community in Scotland*. Aldershot: Ashgate.

Webster, C. (1995) *Youth Crime, Victimisation and Racial Harassment: The Keighley Crime Survey*. Centre for Research in Applied Community Studies, Bradford: Bradford and Ilkley Community College Corporation.

Webster, C. (1996) 'Local Heroes: Violent Racism, Spacism and Localism Among White and Asian Young People', *Youth and Policy*, 53: 15–27, Summer.

Webster, C. (1997) 'The Construction of British "Asian" Criminality', *International Journal of the Sociology of Law*, 25: 65–86.

Webster, C. (2001) 'Representing Race and Crime', *Criminal Justice Matters*, 43 (Spring): 16–17.

Webster, C. (2003) 'Race, Space and Fear: Imagined Geographies of Racism, Crime, Violence and Disorder in Northern England', *Capital and Class*, 80: 95–122.

Webster, C. (2004) 'Policing British Asian Communities', in R. Hopkins Burke (ed.) *Hard Cop/Soft Cop: Dilemmas and Debates in Contemporary Policing*. Cullompton: Willan Publishing.

Webster, C., Simpson, D., MacDonald, R., Abbas, A., Cieslik, M. and Shildrick, M. (2004) *Poor Transitions: Social Exclusion and Young Adults*. Bristol: The Policy Press.

Whitfield, J. (2004) *Unhappy Dialogue: The Metropolitan Police and Black Londoners in Post-war Britain*. Cullompton: Willan.

Williamson, H. (1997) 'Status Zero, Youth and the "Underclass"', in R. MacDonald (ed.) *Youth, the 'Underclass' and Social Exclusion*. London: Routledge.

Gender, Youth Crime and Justice

Loraine Gelsthorpe and Gilly Sharpe

Introduction

In this chapter we focus on patterns of girls'[1] offending and responses to it, as well as historical and contemporary explanations for female juvenile delinquency. We argue that the regulation of acceptable gender-role behaviour has long been a key feature of the criminal justice system's response to offending by girls, and that such regulation is still in evidence in the rhetoric and practice of youth justice in the twenty-first century. We also examine changing perceptions of girls' behaviour and concomitant shifts in their social regulation. In particular, we analyse recurring moral panics regarding girls' behaviour, which seem to have shifted their focus in recent years – from girls' sexuality and 'status' offending, to their apparently increasing violence and alcohol use – and dwell on the resultant punitive turn towards girls and young women.

Whilst we should avoid taking the youth justice system's treatment of boys to be either the norm or acceptable, our chief concern in this chapter is to describe and reflect on policies and practices that particularly affect *girls*, first because girls have tended to be overlooked in youth justice discourse, and second due to the symbolic import of changes, within society in general and the youth justice system in particular, which have affected girls in recent years.

As a consequence of interventionist policies, girls are being increasingly drawn into the criminal justice system, with the consequential effects of a criminal

---

1. We use 'girls' throughout to refer to girls and young women aged 10–17 years.

record, in spite of limited evidence of their increased criminality in recent years. Measures which in the past served to divert the majority of girls from the criminal justice system altogether have been replaced by early intervention, as well as a sharp rise in the use of community penalties and a disproportionate increase in the number of girls – as compared with boys – in custody.

In part this may reflect the increasing visibility of girls, with the 'culture of the bedroom' (as a place for girls to meet, listen to music, talk and so on, see Frith, 1983) having been replaced by a construction of adolescence that revolves around out-of-home activities. Thus moral panics about girls and their changing behaviour have been fuelled by conspicuous consumption among the young, and leisure pursuits of 'pubbing and clubbing' which involve a more conspicuous street presence.

Traditional forms of regulating girls' social behaviour

Numerous historical sketches reveal both public and governmental concern about the behaviour of girls, and there have been frequent and vociferous claims that delinquent girls, like their older sisters, are 'worse' than boys (Carpenter, 1853). Whilst the youth justice system did not distinguish between girls and boys in terms of sentencing and services in its early development, we can discern different attitudes and perceptions with regard to girls and boys over time, which span policy, practice and academic discourses. These attitudes persist to the present day.

Analysis of the youth justice system and related institutions since their inception reveals the existence of a dual image of girls, who were thought simultaneously to be more vulnerable than boys and to need a lot of care, whilst their delinquent behaviour was seen as 'worse' than that of boys: offending girls were generally considered to be breaking not only the law, but also gender role expectations, with girls conforming to the stereotype of femininity most likely to be dealt with by means of the care system as opposed to the 'criminal justice system' (Gelsthorpe, 1989). Despite various nineteenth-century observations and claims that girls were more difficult to 'rescue' than boys, the main aim of the missions and societies for delinquent girls was not to straightforwardly punish them, but to instil good virtues, and to 'rouse a consciousness' in them. Mary Carpenter (1853: 83), inveterate critic of the nineteenth-century penal system adopted for juvenile delinquents, argued that practices whereby many juveniles were imprisoned were especially iniquitous when used for girls and that the system needed for girls was a 'wise and kind' one. Thus the voluntary sector, prominent in early developments in juvenile justice, played a distinctive role in regulating girls' behaviour in ways which reflected contemporary social, political and cultural norms and expectations (Cox, 2003). The reasons for girls' admission to residential care, continuing until well into the second half of the twentieth century, were predominantly to do with 'status offending': being beyond parental control, in 'moral danger', at risk of abuse, absconding, and so on. In residential homes, borstals and approved schools more generally, girls were thought in many cases to need medical treatment and emotional security which would divert their attention from sexual activities. Girls were thought to appreciate the value of a homely atmosphere (Cox, 2003; Gelsthorpe, 1989; 2005).

Later in the twentieth century, while the Criminal Justice Act of 1982 led to the revitalisation of detention centres for boys with the introduction of a 'short, sharp shock' type of regime, for example, the one such centre for girls was closed. Indeed in the White Paper, *Crime, Justice and Protecting the Public* (Home Office, 1990), which preceded the Criminal Justice Act 1991, the Conservative government suggested that the number of girls under the age of 18 years sentenced to custody by the courts was so small that the abolition of detention in a young offender institution for this group might be feasible. Apart from the very few who had committed especially serious offences and who could be dealt with by means of section 53 detention (sections 90–91 of the Powers of Criminal Courts (Sentencing) Act 2000), it was thought that the 150 or so girls sent to custody each year (compared with over 7,000 boys) could be dealt with quite adequately by the 'good, demanding and constructive community programmes for juvenile offenders who need intensive supervision' (Home Office, 1990: 45).

Prevailing beliefs as to what constituted suitable responses to delinquent girls throughout the twentieth century were determined largely by contemporary explanations of girls' offending, which are discussed later in this chapter. Walker (1962), for instance, clearly saw girls as 'less criminally inclined' than boys, as 'vulnerable' and 'at risk' of contamination from the more hardened delinquent boys in residential care. Such themes are echoed in other writings on girls' admission to the youth justice system and approved schools. Hoghughi (1978: 57), studying disturbed juvenile delinquents in the 1970s, claimed that girls were 'more emotionally and socially immature' and 'stubborn and emotionally unstable'. Both Ackland's (1982) study of girls in care and Petrie's (1986) research on girls in residential care similarly describe the importance of the 'social care' model for girls, with an emphasis on addressing their assumed inadequate socialisation, rather than straightforward misbehaviour.

Thus youth justice system responses to girls and young women have been significantly influenced by broad socio-political and religious expectations of 'appropriate' female behaviour. Teachers, social workers, probation officers and voluntary sector workers have influenced decisions within the system by raising concerns about girls' sexuality and independence – their 'passionate and wilful' behaviour (Alder, 1998). Feminist research on girls has revealed that the role of girls' own families has been particularly important in policing girls' behaviour and sexuality (Cain, 1989). Double-standards have continually been applied with regard to girls' and boys' sexual behaviour – with girls being subject to scrutiny and social regulation in a way that boys have not been. Girls have perhaps also sometimes been viewed as uncontrollable, and worse than boys simply because of unreasonably high expectations of their behaviour. At the same time they have been considered more psychiatrically disturbed than boys, which may well reflect the normal discourses of pathology in which women's behaviour is defined (Worrall, 1990).

It is perhaps precisely because of confused and conflicting perceptions of their behaviour that girls have tended to experience both the advantages and disadvantages of 'welfarism' to a greater extent than boys – on the grounds that they are 'at risk', in 'moral danger' and 'in need of protection'. The advantages have included diversion from the formal juvenile justice system, whilst the disadvantages have included sentence up-tariffing (Harris and Webb, 1987), in particular where girls' offending is contrary to conventional gender-role stereotypes, for example, violent offending, a trend which is particularly apparent today, as we discuss in more detail later in this chapter. Recent critiques of juvenile justice, including feminist critiques, have resulted in moves towards a more 'equitable justice' between girls and boys, but as a result of this we have witnessed a greater tendency to categorise girls' behaviour as *criminal* rather than merely *problematic*, and the resultant net-widening effect has meant that more girls and young women than hitherto are being brought within the remit of the criminal justice system (Worrall, 2001). Compulsory early intervention measures introduced by the Crime and Disorder Act 1998, and the concomitant demise of repeat cautioning and the conditional discharge, have contributed to the widening of the youth justice net (Goldson, 2000). Furthermore, voluntary 'prevention programmes' for girls 'at risk' of offending, such as Youth Inclusion and Support Panels and Youth Inclusion Programmes, may influence police or sentencing decisions should a girl subsequently be arrested. Perhaps of most concern, in view of current moral panics surrounding young women's consumption of alcohol and alleged increases in their rowdy and unfeminine behaviour, is the narrowing conception of what is considered to be socially acceptable youthful behaviour, with Anti-social Behaviour Orders being increasingly used as a tool to control and criminalise young people's lifestyles, language and even their dress.

Patterns of offending by girls and system responses

Historically, girls and women offend less than boys and men, and those females who do offend tend to start later, desist sooner, and commit less serious offences than their male counterparts. Eighty per cent of female offenders, compared with 55 per cent of males, have criminal 'careers' lasting less than a year (Home Office, 2003). Official statistics for England and Wales indicate that the peak age of recorded offending is 15 for females and 18 for males (Home Office, 2004). Female juvenile offending is largely restricted to relatively minor offences, with the gender gap amongst 10–17-year-olds being smallest for theft and handling stolen goods, and assault (Home Office, 2004).

Any attempts to analyse trends in either female youth offending or in the treatment of girls and young women by the criminal justice system are hampered by significant difficulties interpreting the available 'evidence'. Variations within offence categories can distort the overall picture of female offending, for example 'violence against the person' can denote anything from murder to a playground fight, and small baseline numbers can mean that even small fluctuations may appear dramatic in percentage terms. Whilst recent data made available by the Youth Justice Board for England and Wales indicate larger increases in recorded female juvenile offences (Youth Justice Board, 2004), there is no necessary corresponding increase in the number of *individual* delinquent girls. Moreover, the reliability of these different data is sometimes questionable. Yet, despite discrepancies in the data sources, the available evidence unanimously indicates a modest increase in female youth offending in recent decades.

This modest increase nevertheless appears to have generated substantial and disproportionate panic (Burman, 2004). Girls are becoming more violent and joining more gangs, we are told, as well as engaging in illegal drug-taking alongside boys. Home Office criminal statistics lend some support to some of these claims. During the 1990s, recorded juvenile crime increased at a faster rate among girls than boys, with notable increases in drug-related and violent crime (Home Office, 2003). The number of arrests of girls for violent offences more than doubled, and is thought to have increased by 250 per cent in the last quarter of the century (Rutter et al., 1998). However, it remains the case that males aged 15–17 are more than twice as likely as their female counterparts to be warned or convicted for theft or handling, and around four times as likely to be warned or convicted for violent offences (Home Office, 2004).

Whilst the 'official' picture of crime may be subject to the ways in which public fears and fantasies affect reporting rates, as well as the exigencies of organisational practice in the light of media influences, and changes in legislation and recording practices, findings from self-report studies may give a more accurate indication of the volume of youth crime committed. Nationally representative self-report surveys conducted in England and Wales by the Home Office have indicated that over half of males and almost one-third of females (aged 14–25) admitted committing at least one offence at some point in their lives, including one in four males and one in eight females during the previous year. Whilst property and violent offending were significantly more prevalent amongst males, the four most common offences were the same for both sexes: buying and selling stolen goods, fighting, shoplifting, and vandalism, and the majority of respondents had committed no more than one or two minor offences in their lives (Flood-Page et al., 2000; Graham and Bowling, 1995). Self-reports also suggest that at ages 12 and 13 there is little difference between males and females in either offending or in drug use or regular drinking (Flood-Page et al., 2000). After age 14, however, the gender difference becomes more marked. Taking all offences together, the male:female ratio increases from just above 1.4:1 at age 14–17 years, to 4:1 at 18–21 years, and 11:1 at 22–25 years (Graham and Bowling, 1995). In sum, girls continue to commit fewer, and on the whole less serious, offences than boys, and to present a lower level of risk of re-offending

(Home Office, 2003). It is notable also that crime is overwhelmingly a youth-related phenomenon for both boys and girls (Jamieson et al., 1999), and perhaps particularly so for girls and young women who, as the available evidence shows, grow – or mature – out of crime rather sooner than their male counterparts.

One key question, of course, is how far changing perceptions of behaviour, actual changes in behaviour and changes in society respectively have led to changes in the nature of criminal justice system responses to girls. Home Office data indicate that females of all ages are more likely than males to receive a caution or a Final Warning for indictable and summary offences (largely under-standable on the basis of the seriousness of offences committed). Between 1994 and 2002, however, the proportion of offenders cautioned for indictable offences, as a proportion of all those cautioned or found guilty in court, fell. This was the case for males and females and for all age groups. The overall number of per-sons aged 10–17 found guilty in court rose between 1994 and 2002, from 33,800 to 42,400 for males and from 4,200 to 6,700 for females, representing rises of 25.4 per cent and 59.5 per cent for male and female young offenders respec-tively. However, recorded female crime amongst this age group *fell* over the period by 30.9 per cent (compared with a 25.1 per cent drop in boys' crime). Thus, there is a curious paradox here. Whilst the rate of diversion has fallen and the rate at which young offenders are found guilty in court has increased (and for girls more so than for boys), actual crime rates, at least as presented in the official statistics, appear to have fallen.

There are other complexities too. Criminal statistics are not disaggregated by age, gender and ethnicity combined, making ethnic monitoring for girls almost impossible. Nonetheless, several studies have found evidence of racial discrimina-tion towards girls by the police, the courts and schools. African-Caribbean, and, in particular 'black other' girls, especially those aged 14 and 15, are up to six times more likely to be prosecuted than similarly placed white females (Feilzer and Hood, 2004). The way in which the police and other criminal justice professionals interact with black girls and young women may of course contribute to the way girls respond to them (Chigwada-Bailey, 2004), and perceptions of black girls' behaviour (which they themselves may consider to be simply sticking up for them-selves) may affect their consequent likelihood of arrest. These values, and resultant behaviour, may contravene expectations of gender-appropriate (for which read white and middle-class) behaviour and thus influence system responses. Moreover, the available evidence suggests that girls have been disproportionately affected by recent (gender-blind) interventionist criminal justice policies.[2]

---

2. This does not seem to stem solely from initiatives introduced by the Crime and Disorder Act 1998, however, since the trend of increasing female juvenile prosecutions, restrictions of police caution-ing, and proportionately greater increases for girls than for boys in the use of supervision orders had already begun in the early 1990s (Home Office, 2003).

Explanations of girls' offending

Criminological theorising about female pathways into crime has been abundant, though often misconceived. Common explanations for girls' criminal behaviour have been well rehearsed and challenged elsewhere (Gelsthorpe, 1989; 2004). The trajectory of theories relating to girls and young women has been unusually conservative compared with those relating to males, however (Scraton, 1990; Smart, 1976), reflecting ideologically informed versions of biological determinism, cultural conceptions of psychological functioning, and social–structural expectations of behaviour.

Several studies of girls and young women in institutions in the 1960s and 1970s, for example, addressed the relationship between psychology and delinquency, pointing – with a common lack of critical reflection on the effects of institutionalisation – to high levels of emotional instability, poor self-image, and psychological disturbance in girls (Cowie et al., 1968; Hoghughi, 1978; Richardson, 1969). Others have attributed delinquency amongst girls to a kind of psychological 'acting out' because of family dysfunction (Blos, 1969), to sexual dysfunction (either being undersexualised or oversexualised) or to obstacles in positive affective relationships (Morris, 1964). Hoffman-Bustamante (1973), in particular, outlined a link between sex roles and girls' lesser participation in criminal activity, suggesting that girls are induced to be more passive and domesticated than boys, who are encouraged instead to be more ambitious, aggressive and extrovert.

There is a common thread in such theories relating to public/private space and social control, and it is perhaps in the direction of control theories that we find particularly useful insights regarding males' and females' differential involvement in crime. Hirschi's (1969) theoretical framework, revolving around attachment, commitment, involvement and belief, has prompted a number of ideas which reflect the differential socialisation of males and females. Focusing on 'deprived families' in Birmingham, Wilson (1980) noted that what differentiated delinquent and non-delinquent children was what she described as the exercise of 'chaperonage', and it is perhaps here that we can discern key differences affecting girls and boys. Hagan and colleagues (1985) came to the conclusion that delinquency was greater amongst males than females because females were more frequently subject to intense and diffuse family control in the private, domestic sphere.

There is empirical support for social control theory from contemporary self-report studies. Graham and Bowling (1995) report that girls were much more closely supervised than boys at the age of 14 to 15, however, gender itself remained an important variable in relation to involvement in crime after controlling for the influences of family, school and other relevant factors. As Graham and Bowling put it: 'among those males and females who are equally closely supervised at home and at school, who are equally attached to their school and their family and who have no delinquent peers, offending remains about twice as common among males as females' (1995: 48). More recent explanations have focused on the broad features of women's and girls' lifestyles and social–structural positions, including women's vulnerabilities in relation to poverty, the stresses and strains that go along with childcare responsibilities, domestic violence and high levels of childhood victimisation (see Gelsthorpe, 2004 for an overview). Widom (1995), for instance, has argued that early exposure to crime as a bystander or victim in families or neighbourhoods can increase one's probability of becoming an offender. But generally the connections between adverse experiences (including histories of victimisation), lifestyle factors, young women's agency and pathways into crime remain under-theorised.

We can gain some important insights from work on desistance. Sampson and Laub's (1993) life-course approach focuses on the structural elements such as relationships, work, and changing location, which may be 'turning points' in a criminal career that can result in desistance. Structural issues are also emphasised in alternative theories such as differential association and social learning (Warr, 2002), strain (Agnew, 1997) and social bonding (Shover, 1996). The more human element of agency is emphasised in approaches focusing on identity change (Maruna, 2001), cognitive scripts, resilience and self-efficacy (Rumgay, 2004), the use of narratives (Bottoms et al., 2004; Maruna, 2001) and cognitive transformations (Giordano et al., 2002). One problem here, of course, is that many of these studies have focused exclusively on males and we do not know what the interplay of factors might be for females.

McIvor et al. (2004) ask whether or not desistance is different for girls, following signs from the various self-report studies that girls desist from crime sooner than boys. Jamieson et al. (1999) found both that a variety of social and cognitive factors may influence decisions to desist and that these factors may differ in their salience between males and females. In this Scottish study, young men tended to couch their explanations of desistance in broadly utilitarian terms, whereas young women more often alluded to the moral dimension of crime. Young women also often felt a profound sense of guilt or shame – in other words, a 'relational' dimension (see Gilligan, 1982). Practical considerations, such as looking after an infant, also had an influence. Thus both the structural and the social are in evidence. As previously indicated, most theories regarding girls' pathways into crime have revolved around the sexual/psychological and the pathological, rather than the structural and social. It remains a serious omission that, in spite of all that we know about the short length of girls' criminal careers, their early desistance and the youthful phenomenon of both male and female crime, explanatory accounts of female youth offending continue to focus on gender-based explanations of their behaviour, whilst boys' behaviour is more commonly conceived in terms of age, or youthful immaturity.

Recent theorising has introduced a new level of analysis, but it is arguable that broad changes in society and the role of women, girls and class are still not sufficiently accounted for. We can at least suggest, if not empirically prove, that reasons for the (small) increase in girls' offending, as well as reactions to it, might include broad structural changes in society.[3] There have been changes in family structures, relationships, attachments and social ties, including a loosening of social regulation via the family. Indeed evidence of a substantial increase in conduct problems amongst British adolescents during the past 25 years (Collishaw et al., 2004) may be explained largely by other significant social changes, including rampant materialism, the development of a global drugs market, and a more prolonged transition into adulthood and financial independence. Consequently, these social and cultural changes may help explain both changes in girls' behaviour – including their violent behaviour – and social reactions to it. The culture of risk (Hudson, 2003) is conceivably one that includes a heightened awareness and fear of crime – particularly crimes committed by those from whom society would not, in terms of gendered socio-cultural expectations, expect.

Violence, moral panic and criminalisation

As previously intimated, stories about girl gangs roaming the streets and randomly attacking innocent victims have been a recurring feature of newspaper headlines and magazines in recent years (see, for example, Kirsta, 2000; Thompson, 2001). Whilst there is *some* support for such claims, the stories are seemingly a distortion of the facts, in the light of our earlier discussion of offending patterns.

A recent self-report survey found that assaults committed by females are more likely to involve a victim they know well, and, somewhat surprisingly perhaps, the victim is more often male then female (Budd et al., 2005). Little is known about the actual nature and seriousness of girls' violent offending. It may be that assault by a girl is more likely to be in anger or self-defence, or against a police officer when arrested (due to physicality of the arrest act where there is a history of abuse, perhaps), or parents, relatives, or members of the public are more likely to bring violent acts committed by girls to the attention of the authorities. Rather than signalling the onset of moral decline amongst our youth, the figures denoting an increase in female juvenile violence seem instead to reflect an increase, in all jurisdictions, in young women charged for non-serious, non-sexual assault. However, it remains unclear whether such changes can be attributed to actual crime rates or to changing responses to girls' behaviour (Alder and Worrall, 2004; Batchelor and Burman, 2004).

Studies focusing on the meaning and context of violence in girls' lives have shown how violence is perceived by many girls and young women as 'normal' and routine, although it is rare for girls to use physical violence on a regular basis

---

3. We would also have to look at demographic changes, but our intention here is to sketch out the social context for offending.

(Phillips, 2003). Girls' aggression and fighting have consistently been found to centre on matters of sexuality (Lees, 1993), physical appearance (Batchelor et al., 2001), and the search for male attention (Artz, 2003). Fighting can result from the sexual policing of girls by other girls, as a means of defending one's sexual reputation or 'saving face' (Phillips, 2003). Violence between girls tends to arise in the context of close 'friendships' and interpersonal relationships, and 'falling out' can have seriously damaging consequences for girls' self-esteem (Batchelor et al., 2001). In terms of the manifestation of aggression and violence by girls, 'relational aggression' – verbal or non-verbal aggression which takes the form of name-calling or 'bitchiness', or the threat of withdrawal of relationship to control the behaviour of others – may be more characteristic of girls than boys (Crick and Grotpeter, 1995). This may partly explain the continuing belief amongst practitioners that girls are 'more difficult to work with' (Chesney-Lind and Belknap, 2004).

Despite many gender similarities, studies have identified key differences in violent school girls' and school boys' relationships with their mothers, fear and experience of physical and sexual abuse, social and interpersonal values and self-concept (in particular in relation to food consumption). Violent girls report significantly higher rates of both fear and experience of sexual assault, coercive sex with boyfriends, and physical assault in the home, than both non-violent girls and violent boys (Silverthorn and Frick, 1999). To represent violent girls simply as victims of circumstance over-simplifies the complexities of female violence, however. This 'rendering them harmless' (Allen, 1998) denies women and girls agency, and risks prioritising individual pathological explanations for violence (Phillips, 2003).

In the context of late modernity, Campbell's (1981) claim is significant that the loosening of social control on girls, who are spending more time out of the home and on the streets, increases the possibility of their becoming involved in delinquent subcultures, especially in urban, working-class areas. A more recent study of boys' and girls' experiences of violence in inner-city estates suggests that, contrary to assumptions that the street is a masculine space, girls – as well as boys – *do* indeed make use of outdoor spaces, often to relieve the pressures generated within over-crowded living spaces, and so they develop knowledge of, and are involved in, 'everyday violence and disorder' in a routinised way (Pearce, 2004: 143). These contextualised and nuanced understandings of violence thus challenge the popular notion that girls are getting 'worse' because they are more violent now than hitherto. Current perceptions of girls' apparent violent behaviour can perhaps be seen as an indication of prevailing societal concerns about morality: girls' purported violence is seen as a threat to the social order, just as during the last century their sexuality was the primary focus of attention (Chesney-Lind and Belknap, 2004). There is some suggestion that concerns about violent behaviour on the part of girls may have replaced the old concerns about girls' status offences – or perhaps that their previously assumed pathological sexuality has been re-categorised as intentioned violence, often fuelled by the consumption of 'unladylike' quantities of alcohol.

Incarceration and institutionalisation

Concern about the continuing shift from welfare to punishment in controlling girls' behaviour is underpinned by reference to the rate at which girls (compared with boys) are sentenced to immediate custody. The 2002 figures for girls aged 10–17 sentenced to custodial orders, for example, represent an increase of 365 per cent over the figures for 1993 (530 girls compared with 114; the increase for boys was 68 per cent). Interestingly, girls are most likely to be serving a custodial sentence for violence against the person, the nature and context of which are unknown. In many cases, as discussed earlier, such violence may involve either fights between peers, or assaults against authority figures, and there seems to be an increasing tendency amongst residential care staff to have recourse to the courts when young people 'lash out', arguably due to stress in the face of discontinuities in their care. Boys of the same age are more likely to be in custody for robbery and burglary (Home Office, 2004).

But beyond concerns about girls (and indeed boys) in custody we need to look at local authority care. Whilst long used as a repository for girls, the proportion of girls admitted to secure accommodation on 'welfare' grounds is increasing: girls made up 24 per cent of the secure children's home population in 2001, rising to 33 per cent in 2004. Most of the children placed in secure accommodation by social services departments on 'welfare' grounds are girls, especially those who have run away from home or institutional care repeatedly (which may be a survival strategy to escape abuse of course) (Goldson, 2002). The Youth Justice Board for England and Wales has aimed to expand provision for girls in this sphere precisely so as to avoid the use of prisons. In practice, however, mixed gender secure units and the mix of 'criminal' and 'welfare' cases make it almost impossible to meet individuals' needs, such that in practice it seems that all children in trouble in secure accommodation are being criminalised rather than treated as children in need of care (Goldson, 2002; O'Neill, 2001). Few would question the sound motives for the avoidance of prisons, but we ought also to question the use of local authority secure accommodation for them, and instead turn our minds (again) to effective diversion and community responses.

Concluding reflections

The changes we have described in this chapter appear to have fuelled the abandonment of traditional welfare-oriented approaches to girls' delinquency and their replacement by an increasing desire to criminalise, punish and lock up what Anne Worrall (2000) captures in her phrase the 'nasty little madams'. Indeed, efforts to control girls and young women's behaviour via a range of formal and informal routes that have stressed their special psychological and other needs, have come under close critical scrutiny, and have given way to more punitive responses. As Worrall puts it:

In the actuarial language that now dominates criminal justice, a group which hitherto has been assessed as too small and too low-risk to warrant attention is now being re-assessed and re-categorised. No longer 'at risk' and in 'moral danger' from the damaging behaviour of men, increasing numbers of young women are being assigned to the same categories as young men ('violent girls', 'drug-abusing girls', 'girl robbers', 'girl murderers' – 'girl rapists' even) and are being subjected to the same forms of management as young men. (2001: 86)

The moral panic generated by the small increase in girls' crime thus contributes to increasing criminalisation of, and punitiveness towards, them. These changes are of no little symbolic significance. It has long been argued that 'youth' is a social category which has the power to carry a deeper message about the state of society. The collective agonising about girls' violence thus perhaps symbolises regrets about the changing social order in late modernity.

References

Ackland, J. (1982) *Girls in Care: A Case Study of Residential Treatment*. Aldershot: Gower.

Agnew, R. (1997) 'Stability and Change in Crime Over the Life Course: a Strain Theory Explanation', in T. Thornberry (ed.) *Developmental Theories of Crime and Delinquency. Advances in Criminological Theory, Vol. 7*. New Brunswick, NJ: Transaction Books. pp. 101–32.

Alder, C. (1998) '"Passionate and Wilful" Girls: Confronting Oractices', *Women and Criminal Justice*, 9(4): 81–101.

Alder, C. and Worrall, A. (2004) 'A Contemporary Crisis?', in C. Alder and A. Worrall, (eds) *Girls' Violence. Myths and Realities*. Albany: State University of New York Press.

Allen, H. (1998), 'Rendering Them Harmless: the Professional Portrayal of Women Charged with Serious Violent Crimes', in K. Daly and L. Maher (eds) *Criminology at the Crossroads: Feminist Readings in Crime and Justice*. New York, NY: Oxford University Press.

Artz, S. (2003) 'To Die For: Violent Adolescent Girls' Search for Male Attention', in D. J. Pepler, K. C. Madsen, C. Webster and K. S. Levene (eds) *The Development and Treatment of Girlhood Aggression*. Mahwah, NJ: Lawrence Erlbaum.

Batchelor, S. and Burman, M. (2004) 'Working with Girls and Young Women', in G. McIvor (ed.) *Women Who Offend*. London: Jessica Kingsley.

Batchelor, S., Burman, M. and Brown, J. (2001) 'Discussing Violence: Let's Hear It From The Girls', *Probation Journal*, 48(2): 125–34.

Blos, P. (1969) 'Preoedipal Factors in the Aetiology of Female Delinquency', *Psychoanalytic Studies of the Child*, 12: 229–49.

Bottoms, A., Shapland, J., Costello, A., Holmes, D. and Muir, G. (2004) 'Towards Desistance: Theoretical Underpinnings for an Empirical Study', *Howard Journal*, 43(4): 368–89.

Budd, T., Sharp, C. and Mayhew, P. (2005) *Offending in England and Wales: First Results from the 2003 Crime and Justice Survey*. Home Office Research Study 275. London: Home Office.

Burman, M. (2004) 'Breaking the Mould. Patterns of Female Offending', in G. McIvor (ed.) *Women Who Offend*. London: Jessica Kingsley.

Cain, M. (ed.) (1989) *Growing Up Good: Policing the Behaviour of Girls in Europe*. London: Sage.

Campbell, A. (1981) *Girl Delinquents*. Oxford: Basil Blackwell.

Carpenter, M. (1853) *Juvenile Delinquents: Social Evils, Their Causes and Their Cure*. London: Cash.

Chesney-Lind, M. and Belknap, J. (2004) 'Trends in Delinquent Girls' Aggression and Violent Behavior. A Review of the Evidence', in M. Putallaz and K.L. Bierman (eds) *Aggression, Antisocial Behavior, and Violence among Girls: A Developmental Perspective*. New York: The Guilford Press.

Chigwada-Bailey, R. (2004) 'Black Women and the Criminal Justice System', in G. McIvor (ed.) *Women Who Offend*. London: Jessica Kingsley.

Collishaw, S., Maughan, B., Goodman, R. and Pickles, A. (2004) 'Time Trends in Adolescent Mental Health', *Journal of Child Psychology and Psychiatry*, 45(8): 1350–62.

Cowie, J., Cowie, V. and Slater, E. (1968) *Delinquency in Girls*. London: Heinemann.

Cox, P. (2003) *Gender, Justice and Welfare: Bad Girls in Britain, 1900–1950*. Basingstoke: Palgrave Macmillan.

Crick, N.R. and Grotpeter, J.K. (1995) 'Relational Aggression, Gender, and Socio-Psychological Adjustment', *Child Development*, 66: 710–22.

Feilzer, M. and Hood, R. (2004) *Differences or Discrimination? Minority Ethnic Young People in the Youth Justice System*. London: Youth Justice Board.

Flood-Page, C., Campbell, S., Harrington, V. and Miller, J. (2000) *Youth Crime: Findings from the 1998/99 Youth Lifestyles Survey*. Home Office Research Study 209. London: HMSO.

Frith, S. (1983) *Sound Effects: Youth, Leisure and the Politics of Rock*. London: Constable.

Gelsthorpe, L. (1989) *Sexism and the Female Offender*. Cambridge Studies in Criminology. Aldershot: Gower.

Gelsthorpe, L. (2004) 'Female Offending: A Theoretical Overview', in G. McIvor (ed.) *Women Who Offend*. London: Jessica Kingsley.

Gelsthorpe, L. (2005) 'Girls in the Youth Justice System', in T. Bateman and J. Pitts (eds) *The RHP Companion to Youth Justice*. Dorset: Russell House Publishing.

Gilligan, C. (1982) *In a Different Voice*. Cambridge, MA: Harvard University Press.

Giordano, P., Cernovich, S. and Rudolph, J. (2002) 'Gender, Crime, and Desistance: Toward a Theory of Cognitive Transformation', *American Journal of Sociology*, 107(4): 990–1064.

Goldson, B. (2000) 'Wither Diversion: Interventionism and the New Youth Justice', in B. Goldson (ed.) *The New Youth Justice*. Dorset: Russell House Publishing.

Goldson, B. (2002) *Vulnerable Inside: Children in Secure and Penal Settings*, London, The Children's Society.

Graham, J. and Bowling, B. (1995) *Young People and Crime*. Home Office Research Study 145. London: HMSO.

Hagan, J., Simpson, J. and Gillis, A. (1985) 'The Class Structure of Gender and Delinquency: Toward a Power–Control Theory of Common Delinquent Behavior', *American Journal of Sociology*, 90: 1151–78.

Harris, R. and Webb, D. (1987) *Welfare, Power and Juvenile Justice*. London: Tavistock.

Hirschi, T. (1969) *Causes of Delinquency*. Berkeley: University of California Press.

Hoffman-Bustamante, D. (1973) 'The Nature of Female Criminality', *Issues in Criminology*, 8: 17–36.

Hoghughi, M. (1978) *Troubled and Troublesome: Coping with Severely Disordered Children*. London: Burnett.

Home Office (1990) *Crime, Justice and Protecting the Public: The Government's Proposals for Legislation*. London: Home Office.

Home Office (2003) *Statistics on Women and the Criminal Justice System: A Home Office Publication under Section 95 of the Criminal Justice Act 1991*. London: Home Office.

Home Office (2004) *Criminal Statistics. England and Wales 2003*. London: Home Office.

Hudson, B. (2003) *Justice in the Risk Society: Challenging and Re-affirming Justice in Late Modernity*. London: Sage.

Jamieson, J., McIvor, G. and Murray, C. (1999) *Understanding Offending Among Young People*. Edinburgh: The Stationery Office.

Kirsta, A. (2000) 'In the Next Ten Seconds the Woman Walking Past is Going to Either … A. Catch a Bus, B. Meet a Friend, C. Violently Attack You and Steal Your Credit Cards', *Nova*, July.

Lees, S. (1993) *Sugar and Spice: Sexuality and Adolescent Girls*. London: Penguin.

Maruna, S. (2001) *Making Good: How Ex-convicts Reform and Rebuild their Lives*. Washington, DC: American Psychological Association.

McIvor, G., Murray, C. and Jamieson, J. (2004) 'Desistance from Crime: is it Different for Women and Girls?', in S. Maruna and R. Immarigeon (eds) *After Crime and Punishment: Pathways to Offender Reintegration*. Cullompton: Willan.

Morris, R. (1964) 'Female Delinquency and Relational Problems', *Social Forces*, 43(1): 82–89.

O'Neill, T. (2001) *Children in Secure Accommodation: A Gendered Exploration of Locked Institutional Care for Children in Trouble*. London: Jessica Kingsley.

Pearce, J. (2004), 'Coming Out to Play? Young Women and Violence on the Street', in C. Alder, and A. Worrall (eds) *Girls' Violence. Myths and Realities*. Albany: State University of New York Press.

Petrie, C. (1986) *The Nowhere Girls*. Aldershot: Gower.

Phillips, C. (2003), 'Who's Who in the Pecking Order? Aggression and "Normal Violence" in the Lives of Girls and Boys', *British Journal of Criminology*, 43: 710–28.

Richardson, H. (1969) *Adolescent Girls in Approved Schools*. London: Routledge and Kegan Paul.

Rumgay, J. (2004) 'Living with Paradox: Community Supervision of Women Offenders', in G. McIvor (ed.) *Women Who Offend*. London: Jessica Kingsley.

Rutter, M., Giller, H. and Hagell, A. (1998) *Antisocial Behaviour by Young People*. Cambridge: Cambridge University Press.

Sampson, R. and Laub, J. (1993) *Crime in the Making: Pathways and Turning Points Through Life*. Cambridge, MA: Harvard University Press.

Scraton, P. (1990) 'Scientific Knowledge or Masculine Discourses? Challenging Patriarchy in Criminology', in L. Gelsthorpe and A. Morris (eds) *Feminist Perspectives in Criminology*. Buckingham: Open University Press.

Shover, N. (1996) *Great Pretenders: Pursuits and Careers of Persistent Thieves*. Boulder, CO: Westview Press.

Silverthorn, P. and Frick, P. (1999) 'Developmental Pathways to Antisocial Behavior: The Delayed-Onset Pathway in Girls', *Development and Psychopathology*, 11: 101–26.

Smart, C. (1976) *Women, Crime and Criminology: A Feminist Critique*. London: Routledge and Kegan Paul.

Thompson, T. (2001) 'Girls Lead the Pack in New Gangland Violence', *The Observer*, 15 April.

Walker, A. (1962) 'Special Problems of Delinquents and Maladjusted Girls', *Howard Journal of Penology and Crime Prevention*, 11: 26–36.

Warr, M. (2002) *Companions in Crime: The Social Aspects of Criminal Conduct*. Cambridge: Cambridge University Press.

Widom, C. Spatz (1995) 'Victims of Childhood Sexual Abuse: Later Criminal Consequences'. Research in Brief. Washington, DC: National Institute of Justice, US Department of Justice.

Wilson, H. (1980) 'Parental Supervision: a Neglected Aspect of Delinquency', *British Journal of Criminology*, 20: 203–35.

Worrall, A. (1990) *Offending Women: Female Lawbreakers and the Criminal Justice System*. London: Routledge.

Worrall, A. (2000) 'Governing Bad Girls: Changing Constructions of Female Juvenile Delinquency', in J. Bridgeman and D. Monk (eds) *Feminist Perspectives on Child Law*. London: Cavendish Publishing.

Worrall, A. (2001) 'Girls at Risk? Reflections on Changing Attitudes to Young Women's Offending', *Probation Journal*, 48(2): 86–92.

Youth Justice Board (2004) *Youth Justice Annual Statistics 2003/04*. London: Youth Justice Board.

PART TWO

Evidence, Policy Rationales and Contemporary Interventions

Youth Crime and Justice: Statistical 'Evidence', Recent Trends and Responses

5

Tim Bateman

Introduction

Perhaps the most common characterisation of contemporary youth justice reforms (particularly in England and Wales), especially by those who have engineered them, is that they are 'evidence led'. Frequently, statistical information is presented as hard incontrovertible 'fact' to back such claims, implying thereby that any commentator who has reservations about the trajectory of current youth justice policy is irrational, or politically motivated. But it is not so clear that the data point unambiguously to the conclusions drawn (principally that youth crime is becoming more serious and more widespread), nor is it obvious that recent trends justify the forms of response around which policy has been, and is being, shaped (primarily increasing modes of intervention and ultimately penal expansion).

The current chapter questions whether statistics can be relied upon to provide an objective account of youth crime, while acknowledging that certain trends may be discernible in the data. It seeks to argue that statistical information might reveal as much about the way that the youth justice system has changed in its treatment of young people who offend as it does about the behaviour of the children themselves. In exploring these themes, claims that the 'new youth justice' (Goldson, 2000) rests upon firm statistical foundations will be subjected to critical scrutiny.

Telling the same story different ways

There is no shortage of data on crime in England and Wales. Criminal statistics are collated regularly and allow analyses at some considerable level of detail. These are supplemented by large-scale victimisation surveys and studies of self-reported offending. Any analysis of recent trends in youth justice has, therefore, plenty of statistical information on which to draw, but there is a problem of interpretation. The data do not in themselves tell an unambiguous story; they can be read in various ways.

In January 2005, on the publication of the quarterly update of crime statistics, to September 2004, the accompanying Home Office press release trumpeted that crime was continuing to fall. The text gave prominence to the claim that violent offending had reduced by 9 per cent over the previous year, and had fallen 36 per cent since its peak in 1995 (Home Office, 2005a). The *Independent* newspaper, however, had a different take, headlining a 'leap in violent crime and gun offences', and noting that, during the relevant quarter, there were 306,200 offences of violence compared with 289,800 over the same period in the previous year (Barrett and Dean, 2005). Meanwhile, *The Guardian* newspaper, perhaps characteristically, took something of an intermediate position, noting that 'violent offences rise, but overall crime is down' (*The Guardian*, 2005).

Such inconsistencies are readily explained. The statistical bulletin, upon which each newspaper account is based, contains two sources of data that point in different directions: offences reported to, and recorded by, the police on the one hand; and victimisation data from the British Crime Survey, based on self-reported experiences of crime, on the other (Allen et al., 2005). The diverse forms of interpretation which the data-sets invoke are not without political and social significance. Thus, prior to the re-election of the New Labour government in May 2005, Michael Howard, then leader of the Opposition, was able to point to police figures showing an increase in crime of 850,000 under Tony Blair's last administration. In turn, the prime minister, drawing on results from the British Crime Survey, asserted a 25 per cent reduction in offending over the same period (Garside, 2004).

The potential to mislead

Explaining how it is possible to use different strands of statistical information to create divergent interpretations is an important matter. In itself, however, this fails to illuminate the 'truth' or actual reality. Indeed, it is not immediately apparent how competing readings of the data might be reconciled and, as one commentator has pointed out, the 'true facts' about youth crime are unknowable in principle (Muncie, 2001; 2002). There are at least five distinct, but interrelated, difficulties.

First, what constitutes an offence varies over time and place. The age of criminal responsibility, for instance, imposes a relatively arbitrary limit on the extent of youth crime: whereas in Scandinavian countries, anyone below the age of 15 years is deemed incapable of committing an offence, in England and Wales a child is held criminally responsible from the age of ten. Until 1998, it was presumed that a child under 14 years of age was incapable of differentiating between right and wrong sufficiently to justify criminal proceedings unless the prosecution was able to adduce evidence to the contrary. This presumption of *doli incapax* was removed by the Crime and Disorder Act 1998, ensuring that large numbers of children aged 10–13 years, who would not previously have received a formal disposal, were exposed to the full rigours of the criminal law (Bandalli, 2000). The inevitable result was to inflate the numbers appearing in the official statistics.

Second, police-recorded crime invariably gives a partial account of offending since, for a variety of reasons, around half of criminal incidents are never reported. Many, for instance, are not brought to police attention because they are considered insufficiently serious, or there is no loss involved (Salisbury, 2003). Conversely, any expansion in private insurance cover has the potential to inflate the number of minor matters that make their way into police statistics, since making a claim is dependent on reporting the offence. By the same token, crimes against those who lack the means to insure their property are likely to be relatively under-represented in sources of official data.

Third, large numbers of offences are committed which either have no obvious direct victim – for instance, possession of cannabis – or never come to the victim's attention – such as thefts from the workplace. Such 'victimless' incidents tend to be bypassed by both police data and the British Crime Survey. Indeed, the direct experience of victimisation is central to what features on the statistical radar. For this reason, official data are likely to understate considerably the volume of white-collar and corporate offences, transgressions which, by their nature, are predominantly committed by professional adults, the wealthy and the powerful, rather than by (predominantly poor, working-class) children.

Fourth, it is obviously impossible to attribute responsibility if no offender is apprehended. 'Clear-up rates' have tended to fall since the 1980s and now stand at just below one in four (23.4 per cent) (Thomas and Feist, 2004). This 'justice gap', between recorded crime and that which results in a substantive disposal, initiates considerable conjecture with regard to the proportion of unsolved offences (75 per cent of the total of all reported and recorded crime) that can reasonably be attributed to young people.

Finally, matters are complicated by the fact that fluctuations in criminal statistics may have little to do with shifts in children's criminality but derive instead from changes in legislation, policy or professional practice. For example, the replacement of cautioning by the final warning scheme in England and Wales, following the implementation of the Crime and Disorder Act 1998, rigidly limited police decision-making discretion following the arrest of a suspect under 18 years of age (Pragnell, 2005). The effect was to expand the use of formal measures to deal with matters which would otherwise have met with an informal response, previously estimated to account for around 10 per cent of all cases involving young people (Audit Commission, 1996). The reform accordingly had an inbuilt tendency to inflate recorded youth crime while at the same time increasing the proportion of children prosecuted for relatively minor offending (Bateman, 2003).

From statistical analysis to youth justice reform

Such difficulties in interpreting the data are not simply limited to abstract theoretical interest. Statistical analysis can promote responses that impinge on children who break the law in a direct fashion. They have material effects. Youth crime has become increasingly politicised, giving rise to a justice system which is arguably ever more punitive in its dealings with children who offend and demonstrates a reduced tolerance for such young people in comparison to adults (Goldson, 2002a). Accordingly, the potential deployment of criminal statistics to support different political agendas is a matter of considerable concern to anybody with an interest in a just, rational and effective youth justice system.

More concretely, the recommendations of the Audit Commission's (1996) influential *Misspent Youth* report, largely credited with providing the blueprint for New Labour's post-1997 youth justice reforms, relied heavily on a particular reading of statistical trends. The report argued that data suggesting a substantial reduction in youth crime since the early 1980s were not persuasive. That conclusion, complemented by a political stance that implied that much youth offending was routinely and unjustifiably minimised, was employed by the incoming Labour government to affirm that there would be *No More Excuses* (Home Office, 1997). Significant change, in the shape of the Crime and Disorder Act 1998 and a swathe of subsequent legislation, followed. Alongside some more welcome reforms (such as the establishment of multi-agency youth offending teams more generously resourced than the services that they replaced), sat other less palatable developments. Forthwith, even a minor infraction of the law, if committed by a child, was to elicit a criminal justice intervention.

As the logic of the interventionist impulse plays out, the limits of the youth justice system have become increasingly blurred. Low-level disorder has become conflated with crime, evidenced by a near obsession with attending to anti-social behaviour, and the development of enforcement measures that target young people disproportionately. Preventive work with children deemed to be 'at risk', who by dint of age or lack of adjudicated offending would previously have been regarded as beyond the purview of criminal justice responses, has become an area of rapid growth. This, despite limited evidence to support such an approach (Armstrong, 2004), and in the face of well-articulated concerns about the 'likely impact of such an early induction into the criminal justice system on the self-perceptions, and subsequent conduct of the children identified' (Pitts, 2005: 9).

The importance of critical engagement with official statistics becomes clear. Making the data useful depends upon asking the right questions, however. Owing to their intrinsic limitations, the data cannot provide an accurate picture of the *volume* of youth crime. Providing that judicious caution is exercised, and proper account is taken of supplementary contextual information, however, it may nonetheless be possible to draw reasonable conclusions about youth crime *trends* in cases where different data-sets point in a consistent direction or, alternatively, inconsistencies in such sets can be analytically explained. Finally, to limit the focus to the behaviour of young people would itself be a mistake, because the statistics are also vulnerable to the impact of systemic change. Any comprehensive account of what youth crime statistics reveal, therefore, will of necessity need to look beyond youth offending itself, to the nature of policy responses and state interventions into the lives of children who transgress the law.

Unwarranted conclusions and consequences

The extent of youth crime

In January 2005, the Home Office published the first results from a new official source, the Crime and Justice Survey, including what proved to be some headline grabbing figures on self-reported offending by young people (Budd et al., 2005). The survey revealed that almost a third of males aged 10–17 years in England and Wales admitted having committed an offence within the past year. According to *The Guardian*, the report 'branded' one in four teenage boys 'a serious offender' (Travis, 2005). It is not difficult to see how such figures, cited out of context, can contribute to a widespread public perception that offending by children is out of control, which in turn requires, and justifies, a tough response (Goldson, 2002b). But a more careful reading of the same statistics, considered contextually, leads to substantially more measured conclusions. In fact, just *17 per cent* of boys aged 10–17 years were classified as having committed a serious offence within the past 12 months. The figure in *The Guardian* headline applied to those defined as serious *or* prolific offenders. The criterion used to demarcate serious criminality also merits attention. A serious offence, for these purposes, means any theft of vehicle, burglary (domestic or commercial), robbery, theft from person, assault resulting in injury (however minor), or selling Class A drugs (whatever the amount, and within a context of most sales being made between friends). While teenage involvement in such activities is no doubt a concern, many of the incidents captured by this measure would almost certainly not correspond to the public's general conception of 'serious'.

Assault occasioning injury, for instance, accounted for the majority of self-reported offences falling within this category of 'seriousness'. Considering that over 10 per cent of boys and girls aged 12–13 years, and 16 per cent of 14–15-year-olds, admitted being responsible for such assaults in the past year, playground fights leading to grazed knees, or bruised arms, are likely to feature highly. Conversely, less than 1 per cent of those under the age of 18 years admitted burglary, robbery or selling Class A drugs, arguably the more genuinely serious of the qualifying offences (although even these cases can include relatively minor infractions).

Perhaps more importantly, findings of high levels of offending are not new. They certainly do nothing to support the contention that youth offending is significantly worse than it has been in the past, or that the youth justice system, prior to 1997, was 'excusing' young people's offending. Pearson's (1983) classic study has shown conclusively that while each generation looks back to a 'golden era' in which young people were less lawless, all attempts to find such a past have proved fruitless. New Labour's reforms of youth justice might reasonably be read as an attempt to reconnect with an earlier period of time (however illusory) within which most young people learned 'respect' and those who broke the law were held to be fully responsible for their actions. But while such a position may yield electoral benefits, it has less justification within a context of 'hard evidence'.

The prevalence of offending revealed in the Crime and Justice survey is similar to, or in some cases lower than, that found in previous self-report studies. Thus Budd et al. (2005: 69) conclude that the 'stability in the offending levels ... might point, then, to a picture of little change in offending by young people'. Similarly, while there are genuine difficulties of comparison over time – statistics are not broken down in the same way – surveys from the 1970s suggest that high levels of self-reported offending by young people are remarkably enduring, and may have been higher in the past. Belson's (1975) survey of schoolboys, for instance, recorded that 70 per cent admitted ever having stolen from a shop, compared with an equivalent figure of 57 per cent for total offending – albeit for both boys and girls aged 14–15 years – in the Crime and Justice survey (Budd et al., 2005).

Self-report surveys do not appear to provide any evidence that youth offending was rising throughout the 1990s and recorded crime figures show a significant, and sustained, decline in children entering the criminal justice system for a period extending over two decades. Between 1980–1990, the number of children aged 10–16 years cautioned or convicted for an indictable offence fell from 175,700 to 110,800 (Rutherford, 1992). The implementation of the Criminal Justice Act 1991 extended the jurisdiction of the youth court (from children aged 10–16 inclusive to those aged 10–17 inclusive) and this makes direct comparisons with the earlier period difficult. Nonetheless, the apparent fall in youth crime continued unabated from 1992 onwards. Ironically, by 1996, when the damning assessment contained in the Audit Commission's *Misspent Youth* report was published, detected youth crime was almost 14 per cent lower than it had been four years earlier. The decline continued at a similar rate up to, and beyond, implementation of the Crime and Disorder Act 1998 (Nacro, 2005a).

As noted above, the Audit Commission (1996) was not persuaded by such data, arguing that the figures might be explained in ways that do not necessarily imply a fall in youth offending. One disputed issue relates to demography. The number of young people aged 10–17 in the overall population has fallen, and a reduction in youth crime might accordingly be anticipated. But from the mid-1980s onwards, detected indictable offences per 100,000 of the population in the relevant age group also fell in line with the decline in absolute numbers (Barclay and Turner, 1991). The Audit Commission was able to argue a contrary position only by assuming that young people acquitted by the courts can legitimately be counted as 'offenders' (Jones, 2001).

As signalled earlier, a second critical question concerns the proportion of offences not reported to the police – or those recorded but undetected – that can reasonably be attributed to young people. The Audit Commission (1996) assumed that if one in four *known* offenders is below the age of 18 years, young people can be considered responsible for a quarter of *all* offending. It followed that, since both the British Crime Survey and police data indicated that overall offending was higher in 1996 than in 1981, youth crime must have risen. Denis Jones (2001), however, in his perceptive critique, provides three convincing arguments for rejecting that assumption. First, the attrition rate (from undetected crime to detected crime) is unlikely to be the same for adults and children since children's offending 'is less sophisticated, less pre-meditated and more liable to detection' (Jones, 2001: 365). Second, there are significant differences in the pattern of adult and youth crime. Children are less likely to commit offences such as fraudulent use of credit cards, theft from employer, and a range of more serious crimes involving firearms, blackmail and murder. They cannot legitimately be considered responsible for a quarter of such incidents. Third, the statistics for detected offending are distorted in ways that ensure young people are over-represented. Policing and the nature of youth crime combine to generate higher arrest rates for children: youth offending is frequently more visible because it tends to occur in public places rather than, for instance, the home or the office; at the same time, police stop and search powers are disproportionately targeted at young people, particularly black youth or those living in areas marked by deprivation and poverty (Goldson and Chigwada-Bailey, 1999).

There are positive reasons too to take seriously the fall in youth offending, evidenced by data on detected crime. Other measures are broadly consistent with such a trend, at least during the 1990s. Police-recorded crime fell every year between 1992 and 1999; moreover, the Home Office attributes subsequent increases to changes in the counting rules and the adoption of more consistent recording practices under the National Crime Recording Standard. The British Crime Survey, which had registered an increase in victimisation up to 1995, also shows sharp reductions in the period since. On this measure, the risk of being a victim is currently at the lowest level since the survey began in 1981 (Finney and Toofail, 2004). Changes in the extent of youth crime cannot, we must conclude, provide an evidential rationale for a more interventionist, or authoritarian, response from the youth justice system.

Growing out of crime

One of the political criticisms levelled at youth justice practice, prior to the post-1997 reforms, was its adherence to the concept that, since juvenile offending was a relatively common feature of adolescence rather than the result of 'individual pathology', the large majority of those committing offences would, if left to their own devices, 'grow out of crime', as part of the maturation process (Rutherford, 1992). The New Labour White Paper *No More Excuses* (Home Office, 1997: Preface) bluntly stated that: 'the research evidence shows that this does not happen'. With this assertion, the government again followed the Audit Commission lead. The *Misspent Youth* report (1996) presented two contra-indicators to the 'growing out of crime' thesis. First, it argued that the known rate of offending by young adult males had risen significantly. Second, it contended that the peak age of known offending by males had increased from '15 years in 1986 to 18 years in 1994' (Audit Commission, 1996: 12). No evidence was offered of a rise in young adult offending, and the claim derives little backing from official data. Between 1984 and 1991, known offending for males aged 17–20 years fell from 119,700 to 111,100 (Home Office, 1987; 1993). The equivalent figures for 18–20-year-olds for 1992 (following the removal of 17-year-olds to the jurisdiction of the youth court) and 1996 (the year of the Audit Commission's report) were 82,700 and 70,500 respectively (Home Office, 1994; 2000).

Similarly, the recorded rise in the peak age of offending for males was not indicative of a gradual process over the period in question, as the Audit Commission account implied. It had already risen to 18 years by 1988 (Barclay and Turner, 1991) and has remained stable in every subsequent year to 2003, with one single exception in 2002 when the peak age fluctuated to 19 years (Nacro, 2005a). Furthermore, a rise in the age at which the occurrence of offending is highest does not necessarily entail a failure to 'grow out of crime'. It is equally compatible with a relative fall in offending by children and young people. Given the reduction in detected youth crime during the 1980s this is indeed a plausible explanation. More concretely, significant decreases in offences of theft and handling stolen goods, offences disproportionately associated with younger children, combined with a relative stability in violent crimes – more prevalent among older teenagers – would be expected to lead to a rise in the peak age for all offences. That is precisely what happened in the mid-1980s (Barclay and Turner, 1991).

Indeed, evidence for the continued relevance of the maturation thesis remains persuasive: most young people will, if given the opportunity to 'survive adolescence without a major sacrifice in life chances' (Zimring, 1978), develop into more-or-less law-abiding adults. The Youth Lifestyles Survey (Flood-Page et al., 2000) confirms that from the age of 18 years, self-reported offending begins to decline, and the fall is both sharper and earlier for violent offences, which appear to be particularly age dependent. The prevalence of property crime remains relatively constant until the late 20s, but there is an important shift in the nature of such offending: shoplifting and handling stolen goods fall, while workplace fraud and theft increase as young adults enter the labour market. If the latter two offence types are excluded, Flood-Page et al. (2000) confirm that boys do 'grow out of crime' as they make the transition to adulthood. The Edinburgh Study of Youth Transitions and Crime, a longitudinal study of 4,300 children who started secondary school in 1998, draws similar conclusions, though more boldly stated, and with an important caveat:

> much youth offending should be treated as natural and normal, and will fade as young people grow into adulthood, provided that there is no drastic response to the offending that is seriously damaging to the teenager. This applies equally to girls and boys. (Smith and McAra, 2004: 21)

The creation of a 'new youth justice' (particularly in England and Wales) was predicated on an assumption that increasing youth lawlessness and a failure to mature out of offending necessitated a radical cultural shift. Criminal behaviour was not to be 'excused' and any child caught offending should expect a formal criminal justice sanction. Early intervention was not, moreover, to be restricted to those who offend and the reach of the youth justice system would extend to children below the age of criminal responsibility and those whose behaviour fell short of adjudicated offending (Goldson, 2005). The argument thus far is that the statistical evidence supposedly underpinning such reform is weak. But the problem goes further than this. It may also be the case, as some have argued, that erroneous and/or distorted readings of crime statistics have served to legitimise drastic responses to young people who offend, of the type that Smith and McAra caution against, and that such interventions are, in themselves, seriously damaging and disfiguring of the maturational process.

Statistical evidence of damaging responses

The punitive turn, alluded to earlier in this chapter, had its roots in the early 1990s, predating New Labour's post-1997 youth justice reforms. Thus the Crime and Disorder Act 1998 reinforced pre-existing policy trends rather than marking a sharp departure from the immediate past. While criminal statistics may have provided no legitimate *basis* for the development of an increasingly authoritarian climate, the material *effects* of that shift are clearly visible in the data. Two features, an increase in the rate of prosecution and a rise in the use of custody, are characteristic of the treatment of all children in trouble in recent years – though they have manifested themselves most acutely in the way that girls are processed through the youth justice system (Gelsthorpe, 2005).

The rate of diversion from court – the proportion of convictions, cautions, reprimands and warnings that result in a pre-court disposal – declined from 73.5 to 55.9 per cent between 1992 and 2003, leading to a consequent proportionate increase in prosecution (Nacro, 2005a). At the opposite end of the system, deprivation of liberty is increasingly common, with black and minority ethnic children hit particularly hard (Kalunta-Crumpton, 2005). Between 1992 and 2003, the number of custodial sentences rose by 55 per cent and the growth would have been much sharper but for a significant fall in the latter year (Nacro, 2005a). On one estimate, and whilst acknowledging that there are difficulties of comparison (Muncie and Goldson, 2006), the level of custody in England and Wales is, relative to the 10–17-years-old population, four times higher than that in France, 10 times higher than that in Spain and 100 times higher than that in Finland (Nacro, 2003a). The growth in the numbers of children locked up is almost entirely due to harsher treatment, rather than changes in the pattern of youth offending and youth crime. For instance, not only are theft and handling stolen goods increasingly more likely to attract a custodial outcome, but the average length of sentence has also risen from 3.9 months in 1993 to 6.1 months in 2003. The equivalent sentence lengths for burglary are 4 and 7.8 months respectively (Home Office, 2005b).

The deleterious effects of custody on the lives of already disadvantaged, and frequently vulnerable, children are well documented (Nacro, 2003b), but two sets of statistics from official sources stand out. The first indicates that attention to evidence would dictate a reduction rather than an increase in the use of detention: 82 per cent of boys released from young offender institutions in 2001 were reconvicted within two years of release. For those with between 3–6 previous convictions, the figure rose to 92 per cent (Home Office, 2004a). The second confirms that penal custody constitutes a 'seriously damaging' response. During 2002, there were 460 recorded incidents of children self-harming in young offender institutions (National Audit Office, 2004). No doubt many lesser incidents go unreported.

Few would doubt the harmful effects of custody, but it is important to acknowledge evidence that prosecution too is harmful. Johnson et al. (2004) have recently reported that formal involvement in the criminal justice system is correlated with increased delinquency, which in turn has negative consequences for children's subsequent life chances. In Northamptonshire, practice has, to date, resisted a rigid application of the final warning scheme's 'three strikes' model, inserting an additional layer of 'informal action' into the pre-court process, on the basis of research findings that prosecution should be delayed beyond the fourth proceedings if it is not to exacerbate the risk of reoffending (Kemp et al., 2002).

Acting on the available evidence then, would imply a set of policy responses serving to expand the practice of diversion and limit the imposition of custodial sanctions. Furthermore, there are additional grounds for developing such an approach. Recent analysis has illuminated an inverse correlation between the rate of diversion and the use of custody (Bateman, 2005; Nacro, 2005b). A clear historical pattern emerges from the statistical data. During the 1980s, the proportion of cases resulting in a caution rose from 44 to 75 per cent, leading to a significant fall in court throughput (Rutherford, 1992). An increase in the *rate* of custody might have been expected as a growing proportion of relatively trivial offences were filtered out at the pre-court stage. In the event, custody as a proportion of convictions remained remarkably stable, leading to a fall in the *absolute number* of custodial disposals in line with the drop in the court population. The 1990s provided a mirror image of that pattern: a decline in the rate of diversion led to an influx of less serious offences into the court arena, generating an overall rise in convictions, despite the fall in known offending. Once again, the *rate* of custody remained relatively stable even though the courts were dealing with a growing proportion of trivial cases. The inevitable result was that, as the pool of children sentenced in court has expanded, so too have the numbers of children consigned to penal institutions.

Why this pattern should obtain is not immediately obvious, but it seems likely that the psychological impact of increases in the court population, particularly against the backdrop of heightened media and political sensitivity to youth offending, is to suggest that youth crime is spiralling upward, and that tough measures are required to combat it. At the same time, early entry to the court system generates a longer 'criminal history' leading to an accelerated, upward, trajectory along the sentencing 'tariff'. Whatever the mechanism, the statistical evidence supports the conclusion that 'the demise of diversion has in effect been a consequence of, but has also contributed to, the punitive environment in which decisions to deprive children of their liberty are taken' (Nacro, 2005b: 29). This finding has a particular contemporary significance. In consulting over what steps youth justice should take in the coming period, the government has signalled its desire to curb the use of custody for young people in England and Wales, but at the same time it has reiterated a commitment to the final warning scheme, in its current, rigid, configuration (Home Office, 2004b). An evidence-led policy would suggest that the two strategies may not be compatible.

Conclusion

Criminal statistics cannot provide a 'true' picture of young people's offending, but to completely disregard their significance on that basis would be unwise. Asking the right questions, while recognising the limitations of the data, has the potential to generate an important body of knowledge with which to inform youth justice policy. In subjecting the data to critical scrutiny, serious questions emerge relating to the legitimacy of the more interventionist and expansionist elements of contemporary youth justice reform. At the same time, such reforms have served to reinforce aspects of a 'new punitiveness' (Goldson, 2002b), and, in so doing, may also have encouraged seriously damaging responses to children in trouble. The statistical evidence suggests that New Labour's 'evidence-driven' youth justice may actually exacerbate the problems of youth crime that it purports to positively address.

References

Allen, J., Dodd, T. and Salisbury, H. (2005) *Crime in England and Wales: Quarterly Update to September 2004*, Statistical bulletin 03/05. London: Home Office.

Armstrong, D. (2004) 'A Risky Business? Research, Policy, Governmentality and Youth Offending', *Youth Justice,* 4(2): 100–16.

Audit Commission (1996) *Misspent Youth: Young People and Crime*. London: Audit Commission.

Bandalli, S. (2000) 'Children, Responsibility and the New Youth Justice,' in B. Goldson (ed.) *The New Youth Justice*. Lyme Regis: Russell House Publishing.

Barclay, G. and Turner, D. (1991) 'Recent Trends in Official Statistics on Juvenile Offending in England and Wales', in T. Booth (ed.) *Juvenile Justice in the New Europe*. Sheffield: Joint Unit for Social Services Research.

Barrett, D. and Dean, N. (2005) 'Leap in Violent Crime and Gun Offences', *The Independent*, 25 January.

Bateman, T. (2003) 'Living with Final Warnings: Making the Best of a Bad Job?', *Youth Justice*, 2(3): 131–40.

Bateman, T. (2005) 'Reducing Child Imprisonment: A Systemic Challenge', *Youth Justice*, 5(2): 91–105.

Belson, W. (1975) *Juvenile Theft: The Causal Factors*. London: Harper and Row.

Budd, T., Sharp, C. and Mayhew, P. (2005) *Offending in England and Wales: First Results from the 2003 Crime and Justice Survey*. Research Study 275. London: Home Office.

Finney, A. and Toofail, J. (2004) 'Levels and Trends,' in T. Dodd, S. Nicholas, D. Povey and A. Walker (eds) *Crime in England and Wales 2003/2004*. Statistical Bulletin 10/04. London: Home Office.

Flood-Page, C., Campbell, S., Harrington, V. and Miller, J. (2000) *Youth Crime: Findings from the 1998/1999 Youth Lifestyles Survey*. Research Study 209. London: Home Office.

Garside, R. (2004) *Crime, Persistent Offenders and the Justice Gap*. London: Crime and Society Foundation.

Gelsthorpe, L. (2005) 'Girls in the Youth Justice System', in T. Bateman and J. Pitts (eds) *The RHP Companion to Youth Justice*. Lyme Regis: Russell House Publishing.

Goldson, B. (2000) *The New Youth Justice*. Lyme Regis: Russell House Publishing.

Goldson, B. (2002a) 'New Labour, Social Justice and Children: Political Calculation and the Deserving–Undeserving Schism'. *British Journal of Social Work*, 32 (September).

Goldson, B. (2002b) 'New Punitiveness; the Politics of Child Incarceration', in J. Muncie, G. Hughes and E. McLaughlin (eds) *Youth Justice: Critical Readings*. London: Sage.

Goldson, B. (2005) 'Taking Liberties: Policy and the Punitive Turn', in H. Hendrick (ed.) *Child Welfare and Social Policy*. Bristol: The Policy Press.

Goldson, B. and Chigwada-Bailey, R. (1999) '(What) Justice for Black Children and Young People?', in B. Goldson (ed.) *Youth Justice: Contemporary Policy and Practice*, Aldershot: Ashgate.

Guardian, The (2005) 'Violent Offences Rise but Overall Crime is Down', 25 January.

Home Office (1987) *Criminal Statistics for England and Wales 1986*. London: HMSO.

Home Office (1993) *Criminal Statistics for England and Wales 1992*. London: HMSO.

Home Office (1994) *Criminal Statistics for England and Wales 1993*. London: HMSO.

Home Office (1997) *No More Excuses: A New Approach to Tackling Youth Crime in England and Wales*. London: The Stationery Office.

Home Office (2000) *Criminal Statistics for England and Wales 1998*. London: The Stationery Office.

Home Office (2004a) *Offender Management Caseload Statistics 2003*. Statistical Bulletin 15/04. London: Home Office.

Home Office (2004b) *Youth Justice – the Next Steps: Summary of Responses and the Government's Proposals*. London: Home Office.

Home Office (2005a) *Crime Continues to Fall.* Press release 015/2005. London: Home Office.

Home Office (2005b) *Sentencing Statistics 2003 England and Wales*. Statistical Bulletin 05/05. London: Home Office.

Johnson, L., Simons, R. and Conger, R. (2004) 'Criminal Justice Involvement and the Continuity of Youth Crime', *Youth and Society,* 36(1): 3–29.

Jones, D. (2001) 'Misjudged Youth: a Critique of the Audit Commission's Reports on Youth Justice', *British Journal of Criminology,* 41: 362–80.

Kalunta-Crumpton, A. (2005) 'Race, Crime and Youth Justice,' in T. Bateman and J. Pitts (eds) *The RHP Companion to Youth Justice*. Lyme Regis: Russell House Publishing.

Muncie, J. (2001) 'The Construction and Deconstruction of Crime', in J. Muncie and E. McLaughlin (eds) *The Problem of Crime*. (2nd edn) London: Sage.

Muncie, J. (2002) 'Official Crime Statistics: Next to Useless?', *Safer Society,* 11 (Winter 2001/2002).

Muncie, J. and Goldson, B. (eds) (2006) *Comparative Youth Justice*. London: Sage.

Nacro (2003a) *A Failure of Justice: Reducing Child Imprisonment.* London: Nacro.

Nacro (2003b) *Counting the Cost: Reducing Child Imprisonment*. London: Nacro.

Nacro (2005a) *Some Facts about Young People who Offend – 2003*. Youth crime briefing. London: Nacro.

Nacro (2005b) *A Better Alternative: Reducing Child Imprisonment*. London: Nacro.

National Audit Office (2004) *Youth Offending: The Delivery of Community and Custodial Sentencing*. London: The Stationery Office.

Pearson, G. (1983) *Hooligan: A History of Respectable Fears*. Southampton: Macmillan.

Pitts, J. (2005) 'The Recent History of Youth Justice in England and Wales', in T. Bateman and J. Pitts (eds) *The RHP Companion to Youth Justice*. Lyme Regis: Russell House Publishing.

Pragnall, S. (2005) 'Reprimands and Final Warnings', in T. Bateman and J. Pitts (eds) *The RHP Companion to Youth Justice*. Lyme Regis: Russell House Publishing.

Rutherford, A. (1992) *Growing Out of Crime: The New Era*. Winchester: Waterside Press.

Salisbury, H. (2003) 'Trends in Crime', in J. Simmons and T. Dodd (eds) *Crime in England and Wales 2002/2003*, Statistical Bulletin 07/03. London: Home Office.

Smith, D. and McAra, L. (2004) *Gender and Youth Offending*. Edinburgh: University of Edinburgh Press.

Thomas, N. and Feist, A. (2004) 'Detection of Crime,' in T. Dodd, S. Nicholas, D. Povey and A. Walker (eds) *Crime in England and Wales 2003/2004*, Statistical Bulletin 10/04. London: Home Office.

Travis, A. (2005), 'One in Four Teenage Boys Branded a Serious Offender', *The Guardian,* 26 January.

Zimring, F. (1978) *Confronting Youth Crime*. New York: Holmes and Meier.

Youth Crime and Justice: Research, Evaluation and 'Evidence'

David Smith

This chapter argues, first, that the youth justice policies of the New Labour governments since 1997, while often claimed to be 'evidence-based', have at best been only partly so. It then suggests that much thinking about the possibility of evidence-based policy is based on misconceptions on the part of policy-makers about the nature of the evidence available, and illustrates the effects of these misconceptions with the example of the 'What Works' movement in probation. The 'failure' of research on initiatives supposedly based on 'what works' principles to provide clear confirming evidence to support the movement led to an official response that what was needed was more rigorously 'scientific' and experimental research, but the chapter argues that there is no reason to believe that, even if such research could be carried out, it would remove current uncertainties and ambiguities. The chapter concludes with an argument for a more modest and realistic view of what research and evaluation can contribute to policy and practice.

New Labour, evidence-based policy and youth justice

An important part of the agenda of New Labour was the 'modernisation' of the processes of government, and this applied at least as forcefully to youth justice as it did to other areas of policy (Muncie, 2002). Modernisation entailed, in particular, greater policy coherence ('joined-up' government) and a commitment to evidence-based policy. The 1999 White Paper on *Modernising Government*, for example, argued that policy must be based on evidence and on what was known about best practice, and must in turn be subjected to evaluation, thus extending the pool of available evidence (Cabinet Office, 1999a). The Cabinet Office (1999b) returned to this theme when arguing for the need for policy-making to become more 'professional': 'policy making must be soundly based on evidence of what works', and government departments needed to improve their openness to and willingness to use evidence. Two years later, the Cabinet Office (2001) reported that policy was now 'more informed by evidence' and that new evidence was being produced, through the review of existing policies, and the piloting and evaluation of new ideas. What this represents, according to Davies (2004), is a move from 'opinion-based' to 'evidence-based' policy, and thus (ideally) from speculation to intellectually rigorous assessment of evidence as the basis for policy choices.

Davies (2004) is an optimist about the possibility of evidence-based policy, but he fully recognises that factors other than evidence are bound to influence government decisions: there will always be resource constraints, for example, lobbyists and pressure groups will demand attention, habit and traditional ways of conceiving problems are hard to change, and political ideologies and considerations of electoral popularity will inevitably enter the decision-making process. That is, the process will never be as 'rational' as the most enthusiastic proponents of evidence-based policy might wish. This is fully apparent in the Labour government's approach to youth justice, in which 'modernisation' turned out to mean a good deal more (or less) than a commitment to joined-up, empirically-based policies. As Jones (2002) demonstrates, the government was able to act as quickly as it did after the 1997 general election because many of the ideas that appeared in the Crime and Disorder Act 1998 had been developed in a series of papers the Labour Party had produced over the previous five years. There were to be 'No more excuses' (Home Office, 1997) for young offenders or for the failures of the system to deal with them effectively; an alleged 'culture of excuse' was to be replaced by a culture of responsibility. This entailed a very specific rejection of the policy and practice of diversion of young people from the formal criminal justice system, as part of what Jones (2002: 15) calls the Youth Justice Board's 'apparent expurgation of all youth justice knowledge and practice prior to 1998'. Whatever *was* to count as evidence, the skills and experience of youth justice practitioners were definitely not.

In reality, it is difficult to see the abandonment of diversion as based on any kind of evidence. In the 1980s, youth justice policies, and, importantly, the informed, reflective and strategic work of practitioners, not only produced a substantial and enduring degree of diversion of young people from the criminal justice system and from custody, but enabled the development of new approaches to direct work with those who could not be diverted. Even critics of the strategy recognised that by the end of the 1980s it had some major achievements to its credit. It had contributed to a reversal of the previous trend to a greater use of custody, its approach to direct work was taken as a model for work with adult offenders, and many projects had the flexibility to diversify into broader social crime prevention or work with victims (Blagg and Smith, 1989; Pitts, 1992). That is, there was a consensus among criminological commentators as well as policy-makers that an approach founded on diversion and the careful avoidance of excessive intervention had helped in the achievement of valued policy aims.

The change in policy that was signalled by the slogan 'no more excuses' was therefore based on considerations that were ideological rather than empirical. According to Tonry (2004), New Labour's penal policies have been evidence-based only when their visibility has been low; high visibility initiatives have invariably been driven by the need to be seen to be tough on crime, whatever the evidence may say. Thus, for example, Butler and Drakeford (1997) argued that the Labour Party had needlessly conceded that youth crime constituted a crisis to which tougher policies were the only solution. Smith (2001) complained that the Crime and Disorder Act 1998 was characterised by a preoccupation with surveillance and control that would lead to excessive intervention in the lives of young people and their families. In a more complex analysis that reflected some of their ambiguities, Muncie (2000: 31) identified the key themes of the new policies as managerialism, communitarianism and populist puni-tiveness, underpinned by 'paternalism, responsibilisation and remoralisation'. Pitts (2001) complained of the 'zombification' of youth justice under the con-trolling spell of the Youth Justice Board for England and Wales, and of the 'Year Zero' style of the Board's rhetoric, with its exaggerated and over-simplified ten-dency to contrast the unadulterated success of policy since 1998 with the unmiti-gated failure of all that preceded it. Instead of diversion, early intervention was promoted; 'net-widening', instead of being an effect to be avoided (Cohen, 1985), became a positively desirable aim of policy. The youth justice system, including the custodial part of it, was redefined as a resource not only for the law-abiding public but for young people in trouble and their families, providing opportunities for reparation, moral development, cognitive therapies, treatment for substance dependence, special education and improved parenting skills.

It is impossible, then, to make sense of the major changes of policy introduced by the Labour government after 1997 in terms of a rational, empirical, evidence-based model. Such evidence as was available pointed to the retention, not the abandonment, of diversion as a policy aim, and to a reduced, not an increased, use of custody (Goldson, 2001). In other, lower profile, areas, the government could reasonably claim that there was an evidence base for what it tried to do: programmes like On Track (Hine, 2005) and Sure Start (Glass, 1999; Tunstill et al., 2005) were based on some evidence of what constituted effective forms of family support and early years intervention. Glass (1999: 260), the civil ser-vant most associated with the origins of Sure Start, wrote that it was an exam-ple of 'joined-up government and evidence-based policy making, with its origins grounded in a thorough analysis of the research literature of "what works"'. Glass's claim arguably errs on the side of optimism, since the relevant evidence comes from a small number of studies conducted in the USA (Karoly et al., 1998), but it also has some substance. Youth justice, however, proved too polit-ically sensitive an issue for the evidence to be allowed to get in the way; New Labour's embrace of evidence as a means of shaping policy was, and remained, selective (Goldson, 2001).

The possibility of evidence-based policy

As often in discussions of evidence-based policy and practice, Davies's (2004) source (Gray, 1997) is concerned with the use of evidence in medicine and health care: evidence-based medicine is taken as a model for the use of evidence to inform policy and practice in other areas. In a well-known definition of evidence-based medicine (EBM), Sackett et al. describe it as:

> the conscientious, explicit and judicious use of current best evidence in making decisions about the care of individual patients, based on skills which allow the doctor to evaluate both personal experience and external evidence in a systematic and objective manner. (1997: 71)

An important feature of this definition (which is echoed by Davies but not by the Youth Justice Board for England and Wales) is that the skills and experience of the practitioner or policy-maker count as a valid basis for decision-making, along with evidence derived from formal clinical trials. The latter, at least when it is based on a sufficient number of trials to allow for a synthesis of the results, is usually and with good reason regarded as 'harder' and more reliable than the kind of evidence available to practitioners of social rather than medical interventions. This is because the trials that form an important basis for EBM consist, or in principle can consist, of the application of a single treatment (the administration of a drug) for a relatively well-defined problem, with relatively well-defined outcomes (the patient either does or does not recover). This is an over-simplification, of course, as few medical treatments have entirely or universally predictable results; but it is certainly the case, as Pawson (2002a: 168) puts it, that 'problem "heterogeneity" remains in EBM but it is not of the same order as in EBP [evidence-based policy], where interventions work through reasoning subjects rather than blinded patients'.

Given the greater controllability and predictability of medical interventions compared with social interventions, it may come as a surprise that advocates of an evidence-based approach to the latter sometimes adopt a more rather than a less restrictive definition, one that excludes the skills of practitioners and their capacity to evaluate their own experiences (Taylor and White, 2002). In the version of what it means to be evidence-based used by the Centre for Evidence-Based Social Services at Exeter University (see www.ex.ac.uk/cebss/), Sackett et al.'s definition becomes: 'Evidence-based social care is the conscientious, explicit and judicious use of current best evidence in making decisions regarding the welfare of those in need.' The author of this definition, Brian Sheldon, thinks that social work has suffered more than other forms of human service from susceptibility to fads and fashions, and it is this (Sheldon, 1998: 16) that justifies the exclusion of practitioners' own knowledge and experience; only thus can they be restrained from falling back on subjective preferences and pet ideas. This assumes that the evidence exists – out there rather than in here – and that it is substantial and accessible enough to enable practitioners to select appropriate 'helping recipes' that should then be applied 'cautiously and within their known scope'.

Whether evidence of this objective, scientific kind exists – or can exist – for social as opposed to medical interventions is problematic. An example that illustrates some of the problems is that of meta-analysis of a large number of results from evaluative studies, which is often viewed as the only valid means of constructing an evidence base for policy (meta-analysis was the basis both for the claim that 'nothing works' in interventions with offenders and for the revival of the belief that something might work (Lipton et al., 1975; McIvor, 1990)). Pawson (2002a and b) identifies two main approaches to meta-analysis – the numerical and narrative approaches – and is critical of both. The numerical approach, he argues, produces a list of 'best buys' identified by an arithmetically expressed 'effect size' that is the product of reiterated averaging and conflation of results from disparate programmes (metaphorically, it fails to distinguish between apples and oranges). The narrative approach allows for a better understanding of the context and process of programmes, but the basis on which it moves from this description to a list of 'exemplars' of good practice is, according to Pawson, unclear and often apparently intuitive. Nor is it clear what the policy-maker is to do with the examples for imitation and emulation, since precise replication is impossible: 'inevitably there are differences in infrastructure, institutions, practitioners and subjects' (Pawson, 2002a: 177; see also Muncie, 2002) that mean that the process of implementation will never be the same from one context to another.

Pawson regards some process like meta-analysis as essential for the development of evidence-based policy, but also believes that 'the issue of finding the precise criterion for making meta-evaluative judgements has yet to be solved' (Pawson, 2002b: 356). His preferred alternative to the existing approaches is 'realist synthesis', in which programmes would be grouped by the 'mechanism' they employ rather than by the problem they seek to address. So rather than grouping (for example) early intervention programmes for children in disadvantaged families, which might use a range of quite different mechanisms for change, programmes could be grouped across diverse problem areas by the change mechanism they use. Pawson's (2002b) main example is of policies that use some form of incentive or reward; other high-level examples, very much not chosen at random, might be the setting of targets, multi-agency partnerships, and the introduction of competition or 'contestability' in service provision. Pawson (2002b: 357) acknowledges that no-one knows how the messages of realist synthesis – typically, 'a tale of caution delivered at a modest level of abstraction' – would be received by policy-makers used to being told what would be the 'best buy', or what models are worthy of attempted replication. Policy-makers long for certainty, for 'one best way' answers (Smith, 2004), and realist synthesis is unlikely to provide them.

Nevertheless, an approach like that advocated by Pawson represents a huge advance in terms of sophistication and potential usefulness over the uncritically positivist understanding of what counts as evidence that continues to dominate official thinking about 'what works' – and what doesn't – in interventions with offenders. This approach can be seen in its purest form in the 'What Works' movement that has developed in the probation service in England and Wales (and in criminal justice social work in Scotland) since the early 1990s, and, according to Mair (2004), was given added impetus by the election of the Labour government in 1997, with its explicit commitment to 'modernisation'. 'Positivism' in this context means the assumption that knowledge in the social sciences is essentially similar in kind to knowledge in the natural sciences, and that if social science is properly conducted, it can produce universal truths that are as stable and reliable as those of, for example, chemistry.

This is a view of social science that has evident attractions for managers and bureaucrats, since it offers certainty, predictability, tidiness and order, in place of the messy, unpredictable and contingent circumstances that make the business of management so difficult (MacIntyre, 1985). It is, however, a view that rests on a mistaken assumption about the social sciences and the nature of the generalisations that can be derived from their empirical findings. Following MacIntyre, I have argued elsewhere (Smith, 2004) that the logic of empirically derived theories in the social sciences is necessarily different from that of theories in the natural sciences, because what happens in the social world can never be made completely predictable. A single observation that disconfirmed the theory of gravity would require that the theory be modified if not abandoned; but in the social sciences a theory can go on being useful even if its specific predictions are quite often disconfirmed, as in MacIntyre's example of the theory of defensible space. As Braithwaite (1993: 386–38) put it, for practical problem-solving purposes, 'it is contextualized usefulness that counts, not decontextualized statistical power'. Positivist social science can enable us to disregard some theories, but we cannot expect it to 'deliver us a unified explanatory edifice' that will answer all our questions. Yet this is what politicians and policy-makers – understandably – want, and what some social scientists have been prepared to claim they have to offer.

The key example of this in current policy, particularly in the probation service but in a less monolithic way in youth justice too, is that of cognitive-behavioural offending-focused groupwork programmes. Meta-analysis had undoubtedly suggested that such programmes represented a promising approach to work with serious and persistent offenders (McGuire, 1995; McIvor, 1990), but Mair (2004) suggests that the evidence only became influential because of a unique combination of a new, modernising government and enthusiastic advocacy of this approach from individuals in key positions in the Home Office and the probation inspectorate. Instead of adopting a stance of cautious and tentative optimism, which would have been a rational response to the research evidence, managers were encouraged to accept these programmes as the unique answer to the question 'What works?', and to ensure that they – and nothing else – became the core of probation practice. Programmes were 'rolled out' with little attention to the questions of context and process which are central to the realist approach to understanding what works, and some basic messages from the original research were ignored or forgotten. For example, the 'risk principle' (Andrews et al., 1990), which specified that the intensity of intervention should be proportional to the assessed risk of reoffending, was in effect abandoned, as cognitive-behavioural programmes were increasingly seen as the best form of provision for everyone, leading the chief inspector of probation to complain of 'programme fetishism' (HM Inspectorate of Probation, 2002; 2004).

The researchers who produced and disseminated the evidence that was interpreted in this fetishistic style could quite legitimately complain that they had never claimed that cognitive-behavioural programmes were the single form of intervention that 'worked', and worked so well that they ought to displace everything else (see for example Raynor, 2004a). The development of the 'What Works' movement is an example not of the failure of research to produce useable evidence but of the problems that can and typically do arise in the process of making sense of the evidence as a basis for policy. This process is inevitably complex and highly politicised, and what is selected as evidence to inform policy depends on factors other than the quality of the evidence (for a classic statement, see Weiss with Bucuvalas, 1980). It is therefore no surprise that Mair should conclude that:

> in spite of the rhetoric, the foundations of What Works cannot be said to be neat, evidence based, carefully considered and well planned ... While we may imagine policy-making to be the result of a detailed, rational sifting of options and decision-making based upon clear evidence, this is certainly not the case with What Works. (2004: 21)

Mair goes on to quote Garland (2001: 26) on how the selection of policy is typically 'driven by value commitments rather than informed instrumental calculation'. This is true of policy areas other than criminal justice, but there are, as argued by Tonry (2004), special political pressures in crime policy that make it especially vulnerable to 'the politics of electoral anxiety' (Pitts, 2000).

In the late 1980s, Raynor (1988) and Roberts (1989) cautiously reintroduced the idea that something might work, after years of 'Nothing works' despondency. These studies were reinforced by McIvor's (1990) overview of sanctions for serious and persistent offenders, and by the later careful evaluation by Raynor and Vanstone (1996; 1997) of a programme adapted from a Canadian model, Reasoning and Rehabilitation. A rational response to the findings reported in this body of work might have been that we now had reasonably strong indicators of what kinds of approach might work better than others with relatively serious offenders, given good staffing and management, a commitment to evaluation, and appropriate continued support after the intensive programme had been completed. The reports that came from the Home Office's own research section were in fact appropriately cautious. Vennard et al. (1997: viii) described the findings as 'positive, but inconclusive', and argued that much remained to be 'known about what type of approach works best, under what conditions and types of setting, with whom'. They found that existing cognitive-behavioural programmes were often delivered by under-trained staff who paid little attention to programme integrity, risk and need principles, or whether the programmes were effective. In a broader-ranging and explicitly policy-oriented collection published by the Home Office in the following year, Vennard and Hedderman (1998: 115) argued that Canadian findings should be treated cautiously when transplanted from their original context and concluded that there had been 'very few well-designed and carefully evaluated studies in this country of the effectiveness of programmes designed to rehabilitate and reduce the risk of reoffending'. They noted the need for more work on the link between risk and level of intervention and on what subsequent work could best sustain any progress made during the course of a programme. Similarly, Underdown (1998) found that while cognitive-behavioural programmes were widespread in the probation service, only a tiny fraction had been subjected to any serious evaluation of their effectiveness.

In a later review of the present state of knowledge of 'what works', Chitty (2005: 77) continued to acknowledge that the main evidence for the effectiveness of cognitive-behavioural programmes 'comes from meta-analytic studies and primary studies of research done abroad ... In Britain, the evidence is mixed and limited.' This is partly a result of problems of implementation, and Chitty (2005: 79) notes that: 'many of the results reported in this volume say a great deal about implementation, its problems and its effects on outcomes rather than the true effects of interventions'. Since any programme can only have effects if it is implemented, it is not clear what this distinction means, though it could be taken as pointing to the need for a theory of intervention, or, in Keat's (1981) terms, a theory of technique, of the kind that realist evaluators would regard as indispensable. For Chitty and her colleagues, however, the answer lies in greater methodological rigour in the design and conduct of research: only randomised controlled trials (RCTs) are robust enough to ensure 'that our knowledge of "what works" is truly improved and the existing equivocal evidence is replaced with greater certainty' (Chitty, 2005: 82). None of the 30 studies reviewed by Chitty and her fellow Home Office researchers approached this standard of rigour and certainty, and most were judged to have fallen far short. In other words, 'we did the wrong kind of research' (Raynor, 2004b: 319).

The difficulties of evaluation in practice

Whether RCTs are actually feasible in the criminal justice field in general, and the youth justice context in particular, remains to be seen; there are evident ethical problems (about denying someone an intervention that might actually be helpful) as well as practical ones (random allocation may not produce comparable groups, for instance). It is also worth considering whether even a successful RCT would deliver the certainty that Chitty (2005) claims it would. The best-known British RCT in the criminal justice field is the IMPACT experiment, whose results were reported by Folkard et al. (1976). This was widely interpreted as showing that intensive probation produced worse results than normal probation, and thus made its own modest contribution to the gloomy faith that 'nothing works'. It is not clear, however, that this interpretation was justified (Pease, 1984), and rather than settling an argument, the IMPACT report generated controversy about just what it had measured and what (if any) messages for practice it conveyed.

No doubt future RCTs of the effectiveness of interventions would be better controlled than IMPACT was, in that they would allow more to be said about the processes that could plausibly be claimed as having produced whatever outcomes are found; even so, as Raynor (2004b: 319) argues, 'it would be unwise to put all our heuristic eggs in this one basket ... Unless we know in detail how outcomes are produced we are unlikely to be able to replicate them.' There is also the issue of implementation, which cannot simply be wished away: 'Pathfinder' evaluations repeatedly encountered practical problems that in some cases meant that numbers were too small for any conclusions about effectiveness to be drawn; for example, very few offenders assessed as having basic skills needs actually started the projects designed for them, and a minute proportion completed them (McMahon et al., 2004).

What can be learned from an evaluation of this kind is therefore more to do with implementation than with the effects of basic skills training on reconviction, and such learning is potentially valuable. But two points are worth noting. First, if the Pathfinder projects are to be regarded as having failed, which seems to be the (premature and over-generalised) view of the Home Office, it is not straightforward to decide whether the failure was one of theory or of implementation, because the two are intimately linked. The theory underlying cognitive-behavioural groupwork does not necessarily have to be abandoned in the light of the failure of the Pathfinder research to find positive results, since the failure may be better explained by a theory of implementation: the conditions in which such groupwork programmes are implemented may reduce the chances of success (if, for example, there is a long waiting period before the programme starts, the members of the group are uncomfortable in each other's company, or the group leaders are unmotivated). Second, implementation is always going to be difficult, especially when projects move beyond the pilot or demonstration stage, because of inevitable variations in management competence, offender motivation, staff skill and interest, the quality and accessibility of the programme site, the mix of personalities in the group, and so on. Ideal implementation is probably unachievable, and certainly cannot be assumed in advance; and there is no reason to believe that an RCT approach to evaluation would not run into exactly the same kind of problems as those encountered in the Pathfinder research.

All this is an elaboration of an apparently straightforward point: that good evaluation research is difficult to do, and will rarely, if ever, produce results that are as clear-cut and unambiguous as governments would like them to be. A glance at the Youth Justice Board's own research reports illustrates the point. The Board has been less committed than the Home Office and the National Probation Service to a particular (cognitive-behavioural) model of intervention, but it has of course been influenced by the same evaluation findings, and one of the seven types of project it specifically sought to support from 1999 was cognitive-behavioural work (Feilzer et al., 2004). As with much of the research commissioned by the Board (cf. Hammersley et al., 2004; Wilcox, 2003), the national evaluation depended upon the work of local evaluators. The three-way relationship between the national evaluators, the local evaluators and the project staff 'was challenging and caused a number of problems for both local and national evaluators' (Feilzer et al., 2004: 5). The data collected by the local evaluators differed across the 23 projects studied (four of which, incidentally, were judged not to be fully cognitive-behavioural in their approach); the evaluation was 'severely limited by the partial data made available to the national evaluators' (Feilzer et al., 2004: 7) – partial because of problems in data collection but also because the numbers of young people referred were lower than expected; the local evaluators of half of the projects felt that questions about how far the projects had achieved their and the Board's aims and objectives were premature, while the evaluators of the other half thought that at least some objectives had been achieved, while providing little evidence to support the claim; and it was not clear how the samples interviewed by local evaluators had been selected, and therefore how representative they were. The evaluation was 'further hindered by the substantial delays in the setting-up and implementation of the projects' (Feilzer et al., 2004: 7).

Conclusions

Presumably ways could be identified of avoiding or minimising some of these problems in future evaluations; for example, agreement could be reached in advance about what data to collect locally, and the purposes and requirements of the evaluation could be better explained to project staff (Wilcox (2003) is optimistic about the Youth Justice Board's capacity to learn from experience). But it is difficult to see how future work of this kind could be free of all such problems. A mix of local and national evaluation is the obvious procedure when more than a handful of projects are being examined, and it is inevitable that the local evaluations will vary in scope and quality. Furthermore, for all its limitations, it would be wrong to regard a study like this as without value. Feilzer et al. (2004) fully recognise the preliminary nature of the study, and suggest that further work should involve the rigorous evaluation, with control groups, of the projects whose work was judged most promising, which would be treated as demonstration projects that might in time come to form a model of good practice. Thus the research process would need to be a long-term, incremental one, rather than producing at a stroke all the answers to the policy-makers' questions. This is the position of Earle et al. (2003); reviewing their experience of evaluating the introduction of referral orders, they conclude:

> An interactive process that involves politicians, policy-makers, practitioners and independent academic researchers in both the design and implementation of policy, is surely the best way of guarding against the dominance of ideology and populist politics in the youth justice system. (2003: 149)

Similarly, Raynor (2004b: 322) concludes his discussion of the evaluation of the probation Pathfinders by noting: 'The business of using research evidence to improve services is more incremental, provisional, iterative and gradual than big gestures would like it to be.' To claim otherwise, for example by arguing that a properly scientific RCT will – at last! – provide all the answers, is to mislead policy-makers about what they can realistically expect to get from research, and reflects a mistaken view of the nature of evaluation and the kind of evidence it can produce, and ultimately of the nature of the social sciences and of human life.

It is unrealistic to expect that youth justice policy, or criminal justice policy in general, will be shaped by research, but it is reasonable to expect that research will be one of the factors that influence and inform it (Raynor, 2003). I have argued that this influence is most likely to be achieved, and to be helpful, if policy-makers are consistently reminded of what they can and cannot expect of research in a field such as youth justice. What they should not expect are universal truths or 'law-like generalisations' (MacIntyre, 1985); what they ought to expect are empirically informed ideas about what looks promising, what, if properly implemented (and what 'properly' means should be specified as far as possible), will 'work', for what people and what purposes, and in what contexts. Researchers therefore have a responsibility not to pander to politicians' and bureaucrats' demands for certainty, for a single right answer. The claims they make for evaluative research should in one sense be more modest, since they will not be concerned with ultimate truths; but in another sense their claims can be more confident, if they avoid the positivist trap of believing that only the most 'scientific' approaches can tell us anything useful.

References

Andrews, D. A., Bonta, J. and Hoge, R. D. (1990) 'Classification for effective rehabilitation: rediscovering psychology', *Criminal Justice and Behaviour*, 17: 19–52.
Blagg, H. and Smith, D. (1989) *Crime, Penal Policy and Social Work*. Harlow: Longman.

Braithwaite, J. (1993) 'Beyond Positivism: Learning from Contextual Integrated Strategies', *Journal of Research in Crime and Delinquency*, 30(4): 383–99.

Butler, I. and Drakeford, M. (1997) 'Tough Guise: the Politics of Youth Justice', *Probation Journal*, 44(4): 216–19.

Cabinet Office (1999a) *Modernising Government*. London: The Stationery Office.

Cabinet Office (1999b) *Professional Policy Making for the Twenty-First Century*. London: Cabinet Office.

Cabinet Office (2001) *Better Policy Making*. London: Cabinet Office.

Chitty, C. (2005) 'The Impact of Corrections on Re-Offending: Conclusions and the Way Forward', in G. Harper and C. Chitty (eds) *The Impact of Corrections on Re-offending: A Review of 'What Works'*. (2nd edn) Home Office Research Study 291. London: Home Office.

Cohen, S. (1985) *Visions of Social Control*. Cambridge: Polity Press.

Davies, P. (2004) 'Is Evidence-Based Government Possible?', the Jerry Lee Lecture 2004, presented at the Campbell Collaboration Symposium, Washington, D.C., 19 February.

Earle, R., Newburn, T. and Crawford, A. (2003) 'Referral Orders: Some Reflections on Policy Transfer and "What Works"', *Youth Justice*, 2(3): 141–50.

Feilzer, M., with Appleton, C., Roberts, C. and Hoyle, C. (2004) *The National Evaluation of the Youth Justice Board's Cognitive Behaviour Projects*. London: Youth Justice Board.

Folkard, M. S., Smith, D. E. and Smith, D. D. (1976) *IMPACT Volume II: The Results of the Experiment*. Home Office Research Study 36. London: HMSO.

Garland, D. (2001) *Culture of Control: Crime and Order in Contemporary Society*. Oxford: Oxford University Press.

Glass, N. (1999) 'Sure Start: the Development of an Early Intervention Programme for Young People in the United Kingdom', *Children and Society*, 13(4): 257–64.

Goldson, B. (2001) 'A Rational Youth Justice? Some Critical Reflections on the Research, Policy and Practice Relation', *Probation Journal*, 48(2): 76–85.

Gray, J. A. M. (1997) *Evidence-Based Healthcare: How to Make Health Policy and Management Decisions*. Edinburgh: Churchill Livingstone.

Hammersley, R., Reid, M., Oliver, A., Genova, A., Raynor, P., Minkes, J. and Morgan, M. (2004) *The National Evaluation of the Youth Justice Board's Drug and Alcohol Projects*. London: Youth Justice Board.

Hine, J. (2005) 'Early Multiple Intervention: a View from On Track', *Children and Society*, 19(2): 117–30.

HM Inspectorate of Probation (2002) *Annual Report 2001–2002*. London: Home Office.

HM Inspectorate of Probation (2004) *Annual Report 2003–2004*. London: Home Office.

Home Office (1997) *No More Excuses – A New Approach to Tackling Youth Crime in England and Wales*. Cm 3809. London: The Stationery Office.

Jones, D. W. (2002) 'Questioning New Labour's Youth Justice Strategy: a Review Article', *Youth Justice*, 1(3): 14–26.

Karoly, L. A., Greenwood, P. W., Everingham, S. S., Houbé, J., Kilburn, R., Rydell, C. P., Sanders, M. and Chiesa, J. (1998) *Investing in our Children: What We Know and Don't Know about the Costs and Benefits of Early Childhood Interventions*. Santa Monica, CA: RAND Corporation.

Keat, R. (1981) *The Politics of Social Theory: Habermas, Freud and the Critique of Positivism*. Oxford: Blackwell.

Lipton, D. S., Martinson, R. and Wilks, J. (1975) *The Effectiveness of Correctional Treatment: A Survey of Treatment Evaluation Studies*. New York: Praeger.

MacIntyre, A. (1985) *After Virtue: A Study in Moral Theory.* (2nd edn) London: Duckworth.

Mair, G. (2004) 'The Origins of What Works in England and Wales: a House Built on Sand?', in George Mair (ed.) *What Matters in Probation.* Cullompton: Willan.

McGuire, J. (ed.) (1995) *What Works? Reducing Reoffending.* Chichester: Wiley.

McIvor, G. (1990) *Sanctions for Serious or Persistent Offenders.* Stirling: Social Work Research Centre, University of Stirling.

McMahon, G., Hall, A., Hayward, G., Hudson, C. and Roberts, C. (2004) *Basic Skills Programmes in the Probation Service: An Evaluation of the Basic Skills Pathfinder.* Home Office Research Findings 203. London: Home Office.

Muncie, J. (2000) 'Pragmatic Realism? Searching for Criminology in the New Youth Justice', in B. Goldson (ed.) *The New Youth Justice.* Lyme Regis: Russell House Publishing.

Muncie, J. (2002) 'Policy Transfers and "What Works": some Reflections on Comparative Youth Justice', *Youth Justice*, 1(3): 27–35.

Pawson, R. (2002a) 'Evidence-Based Policy: in Search of a Method', *Evaluation*, 8(2): 157–81.

Pawson, R. (2002b) 'Evidence-Based Policy: the Promise of "Realist Synthesis"', *Evaluation*, 8(3): 340–58.

Pease, K. (1984) 'A Five Year Plan for Probation Research', in Paul Senior (ed.) *Probation: Direction, Innovation and Change in the 1980s.* London: National Association of Probation Officers.

Pitts, J. (1992) 'The End of an Era', *Howard Journal of Criminal Justice*, 31(2): 133–49.

Pitts, J. (2000) 'The New Youth Justice and Politics of Electoral Anxiety', in Barry Goldson (ed.) *The New Youth Justice.* Lyme Regis: Russell House Publishing.

Pitts, J. (2001) 'Korrectional Karaoke: New Labour and the Zombification of Youth Justice', *Youth Justice,* 1(2): 3–16.

Raynor, P. (1988) *Probation as an Alternative to Custody.* Aldershot: Avebury.

Raynor, P. (2003) 'Research in Probation: from Nothing Works to What Works', in Wing Hong Chui and Mike Nellis (eds) *Moving Probation Forward.* London: Pearson Longman.

Raynor, P. (2004a) 'Seven Ways to Misunderstand Evidence-Based Probation', in David Smith (ed.) *Social Work and Evidence-Based Practice.* London: Jessica Kingsley.

Raynor, P. (2004b) 'The Probation Service "Pathfinders": finding the Path and Losing the Way?', *Criminal Justice,* 4(3): 309–25.

Raynor, P. and Vanstone, M. (1996) 'Reasoning and Rehabilitation in Britain: the Results of the Straight Thinking on Probation (STOP) Programme', *International Journal of Offender Therapy and Comparative Criminology,* 40: 279–91.

Raynor, P. and Vanstone, M. (1997) *Straight Thinking on Probation (STOP): The Mid-Glamorgan Experiment.* Oxford: Centre for Criminological Research, University of Oxford.

Roberts, C. (1989) *Hereford and Worcester Probation Service Young Offender Project: First Evaluation Report.* Oxford: Department of Social and Administrative Studies, University of Oxford.

Sackett, D. L., Richardson, W. S., Rosenberg, W. and Haynes, R. B. (1997) *Evidence-Based Medicine: How to Practise and Teach EBM.* Edinburgh: Churchill Livingstone.

Sheldon, B. (1998) 'Evidence-Based Social Services: Prospects and Problems', *Research Policy and Planning*, 16(2): 16–18.

Smith, D. (1987) 'The Limits of Positivism in Social Work Research', *British Journal of Social Work,* 17(4): 401–16.

Smith, D. (2004) 'The Uses and Abuses of Positivism', in George Mair (ed.) *What Matters in Probation*. Cullompton: Willan.

Smith, R. (2001) 'Foucault's Law: the Crime and Disorder Act 1998', *Youth Justice,* 1(2): 17–29.

Taylor, C. and White, S. (2002) 'What Works About What Works? Fashion, fad and EBP', *Social Work and Social Sciences Review,* 10(1): 63–81.

Tonry, M. (2004) *Punishment and Politics: Evidence and Emulation in the Making of English Crime Control Policy.* Cullompton: Willan.

Tunstill, J., Allnock, D., Akhurst, S., Garbers, C. and NESS Research Team (2005) 'Sure Start Local Programmes: Implications of Case Study Data from the National Evaluation of Sure Start', *Children and Society,* 19(2): 158–71.

Underdown, A. (1998) *Strategies for Effective Supervision: Report of the HMIP What Works Project.* London: Home Office.

Vennard, J. and Hedderman, C. (1998) 'Effective Interventions with Offenders', in P. Goldblatt and C. Lewis (eds) *Reducing Offending: An Assessment of Research and Evidence on Ways of Dealing with Offending Behaviour*. Home Office Research Study 187. London: Home Office.

Vennard, J., Sugg, D. and Hedderman, C. (1997) *Changing Offenders' Attitudes and Behaviour: What Works?*. Home Office Research Study 171. London: Home Office.

Weiss, C. H. with Bucuvalas, M. J. (1980) *Social Science Research and Decision-Making.* New York: Columbia University Press.

Wilcox, A. (2003) 'Evidence-Based Youth Justice? Some Valuable Lessons from an Evaluation for the Youth Justice Board', *Youth Justice*, 3(1): 18–33.

Actuarialism and Early Intervention in Contemporary Youth Justice

Roger Smith

Introduction

Accepted wisdom in the context of child welfare and youth justice holds that early intervention has an enormous contribution to make to the achievement of positive outcomes (for example, Home Office, 1997; Chief Secretary to the Treasury, 2003; Department for Education and Skills, 2004; Sutton et al., 2004). This is partly fuelled by influential initiatives such as the Perry Pre-School programme originating in the United States in the 1960s (see, for example, Schweinhart, 2001), and partly from a rather more intuitive assumption that 'prevention is better than cure'. However, there are also more deep-rooted forces informing such beliefs. The initial aim of this chapter will be to explore some of these ideas, and to consider their implications for policy and practice in youth justice. Following this, the chapter will explore the applications of the prevailing commitment to 'nipping crime in the bud – stopping children at risk from getting involved in crime' (Home Office, 1997: 2), and applying interventions which ensure 'responsible' and law-abiding behaviour. The limitations of this perspective will be explored, and the consequences for young people considered. Finally, there will be a discussion of alternative perspectives on 'early intervention', and the value of practice which is holistic and inclusive, reflecting a genuinely child- and young person-centred strategy.

The emergence and consolidation of 'actuarialism'

The presence and representation of youth crime in contemporary societies are typically characterised by public fears about threat and danger (Pearson, 1983), and the long-standing preoccupation with methods of intervention designed to pre-empt the development of delinquent careers is unsurprising (Pitts, 1988). Recent developments in policy and practice, however, suggest that there has been a significant shift in the way in which these concerns are conceptualised, leading to an emphasis on a particular kind of approach – namely, 'actuarialism' (Feeley and Simon, 1994; Kempf-Leonard and Peterson, 2002; Young, 1999). In brief, actuarialism has been defined as an approach to crime control and management which dispenses with concerns about the meaning or motives behind offending and replaces these with an emphasis on 'technologies' of 'risk minimisation' and the elimination of potential threats to social order (Feeley and Simon, 1994).

Whilst crime and punishment represent a particularly resonant context for this emergent emphasis on the 'machinery' of control (Foucault, 1979), it is also, arguably, derived from broader social, political and ideological movements, associated with 'modernisation', and the 'risk society' (Beck, 1992). Young, for one, is surprised that this link has not been made more explicit:

> It is extraordinary that the academic discourse on actuarial justice develops separately from the rich vein of scholarship concerning the nature of a 'risk society'. (1999: 68)

Hudson (2003), however, has attempted to illuminate the connections between the so-called 'risk society' and the strategies which have become prevalent in criminal justice for managing problem behaviour, including the capability to predict 'risk', and the capacity to take action to control or minimise it. Alongside the notion of 'risk', two further important characteristics of youth justice systems in 'late modern' societies might also be identified (Hudson, 2003: 42). First, the attempt to perfect *scientific* means of quantifying the potential for the commission of offences, and second, the application of *managerial* techniques to control the threat to the community thus identified. 'Actuarialism' is, therefore, to be viewed both as a means of conceptualising youth crime, and as a mode of intervention.

Muncie (2004) makes this link explicit, arguing that 'managerialism' in practice is entirely consistent with an actuarial philosophy. The de-humanising assumptions underpinning this set of beliefs (Kempf-Leonard and Peterson, 2002) are translated into a 'significant lowering of expectations in terms of what the youth justice system can be expected to achieve' (Muncie, 2004: 273). Objectives such as reform and rehabilitation become subsumed to mechanical functions such as measurement and classification of risk and efficient deployment of resources to minimise the threat of harm. Information sharing and the 'flagging up' of early concerns about children's well-being and/or 'risk factors' have thus become central to government strategy and policy formation (Chief Secretary to the Treasury, 2003: 53).

The increasing prominence of this approach to youth crime (and anti-social behaviour) can be identified in a number of aspects of government policy, especially since 1997. The establishment of the prevention of offending as the principal 'statutory aim' of the youth justice system is a prime example (Home Office, 1997: 7). In 2003, the government consolidated the 'preventive' imperative by extending the principle to apply to courts in the exercise of their sentencing powers (Home Office, 2003: 4). Other aspects of government policy have become infused with actuarial objectives. The prevailing approach to prevention is based on assumptions about the possibility of quantifying and targeting 'risk factors' on a number of levels (Smith, 2003: 53). A trail can be mapped out, beginning with broad measurements of 'social exclusion' (Social Exclusion Unit, 1998), passing through community-wide initiatives such as 'crime audits' (Fox and McManus, 2001) and leading to specific measures aimed at controlling individuals or groups of young people, such as 'dispersal orders', whereby police are enabled to disperse groups of 'two or more' people from areas where 'anti-social behaviour is prevalent' (National Centre for Policing Excellence, 2005: 3). As Hudson (2003) and Goldson (2005) have noted, because such inter-ventions are based on risk estimates and predictions of future behaviour, they do not require substantive evidence of wrong-doing to justify intervention.

This multi-level approach to risk management in policy has been translated into a (substantial) number of specific practical programmes and modes of intervention. 'Generalised' programmes such as Sure Start[1] and Connexions[2] are conceptualised partly in terms of their ability to reduce youth crime, whilst 'targeted' and 'individualised' interventions – including On Track,[3] the Youth Inclusion Programme,[4] and the 'Splash'[5] summer activity schemes – require the prior identification of groups or individuals who are likely to offend (Smith, 2003). The Youth Inclusion Programme was set up in 2000 by the Youth Justice Board for England and Wales (Audit Commission, 2004: 95), and its aims were to 'target the 50 most "at risk" 13–16 year olds in the [local] area', to provide them with 'constructive activities', and thereby to reduce arrest rates by 60 per cent. The principle of targeting was subsequently extended to 9–12-year-olds for the 'Splash' schemes operating in England and Wales (New Opportunities Fund, 2003; Splash Extra National Support Team, 2003). The emergence of the confusingly-titled Youth Inclusion and Support Panels[6] cemented this early iden-tification strategy (Children and Young People's Unit and Youth Justice Board,

---

1. Sure Start is the UK government's national early years (0–5) programme to promote parenting support and child development.
2. Connexions is the government's youth support programme, providing careers guidance, personal support and mentoring to young people (13–19, and sometimes up to 25).
3. On Track was the Home Office initiated crime reduction programme aimed at 4–12 year olds.
4. The Youth Inclusion programme is a 'tailor-made' intervention for young people aged 13–16, involved in or 'at risk' of offending.
5. Splash summer holiday activity schemes were initially funded by the Home Office, with the aim of diverting 13–17-year-olds from crime and anti-social behaviour.
6. YISPs were piloted, then 'rolled out' in 2003, and they aim to identify those 8–13-year-olds most likely to offend and to work with them to prevent them becoming involved in crime.

2002). Similar initiatives are also evident in Scotland, despite its very different youth justice system (Scottish Executive, 2002).

The use of actuarial 'risk instruments' in this context is problematic, however, as Hudson (2003: 49) notes:

> To the extent that they still incorporate factors such as employment, sub-stance abuse, educational levels and criminal records of family members ..., these techniques continue to use actuarial assessments as though they were clinical assessments, that is, they are using descriptions of the characteristics of populations of offenders to predict the likelihood of reoffending of individual offenders. (2003: 49)

Generalised tools that indicate population-wide probabilities have been translated through the government's early intervention strategy into a series of predictive mechanisms that operate at the level of *individual* children and young people. The attempt to predict future risk by identifying young people as members of 'problem groups' (and sometimes as a problem group *per se*) takes priority over the evidence (or lack of it) of current offending behaviour. Indeed, many of the intervention strategies targeted at anti-social behaviour consciously and deliberately dilute the burden of proof otherwise required to justify coercive intervention (National Centre for Policing Excellence, 2005: 12). As a result, the line between offending and 'pre-offending' becomes increasingly blurred (Tarling et al., 2004). This point is further underlined by Goldson (2005: 279), who points out the inconsistencies of applying coercive interventions to children under the age of ten and, therefore, below the age of criminal responsibility (in England and Wales).

Included within the actuarial context are the range of court disposals and statutory orders alongside other policy and practice initiatives that may not have a specific legislative basis. Thus, Parenting Orders, Child Safety Orders and Anti-Social Behaviour Orders fall into the former category, whilst mentoring schemes and the Identification, Referral and Tracking (IRT) initiative (Department for Education and Skills, 2003) are located within the latter. The common strand, however, is the identification of individualised 'risk factors', and associated interventions to control and address such 'risk'. The proposed 'information hub', for example, through which IRT[7] is operationalised, provides for sharing of 'concerns' across professional boundaries:

> there is a strong case for giving practitioners the ability to flag on the system early warnings when they have a concern about a child which in itself may not be a trigger or meet the usual thresholds for intervention. (Department for Education and Skills, 2003: 53)

---

7. The IRT initiative is also known by the term Information Sharing and Assessment (ISA), possibly as an attempt to mitigate some of the rather more coercive and intrusive connotations of 'tracking' vulnerable children.

For Hudson (2003: 48), this is a predictable consequence of a shift of emphasis from 'risk management' to 'risk control'. Combined with the scientistic and managerialist assumptions mentioned earlier, this leads to an intervention strategy which justifies action on the basis that the individual possesses 'characteristics associated with offending', as distinct from any concrete evidence of actual wrong-doing. 'Actuarial justice' then, represents a kind of calculative logic which transforms crime control to a process based on prediction and pre-emption (Feeley and Simon, 1994). Offenders are no longer considered as distinctive individuals, but merely as representatives of particular problems:

> This does not mean that individuals disappear in criminal justice. They remain, but increasingly they are grasped not as coherent subjects, whether under- stood as moral, psychological or economic agents, but as members of partic- ular subpopulations and the intersection of various categorical indicators. (Feeley and Simon, 1994.: 178)

The concern is to identify risks in terms of the probability of certain outcomes occurring amongst the group as a whole. This then justifies an approach based on identification, surveillance, and preventive action to protect the 'safety of the community' (ibid.: 180).

Catching 'em young: Actuarial practice

So far the focus has been on the theoretical, strategic and policy aspects of actuarial justice. It will be helpful now to consider a number of innovations which give practical substance to some of these ideological shifts. This is not to suggest that actuarialism is the only conceptual framework to influence the practice of early interventions. Muncie (2002: 156), for example, has suggested that a number of parallel and competing rationales impact upon contemporary youth justice policy and practice, of which actuarial 'risk assessment' and 'man- agerialism' are just two. Nevertheless, the influence of actuarialism is assuming increasing significance as can be seen with regard to at least four specific aspects of early intervention in the youth justice system: assessment; preventive programmes; Anti-Social Behaviour Orders; and 'first encounters' involving the formal processing of offences.

(a) Assessment (ASSET and ONSET)

The use of formalised and routinised instruments of assessment represents a particularly clear-cut application of actuarial principles in the youth justice system. In England and Wales, the introduction of the 'ASSET' form (Smith, 2003) has attempted to insert a relatively basic model of risk assessment as a core element underpinning all aspects of work with a young person, as specified in the first version of National Standards for Youth Justice Services (Youth Justice Board, 2000: 9), and reiterated in the revised 2004 version:

> All children and young people entering the youth justice system should benefit from a structured needs assessment. The assessment process is designed to identify the risk factors associated with offending behaviour and to inform effective intervention programmes. The Youth Justice Board has developed the *Asset* common assessment profile for this purpose. (Youth Justice Board, 2004b: 27)

ASSET is the primary assessment and decision-making tool for all young people identified as offenders, at whatever stage in the justice system, although in a shortened version for final warnings. ASSET incorporates a standard menu of offence-related and social and personal factors which are to be scored and aggregated, providing the basis for predicting future behaviour and planning 'appropriate' interventions.

Although equivocal about its use and value, research into the first two years of ASSET's implementation claims that it has been reasonably accurate as a predictive tool, with a 67 per cent success rate in forecasting reconvictions (Baker et al., 2004: 6). This prompted the development of a related document, the ONSET form (Youth Justice Board, 2003b), which is designed for use at the pre-offending stage by Youth Inclusion and Support Panels, where children may be judged 'at risk' of criminal involvement. 'Concerns' may be identified in respect of: 'living and family arrangements'; 'statutory education'; 'neighbourhood and friends'; 'substance misuse'; 'emotional and mental health'; 'perception of self and others'; 'thinking, behaviour and attitudes'; 'motivation/positives'; 'child's vulnerability'; and 'risk of harm by child'. Similar scoring mechanisms are incorporated. Thus, 'soft' information, such as perceptions of attitudes and emotional well-being, becomes quantifiable, offering a seemingly authoritative basis for significant decisions about state intervention with children and young people, who have not necessarily committed any criminal offences. Of course, the scope for negative assessment based upon appearance, attitude, or simply 'being in the wrong place at the wrong time' is enormous, with associated implications for the institutionalisation of oppressive practices and discrimination.

(b) Preventive work

Recent years have seen a proliferation of policy initiatives and practical interventions promoting early preventive intervention (including Youth Inclusion Programmes, Youth Inclusion and Support Panels and Splash schemes). Their actuarial character is partly reflected in the referral process by which young people are initially identified (some might say 'conscripted') and it also determines aspects of programme delivery. Increasingly formalised assessment processes, such as ONSET, are used to identify those 'at risk', and programmes are typically 'targeted' at young people who are thought to meet core criteria:

> The starting point should be for the YISP members and other agencies to examine their records to identify children who are vulnerable of becoming involved in offending or repeat offending e.g. children involved or exposed to 4 or 5 risk factors associated with predicting offending. (Youth Justice Board and Children and Young People's Unit, 2002: 7)

The aims for children who participate in such programmes are to:

> reduce offending and anti-social behaviour by providing Integrated Support Plans (ISP[8]) and or an Acceptable Behaviour Contract (ABC[9]) with key worker support. (ibid.: 3)

The focus is very much on 'risk control' (Hudson, 2003: 50). As if this is not clear enough, the coercive aspects of the programme are spelt out further:

> In appropriate cases an ISP should be integrated with an ABC to address the underlying causes of anti-social behaviour and to *reinforce* an individual's and parent's or carer's responsibilities ... It is expected that if the child's behaviour does not improve ... the panel [YISP] could have a role in making recommenda-tions and providing evidence to the police and local authority for an ASBO [Anti-Social Behaviour Order] application or other *enforcement* action. (Youth Justice Board and Children and Young People's Unit, 2002: 4, emphases added)

'Prevention' thus has a distinctive character under these conditions. The prioritisation of risk control leads to the establishment of a framework which focuses on potentially problematic behaviour, at the expense of welfare need or personal and social development. Outcomes are prioritised, so that crime reduction and behaviour change are the paramount indicators of success or failure. In this way, the Youth Justice Board for England and Wales (2005) expects Youth Inclusion Programmes to reduce arrest rates amongst the target population by 70 per cent over a twelve-month period. Indeed, detailed targets are specified by government for all aspects of crime reduction (Partnership Performance and Support Unit, 2004). Thus, the actuarial approach to early intervention is explic-itly aligned with 'managerialist' operating principles, such as performance mea-surement and cost-effectiveness (Muncie, 2002: 156).

These priorities will inevitably determine the content of interventions, which will be concerned primarily with surveillance and control, behaviour management,

---

8. The Integrated Support Plan is an agreed programme of intervention produced by the participants in the Youth Inclusion and Support Panel in relation to a particular young person
9. An Acceptable Behaviour Contract is a 'voluntary' written agreement between someone who has been responsible for anti-social behaviour and one or more agencies whose duty it is to prevent such behaviour.

and attendance, rather than the intrinsic quality of the intervention and/or the experience for the child/young person (Splash Extra National Support Team, 2003).

(c) ASBOs

The introduction of Anti-Social Behaviour Orders was initially believed to be something of a publicity stunt (Burney, 2002), but extended powers, government prompting, and their supposed popular appeal have resulted in a dramatic upturn in their use (1,323 in the year to March 2004; Home Office, 2004a), with wide-ranging prohibitions being imposed on young people, based on 'hearsay' and perceived risk, rather than evidence and 'hard facts' (Home Office, 2004b). ASBOs are largely speculative and pre-emptive, rather than evidence-based or offence-related:

> Anti-Social Behaviour Orders (ASBOs) are civil orders that were designed to deter anti-social behaviour and prevent the escalation of such behaviour without having to resort to criminal sanctions ... (Campbell, 2002: 2)

In actuarial terms, the significant aspects of ASBOs are their relationship to 'risk control' (Clear and Cadora, 2001; Hudson, 2003), and 'selective incapacitation' (Feeley and Simon, 1994). The aim is to use predictive mechanisms to determine the likelihood of further episodes of unacceptable behaviour (which may or may not be criminal). Measures such as Acceptable Behaviour Contracts are then imposed to exercise appropriate constraints. Such strategies aim to use classificatory techniques to:

> identify high-risk offenders and to maintain long-term controls over them while investing in shorter terms and less intrusive control and surveillance over lower risk offenders. (Feeley and Simon, 1994: 175)

As Walsh (2003) has commented, the introduction and subsequent statutory strengthening of the ASBO have occurred notwithstanding available evidence which indicates little change in public concern about young people's behaviour. Indeed, measures of control such as the ASBO and the dispersal order may themselves contribute to rising fear of crime, by heightening public awareness (Walsh, 2003: 110).

(d) Pre-court disposals

Actuarialism is also a feature of pre-court disposals (Reprimands and Final Warnings).[10] Considerable emphasis is placed upon apparent evidence that

---

10. Reprimands and Final Warnings are the options made available to the police by the Crime and Disorder Act 1998 for dealing with offences without resorting to prosecution.

re-offending rates are low with regard to children and young people made subject to these sanctions, and have apparently declined since the full implementation of these disposals in 2000 (Youth Justice Board, 2003a). Actuarialism depends on the efficient and effective measurement of risk and the imposition of the least costly intervention consistent with this assessment. Even progressive youth justice principles of minimum necessary intervention may be reflected in actuarial practices, albeit in distorted fashion:

> While the ... juvenile justice aim of employing the least restrictive alternative ... is upheld by new risk management strategies, the difference is that the goal of the process may have shifted from the best interests of the child to the best interests of a more cost-effective system. (Kempf-Leonard and Peterson, 2002: 438)

Linked to this is the notion of the sentencing 'tariff', well-established in criminal justice, which also fits neatly with actuarial assumptions. The Audit Commission (2004: 17) stresses the importance of applying 'gravity factor' analysis, whilst ensuring that early 'one-off' disposals are not used repeatedly. The idea of progressive and selectively applied disposals suggests a pattern of 'graded' (Foucault, 1979) interventions, allied with a concern to apply cost-effective risk control methods.

The preoccupation with control is further exemplified by research into the implementation of the Final Warning (Holdaway and Desborough, 2004). The decision as to whether or not to administer a Final Warning rests on the outcome of a mechanistic assessment of offending history and 'gravity score'. Interventions are mandated accordingly, so that a score of 1 or 2 merits a reprimand, 3 equates to a Final Warning and 4 should result in a decision to charge the young person. Whilst warnings may be delivered in a variety of ways, including 'restorative conferences':

> the overriding presumption must be on delivering reprimands in a way that will be most effective in preventing reoffending and in considering the views of the victim. (Home Office, 2000b: para 7)

The emphasis on 'risk control' here is further underlined by the insistence of the Youth Justice Board for England and Wales that Final Warnings be supported by intervention programmes in at least 80 per cent of cases (Youth Justice Board, 2004a: 20); although, ironically, researchers have been unable to find any link between the delivery of such interventions and re-offending rates (Hine and Celnick, 2001).

The problems of actuarialism

Following the emergence of actuarial principles as central tenets of the 'new youth justice' (Goldson, 2000a), two key questions arise. First, does 'actuarial justice' actually 'work'?; in other words, does it achieve the objectives of identifying and reducing the risk of young people (re-)offending? Second, is 'actuarialism' a legitimate or desirable strategic aim; that is, can it be justified in principle?

Actuarialism does achieve certain symbolic ideological ends by creating a sense of reliability and certainty, through the instruments and machinery generated for predicting, assessing and intervening with young people whose behaviour gives cause for concern; and it therefore suggests the possibility of offering definitive solutions to the problematic issue of troublesome youth. In this sense, it provides a justifiable and intelligible means of satisfying pressures for 'something to be done'. Thus, ASBOs and their attendant paraphernalia – such as Acceptable Behaviour Contracts and Parental Responsibility Contracts[11] – offer reassurance that definitive responses have been put in place, for example, to ensure that the risk of youth crime is reduced (Bullock and Jones, 2004; Government Office for the West Midlands, undated; Home Office, 2000a; 2004a).

Despite this, the sense of certainty offered is illusory (Giddens, 1992). We must acknowledge the procedural and epistemological limitations of actuarial practices. For example, indicators of 'risk' are based on subjective and contested judgements. It is acknowledged even by those who promote a 'risk-focused prevention paradigm' that:

> There are methodological as well as ethical difficulties to using current knowledge of relevant risk factors to target individual children ... (Youth Justice Board, 2001: 25)

This is exemplified by attempts to operationalise and implement such 'risk factors' (Hill et al., 2004). For example, 'parenting difficulties' and 'non-constructive spare time/easily bored', are two of the indicators of concern which can be used to trigger interventions in respect of children. These are vague terms which apply to most of the population at one time or another! In addition, it should be noted that even strong proponents of evidence-based approaches are cautious about the efficacy of predictive tools. For example:

> By the age of 17, only half the children behaving anti-socially at age 8 will have grown into anti-social adolescents. (Sutton et al., 2004: 11)

Even if we overlook the intrinsically problematic nature of the term 'anti-social adolescent', there are serious practical difficulties. Predictive tools such as ASSET are also beset with limitations. Not only do they contain a number of subjective components, but they are also highly geared towards emphasising negative aspects of children's lives at the expense of 'protective factors' (Smith, 2003). In addition, there is little evidence that they are used consistently, or that they provide a sound basis for predicting future behaviour (Baker et al., 2004).

---

11. Parental Responsibility Contracts are recommended by the Home Office (2000a) as a means of requiring that parents take full responsibility for preventing the anti-social behaviour of children under the age of 10.

ASSET is reported as having the potential for predicting the likelihood of reconviction accurately in 70 per cent of cases (Baker et al., 2004: 68). Bearing in mind that 50 per cent accuracy would be the equivalent of tossing a coin, this suggests very high rates of both 'false positives' and 'false negatives'.

At best, apparently authoritative decision-making is likely to be based on unreliable information and subjective judgements. But, is the cost of applying the technologies of assessment and classification by an 'army of experts' in youth crime (Foucault, 1979) nonetheless justifiable? Is routine error just an unfortunate by-product of scientistic logic? Knowing the limitations of science (Giddens, 1990), do we consider it acceptable to 'get it wrong' sometimes in order to manage and control risk? Cost-benefit analyses of the kind undertaken by the Audit Commission (2004) tend not to address these moral and political questions, although it is argued that they demonstrate some insight into the massive human and financial waste resulting from the failures of pre-emptive and excessive interventions (Sutton et al., 2004). It is well known that criminogenic 'labelling' is damaging and counter-productive (Goldson, 2000b), and in contrast to speculative risk-based approaches, it might be argued that:

> there must be a strong presumption in favour of preventive services presenting and justifying themselves in terms of children's existing needs and problems, rather than the future risks of criminality. (Utting, 2004: 99)

There are other questions to be asked of actuarial strategies of youth justice. Clearly, it is important to consider the impact of such interventions on re-offending rates. Whilst grandiose claims have been made for interventions such as Final Warning programmes (Youth Justice Board, 2004a), more considered evidence is, at best, equivocal (Bateman, 2003; Hine and Celnick, 2001; Holdaway and Desborough, 2004: 38). At the same time, community prevention programmes based on 'targeting' those at risk are claimed only to have a limited effect on further offending rates (France et al., 2004; Splash Extra National Support Team, 2003), and even this could be attributable to factors associated with a general decline in recorded crime, or the influence of age (Home Office, 2004b; Powell, 2004). At their most benign, many of the 'new' modes of early intervention resemble nothing more than well-established best practice in youth work, the value of which has been recognised for many years (Bamforth, 2004; Sutton et al., 2004). At their most problematic, risk-oriented and individualised anti-social behaviour interventions seem to have positively criminogenic tendencies, to the extent that young people found in breach of them become liable to punitive interventions (even custody) for behaviour which falls short of criminal activity (Campbell, 2002).

Actuarialism: A moral failure

Aside from the practical deficiencies of actuarial practice, it is also important to recognise moral and political inadequacies. The problem of dealing with uncertainty associated with 'modernity' (Beck, 1992) may lead to a suggestion that a degree of injustice is acceptable, in the interests of the protection of the public. The criticism that actuarial justice is ineffective may be resisted on the basis that it cannot deliver a perfect system, but that it is capable of improvement and progressive refinement (Baker et al., 2004; Youth Justice Board, 2001). In any case, it may be argued, it is 'better to be safe than sorry'. This is a dangerous road to follow, however:

> the perception of community safety has surpassed concern for the needs of the youth, and the unlimited discretionary procedures that ... prevail make almost anything possible. (Kempf-Leonard and Peterson, 2002: 435)

The consequences of this line of argument are highly questionable, and from both a children's rights and a child welfare perspective it raises very significant concerns. 'Targeting' individuals and communities leads to an undue focus on young people from specific class and ethnic backgrounds (Smith, 2003), and the very act of shining a spotlight selectively in this way leads to an over-emphasis on their behaviour. Why, indeed, should young people 'hanging around' be considered any more anti-social than owners who allow their dogs to foul the pavement? (see crimereduction.gov.uk, 2004).

Equally, the preoccupation with 'risk' at the expense of 'need' has been a perennial feature of children's services in general (Smith, 2005), and it is clearly problematic if youth justice interventions concentrate solely on the former aspect of young people's behaviour. This, in turn, raises the question as to whether it is appropriate for initiatives such as 'Splash' and Youth Inclusion Programmes to be driven by indicators and priorities associated almost exclusively with crime prevention, which may distort service delivery. Much concern was expressed at the time, for example, over the government's decision to divert 25 per cent of Children's Fund[12] budgets towards specific measures related to youth crime and anti-social behaviour. Project evaluations have highlighted the drawbacks:

> The stigmatisation of participating in projects has led to low numbers of take-up for young people either at risk or on pre-court disposals. Involvement in some programmes is seen to 'label' young people as an offender, whether this is in the eyes of the young person or the community in which they live. (Powell, 2004: 40)

Such processes of exclusion work negatively in at least three ways. First, they can contribute to young people's perceptions of themselves as 'offenders' and

---

12. The Children's Fund was a Treasury initiative, prompted by consultation with voluntary children's organisations, and the 2000 public spending review, resulting in the investment of an initial sum of £450 million in new projects to promote *child welfare*.

thus consolidate deviant identities (Becker, 1963). Second, because children are 'objectively' identified as potential offenders, this creates the possibility for the community and justice agencies to categorise them as criminal (Foucault, 1979). Third, the presumption of criminality may lead to children's rights being compromised (Goldson, 2000b).

Indeed, actuarialism invokes a 'culture of control' (Garland, 2001). The prioritisation of the identification, management and control of risk is a product of a changing social climate, which is characterised by fear of children and young people because of the threat they are reputed to represent. The 'achievement' of actuarialism in youth justice is to render these arbitrary and discriminatory practices acceptable, and apparently rational. They are cloaked in respectability accorded by ostensibly scientific means of identifying and measuring risk. On this basis, it is justifiable to construct systematic planned interventions, and to routinise delivery in the form of quantifiable inputs, targets and performance measures, against which effectiveness might be evaluated. Furthermore, it is acceptable to dispense with traditional concerns of justice, such as fairness and due process, in the interests of eradicating *potential* threats, which, by their nature, cannot be precisely known. These spectral fears seem to permit aggressive pre-emptive interventions in children's lives:

> The punitive turn that takes liberties and violates rights is underpinned by an intolerance and contempt for troubled, even if troublesome, children. (Goldson, 2005: 283)

In the final analysis, two fundamental concerns emerge. First, actuarial justice is based on speculative and unsupportable assumptions: about the source and nature of risk, the potential for measuring risk, and the desirability and feasibility of intervention strategies based on risk control. Second, the increasing dominance of such conceptual rationales and applied practices diminishes the influence of more legitimate approaches to early intervention.

Alternatives to actuarialism: 'Real' preventive policy and practice

Whilst risk control appears to have become the predominant characteristic of youth justice, at least in the domain of early intervention, other principles and objectives have not been totally excluded. The contributions made by some locally-based initiatives and creative practitioners in sustaining alternatives must be acknowledged, and through the development of imaginative practice a progressive role for youth justice work might be preserved and developed. In this way it is important to contrast the target-driven (and targeted) preventive approach to one which is inclusive and genuinely concerned with the engagement and participation of young people. The relatively straightforward but significant step of extending the opening hours of community leisure services in one area may engage several hundred young people, offering them something to do other than hanging around on street corners. One application of such an initiative appears to have contributed to a substantial (23 per cent) reduction in calls to the police during its hours of operation (Bamforth, 2004).

Likewise, it seems that in practice many of the 'Splash Extra'[13] schemes, which were intended to target young people 'at risk of offending', did not do so, preferring instead to avail their programmes to the community as a whole (New Opportunities Fund, 2003). In these instances, actuarial aims were subsumed under more traditional and universal youth work objectives. It is important, too, to draw the right lessons. Reductions in crime and improvements in the quality of community life are at least as likely to be attributable to the investment of resources and staffing in activities for young people collectively as they are to 'targeting' those at risk.

Concerns about targeting have permeated other aspects of the youth justice system. The enthusiasm of government and the media for Anti-Social Behaviour Orders cannot disguise disquiet amongst agencies and practitioners, who are concerned that this obsession with risk control will have a counter-productive and damaging impact. There is clearly a great deal less enthusiasm for these measures in some geographical areas than others (Clark, 2004; crimereduction.gov.uk, 2005). Indeed, the notion of 'diversion' has re-emerged as an operating principle, with the elaboration of strategies such as 'pathways to prevention', and an emphasis on developmental needs rather than crime (or behaviour) control (Government Office for the West Midlands, undated; Wong, 2003; Welsh Assembly Government and Youth Justice Board, 2004). The Youth Justice Board of England and Wales has also done something of a *volte face*, in promoting the greater use of diversionary interventions, although only for 'minor, low-risk' infringements (Morgan, 2004). Whilst the language of 'risk' still exerts an influence, the re-discovery of other rationales, principles and purposes is apparent.

In addition, it is important to stress the value of a 'rights' perspective. It is not just that this restates the significance of principles such as proportionality and due process, which are simply discounted in risk-based, prospective strategies, where notions of 'guilt' or culpability are ultimately rendered irrelevant (Goldson, 2005: 279). The ideology of children's rights is of greater worth, because it provides a positive frame for engagement with young people in general. It offers the possibility of participative dialogue, rather than conflict and control. It has been suggested that a 'rights-based agenda' can engage young people in addressing the problems associated with their behaviour without compounding prior experiences of

---

13. Splash Extra was an extension of the initial Splash summer activity scheme as part of the government's 2002 Street Crime and Robbery initiative targeted at 9–17-year-olds in high crime areas.

inequality or discrimination (Scraton and Haydon, 2002). Initiatives within the field of youth justice that seek young people's views, that value them, and that act on them, provide an effective antidote to the alienating tendencies of actuarialism. Equally, a preventive strategy undertaken by criminal justice agencies such as the police 'can only be effective as part of [an] overall youth strategy' (Clark, 2004); and this in turn requires open and honest partnership working between agencies, and with young people themselves.

It is unsurprising that policy and practice in youth justice should be characterised by differing and sometimes competing aims and objectives. As Hudson (1987) has observed, conflicts between advocates of 'welfare' and 'justice' typified debates in a previous era. However, the advent of actuarialism has represented a significant shift, not least because it is speculative, relying on techniques of prediction and incapacitation. Whilst it might also be suggested that other more child-centred and benign perspectives such as 'developmentalism' (Rutherford, 1992) share the characteristic of being future-oriented, and geared to optimising outcomes for young people, there is little else in common between them.

Indeed, it is the very powerful contradiction between actuarial approaches, and those based on other principles (such as diversion, rights, or restoration), which suggests that serious problems lie in store for those involved in delivering youth justice, as well as the children and young people caught up in the process. The superficial attractiveness of standardised procedures and consistent service delivery is apparent (Kempf-Leonard and Peterson, 2000: 85), but at the same time, these very processes obscure a range of more insidious effects. Standardisation, for example, may serve to legitimate institutional discrimination (Bowling and Philips, 2002); complex community interests are subsumed under generalised risk control strategies; children's rights are overridden in the interests of security and certainty; and longer-term developmental objectives are overlooked in favour of the quick fix needed to meet targets and satisfy performance indicators:

> The new systems of risk control violate some of the fundamental tenets of due process. The principles of no punishment without conviction, and proportionality of punishment to harm done, are set aside by the new technologies of risk. (Hudson, 2003: 67)

Ultimately, actuarial principles and methods are incompatible with aspirations towards a youth justice system which is rooted in the complex dynamics and systemic inequalities which characterise many young people's lives. Indeed, the only encouragement to be taken from this discussion is that, at the level of practice, actuarial techniques are regularly being resisted (for example, Baker et al., 2004: 73; New Opportunities Fund, 2003: 8) in favour of interventions which are centred on the experiences, aspirations and needs of young people.

References

Audit Commission (2004) *Youth Justice 2004*. London: Audit Commission.

Baker, K., Jones, S., Roberts, C. and Merrington, S. (2004) *ASSET: The Evaluation of the Validity and Reliability of the Youth Justice Board's Assessment for Young Offenders*. London: Youth Justice Board.

Bamforth, A. (2004) 'Positive Activities that Deal with Youth Disaffection: Lessons Learned from the Youth Only Zone, Sefton', paper presented at the 5th Annual ACPO Youth Justice Conference, Liverpool.

Bateman, T. (2003) 'Living with Final Warnings: Making the Best of a Bad Job?', *Youth Justice*, 2(3): 131–40.

Beck, U. (1992) *Risk Society*. London: Sage.

Becker, H. (1963) *The Outsiders*. New York: Free Press.

Bowling, B. and Phillips, C. (2002) *Racism, Crime and Justice*. Harlow: Longman.

Bullock, K. and Jones, B. (2004) *Acceptable Behaviour Contracts: Addressing Antisocial Behaviour in the London Borough of Islington*. London: Home Office.

Burney, E. (2002) 'Talking Tough, Acting Coy: What Happened to the Anti-Social Behaviour Order?', *The Howard Journal*, 41(5): 469–84.

Campbell, S. (2002) *Implementing Anti-social Behaviour Orders: Messages for Practitioners*. London: Home Office.

Chief Secretary to the Treasury (2003) *Every Child Matters*, Cm 5860. London: The Stationery Office.

Children and Young People's Unit and Youth Justice Board (2002) *Use of Children's Fund Partnership Funding for Crime Prevention Activities Jointly Agreed with Youth Offending Teams Guidance*. London: Children and Young People's Unit.

Clark, C. (2004) 'Pre Crime Prevention: Helping Those in Need', paper presented at the 5th Annual ACPO Youth Justice Conference, Liverpool.

Clear, T. and Cadora, E. (2001) 'Risk and Community Practice', in K. Stenson and R. Sullivan (eds) *Crime, Risk and Justice*. Cullompton: Willan. pp. 51–67.

crimereduction.gov.uk (2004) 'How ASBOs have Worked – Case Studies'. http://crimereduction.gov.uk/asbos8.htm – accessed 14 October.

crimereductionuk.gov.uk (2005) 'Anti-Social Behaviour Orders: Statistics'. http://crimereduction.gov.uk/asbos2.htm – accessed 3 May.

Department for Education and Skills (2003) *Every Child Matters*. London: The Stationery Office.

Department for Education and Skills (2004) *Every Child Matters: The Next Steps*. London: The Stationery Office.

Feeley, M. and Simon, J. (1994) 'Actuarial Justice: the Emerging New Criminal Law', in D. Nelken (ed.) *The Futures of Criminology*. London: Sage. pp. 173–201.

Foucault, M. (1979) *Discipline and Punish*. Harmondsworth: Peregrine.

Fox, C. and McManus, J. (2001) *The Nacro Guide to Crime Audits*. London: Nacro.

France, A., Hine, J., Armstrong, D. and Camina, M. (2004) *The On Track Early Intervention and Prevention Programme: From Theory to Action*. London: Home Office.

Garland, D. (2001) *The Culture of Control*. Oxford: Oxford University Press.

Giddens, A. (1990) *The Consequences of Modernity*. Cambridge: Polity Press.

Giddens, A. (1992) *Modernity and Self-Identity*. Cambridge: Polity Press.

Goldson, B. (ed.) (2000a) *The New Youth Justice*. Lyme Regis: Russell House Publishing.

Goldson, B. (2000b) 'Wither Diversion? Interventionism and the New Youth Justice' in B. Goldson (ed.) *The New Youth Justice*. Lyme Regis: Russell House Publishing. pp. 35–57.

Goldson, B. (2005) 'Taking Liberties: Policy and the Punitive Turn,' in H. Hendrick (ed.) *Child Welfare and Social Policy*. Bristol: Policy Press. pp. 271–87.

Government Office for the West Midlands (undated) *Best Behaviour: Shared Learning from the West Midlands on Anti-Social Behaviour and Young People*. Leicester: National Youth Agency.

Hill, R., Jones, S., Roberts, C. and Baker, K. (2004) *An Evaluation of the Early Application and piloting of RYOGENS*. Oxford: Oxford University Press.

Hine, J. and Celnick, A. (2001) *A One-Year Reconviction Study of Final Warnings*. Sheffield: University of Sheffield Press.

Holdaway, S. and Desborough, S. (2004) *Final Warning Projects: The National Evaluation of the Youth Justice Board's Final Warning Projects*. London: Youth Justice Board.

Home Office (1997) *No More Excuses*, Cm 3809. London: The Stationery Office.

Home Office (2000a) *Anti-Social Behaviour Orders: Guidance on Drawing up Local ASBO Protocols*. London: Home Office.

Home Office (2000b) *The Final Warning Scheme – Guidance for Youth Offending Teams*. London: Home Office.

Home Office (2003) *Youth Justice – The Next Steps*. London: Home Office.

Home Office (2004a) 'Anti-Social Behaviour Orders and Acceptable Behaviour Contracts' http://www.homeoffice.gov.uk/crime/antisocialbehaviour/orders/ – accessed 14 October.

Home Office (2004b) *Crime in England and Wales 2003–04*. London: Home Office.

Hudson, B. (1987) *Justice Through Punishment*. Basingstoke: Macmillan.

Hudson, B. (2003) *Justice in the Risk Society*. London: Sage.

Kempf-Leonard, K. and Peterson, E. (2000) 'Expanding Realms of the New Penology: the Advent of Actuarial Justice for Juveniles', *Punishment & Society*, 2(1): 66–97.

Kempf-Leonard, K. and Peterson, E. (2002) 'Expanding Realms of the New Penology: the Advent of Actuarial Justice for Juveniles' in J. Muncie, G. Hughes and E. McLaughlin (eds) *Youth Justice: Critical Readings*. London: Sage. pp. 431–51.

Morgan, R. (2004) 'Keynote Address', paper presented to 5th ACPO Youth Justice Conference, Liverpool.

Muncie, J. (2002) 'A new Deal for Youth? Early Intervention and Correctionalism', in G. Hughes, E. McLaughlin and J. Muncie (eds) *Crime Prevention and Community Safety: New Directions*. London: Sage. pp. 142–62.

Muncie, J. (2004) *Youth and Crime*. (2nd edn) London: Sage.

National Centre for Policing Excellence (2005) *Practice Advice on Part 4 of the Anti-Social Behaviour Act 2003 (Police Powers to Disperse Groups): 2005*. ACPO Centrex.

New Opportunities Fund (2003) *Delivering Summer Activities in High Crime Neighbourhoods: The Intensive Evaluation of Splash Extra 2002*. London: New Opportunities Fund.

Partnership, Performance and Support Unit (2004) *Negotiating Crime and Disorder Reduction Targets*. London: Home Office.

Pearson, G. (1983) *Hooligan: A History of Respectable Fears*. Basingstoke: Macmillan.

Pitts, J. (1988) *The Politics of Juvenile Crime*. London: Sage.

Powell, H. (2004) *Crime Prevention Projects: The National Evaluation of the Youth Justice Board's Crime Prevention Projects*. London: Youth Justice Board.

Rutherford, A. (1992) *Growing Out of Crime: The New Era*. Winchester: Waterside Press.

Schweinhart, L. (2001) 'How the High/Scope Perry Preschool Study has Influenced Public Policy', paper presented at the Inter-disciplinary Evidence-Based Policies and Indicator Systems Conference, Durham, unpublished.

Scottish Executive (2002) *Youth Crime Review*. Edinburgh: Scottish Executive.

Scraton, P. and Haydon, D. (2002) 'Challenging the Criminalization of Children and Young People: Securing a Rights-Based Agenda', in J. Muncie, G. Hughes and E. McLaughlin (eds) *Youth Justice: Critical Readings*. London: Sage. pp. 311–28.

Smith, R. (2003) *Youth Justice: Ideas, Policy, Practice*. Cullompton: Willan.

Smith, R. (2005) 'Welfare vs Justice – Again!', *Youth Justice*, 5(1): 3–16.

Social Exclusion Unit (1998) *Bringing Britain Together: A National Strategy for Neighbourhood Renewal*. London: The Stationery Office.

Splash Extra National Support Team (2003) *Splash Cymru 2002/3 Final Report*. Woking: CapGemini Ernst & Young.

Sutton, C., Utting, D. and Farrington, D. (2004) 'Introduction', in C. Sutton, D. Utting and D. Farrington (eds) *Support From the Start*. London: DfES, pp. 9–20.

Tarling, R., Davison, T. and Clarke A. (2004) *Mentoring Projects: The National Evaluation of the Youth Justice Board's Mentoring Projects*. London: Youth Justice Board.

Utting, D. (2004) 'Overview and Conclusions', in C. Sutton, D. Utting and D. Farrington (eds) *Support From the Start*. London: DfES, pp. 89–100.

Walsh, C. (2003) 'Dispersal of Rights: A Critical Comment on Specified Provisions of the Anti-Social Behaviour Bill', *Youth Justice*, 3(2): 104–11.

Welsh Assembly Government and Youth Justice Board (2004) *All Wales Youth Offending Strategy*. Cardiff: Welsh Assembly Government.

Wong, K. (2003) 'Rethinking prevention', *Community Safety Practice Briefing*. London: Nacro.

Young, J. (1999) *The Exclusive Society*. London: Sage.

Youth Justice Board (2000) *National Standards for Youth Justice*. London: Youth Justice Board.

Youth Justice Board (2001) *Risk and Protective Factors Associated with Youth Crime and Effective Interventions to prevent it*. London: Youth Justice Board.

Youth Justice Board (2003a) *Annual Review 2002/03: Gaining Ground in the Community*. London: Youth Justice Board.

Youth Justice Board (2003b) *ONSET Guidance Notes*. London: Youth Justice Board.

Youth Justice Board (2004a) *Annual Review 2003/04: Building in Confidence*. London: Youth Justice Board.

Youth Justice Board (2004b) *National Standards for Youth Justice Services*. London: Youth Justice Board.

Youth Justice Board (2005) 'Youth Inclusion Programme (YIP)'. http://www.youth-justice-board. gov.uk/YouthJusticeBoard/Preventaion/YIP/accessed 16 Jan 2006.

Youth Justice Board and Children and Young People's Unit (2002) *Establishing Youth Inclusion and Support Panels (YISPS)*. London: Youth Justice Board.

Restorative Approaches, Young People and Youth Justice

Kevin Haines and David O'Mahony

Restorative justice has become a core element of much youth justice policy and practice internationally. Within the UK, it has been incorporated into several aspects of the youth justice system, notably through new police cautioning procedures and referral orders. In this chapter we critically analyse restorative approaches to youth justice, focusing on the UK, and question how they fit within a system that attempts to deliver 'justice' for children. We start by looking at definitions of restorative justice before considering some examples of restorative approaches, how they have been incorporated into policy and practice and the evidence as to whether such schemes achieve their objectives. We then move on to question how restorative justice is located within traditional and punitive models of justice and how the needs of children are incorporated into restorative approaches.

Defining restorative justice

Restorative justice has been described as 'a process whereby all the parties with a stake in a particular offence come together to resolve collectively how to deal with the aftermath of the offence and its implications for the future' (Marshall, 1999). It is often seen as an approach that seeks to repair relationships through a 'healing' process that is designed to meet the needs of the victim and which seeks to 'reintegrate' the offender. Thus restorative justice conceptualises offending, primarily as a breakdown in relationships between individuals, and only secondly as a violation of the law. The retributive focus of the traditional justice system and concern with just deserts are questioned within models of restorative justice. Indeed, these are seen as ineffective, even undesirable and can be counterproductive in meeting the needs of those most affected by crime

(McCold, 1996). Rather the restorative process seeks to repair the injuries caused; restore relationships and address the needs of the victim and the offender (Claassen, 1996). In practice, for many, a major part of the appeal of restorative justice is the restoration of the centrality of the victim (Shapland et al., 1985) and its utility in forcing offenders to take responsibility for their actions (Dignan and Lowey, 2000; Umbreit, 1994).

Zehr and Mika (2003) have provided a more detailed definition of restorative justice and they suggest it comprises a number of critical elements. The first is that crime is a fundamental violation of people and interpersonal relationships. As such the restorative process should seek to maximise the search for 'restoration, healing, responsibility and prevention' (ibid.: 41). Second, violations create both obligations and liabilities. So offenders are obliged to put things right as much as possible and to understand the harm they have caused. They are further obliged to be active participants in addressing their own needs. The broader community also has obligations to victims and to offenders and for the general welfare of its members. Third, restorative justice seeks to 'heal' and put right the wrongs, so the needs of the victim are the starting point and offenders are encouraged to repair the harm insofar as possible. In this process there should be an exchange of information, dialogue and consent that provides for forgiveness and reconciliation. Thus the process should be rooted in, and belong to, the community (Zehr and Mika, 2003).

However, arriving at an agreed definition of restorative justice has proved extremely problematic (Roche, 2001), not least because in reality it deals with both practices and processes, which themselves vary. In effect restorative justice is seen by some as meaning 'all things to all people' (McCold, 1996). Restorative justice programmes worldwide vary considerably in terms of what they do and how they do it. Practice differs according to the specific situation, the way programmes have developed in local areas and the extent to which restorative principles are accepted and integrated within the criminal justice system. It is therefore probably more convenient to think of restorative justice as an encompassing concept which has diverse practical implications that are theoretically derived from a number of key principles. Van Ness and Strong (1997) describe these as 'encounter, reparation, reintegration and participation', while Daly (2002) suggests they emphasise the role of the victim; the involvement of relevant parties to discuss the impact of the offence, its impact and what should be done about it; and decision-making that is carried out by both lay and legal actors.

What does all of this mean for criminal justice policy and specifically the practice of delivering youth justice? One obvious result is that restorative justice encompasses a very open set of principles that can impact upon practice in many different ways, with many possible outcomes. While Braithwaite supports this wide-ranging model as necessary, as 'standards must be broad if we are to avert legalistic regulation of restorative justice, which is at odds with the philosophy of restorative justice' (Braithwaite, 2002: 15), McCold laments the lack of clarity, stating: '[i]f restorative justice is to emerge as a justice paradigm a shared vocabulary and parameters of the theory needs to be established ... [as] theory, research and practice cannot proceed without a shared understanding ...' (McCold, 1996: 359).

Researching restorative justice

Despite the proliferation of restorative justice measures in recent years, there remains relatively little evaluative research in the UK and very many more questions than answers are to be found. We focus on three main expressions of restorative justice practice here: youth offender panels; police-led restorative cautioning; and restorative conferencing, each of which relate to children and young people.

Youth offender panels

Youth offender panels were established in England and Wales under the provisions of the Youth Justice and Criminal Evidence Act (1999) as part of the referral order (Goldson, 2000; Haines, 2000). The orders are available to the youth courts as a primary court disposal for first-time offenders between the ages of 10–17 years in England and Wales. The main aim of the panels is to provide first-time offenders with 'opportunities to make restoration to the victim, take responsibility for the consequences of their offending and achieve reintegration into the law-abiding community' (Home Office, 2002).

When a young person is referred by the court to a youth offender panel, the panel itself decides how the offending should be dealt with and what form of action is necessary. If the victim wishes, they may attend the panel meeting and describe how the offence affected them. Parents are required to attend the panel meeting (if the young person is under the age of 16) and meetings are usually held in community venues. Government guidelines state that young people should not have legal representation at panel meetings, as this may hinder their full involvement in the process, but if a solicitor is to attend, they may do so as a 'supporter' (Home Office, 2002).

The panel has to decide on an agreed plan which can provide reparation to the victim or community and include interventions to address the young person's offending. This can include victim awareness, counselling, drug and alcohol interventions and forms of victim reparation. The length of the order should be based on the seriousness of the offence, but panels are free to determine the nature of intervention necessary to prevent further offending by the young person (Home Office, 2002). The young person must agree to the plan. However, if they refuse they will be referred back to the court for sentencing. Once a plan is agreed, it is monitored by the Youth Offending Team and if the young person fails to comply with its terms they may be referred back to court for sentencing.

Referral orders were piloted in 11 areas across England and Wales between March 2000 and August 2001. Research concluded that, in the main: 'within a relatively short time youth offender panels have established themselves as constructive, deliberative and participatory forums in which to address young people's offending behaviour' (Newburn et al., 2002). The orders were 'rolled out' across the rest of England and Wales in April 2002 and in 2003/04 there were over 27,000 referral orders made, 25 per cent of all court disposals (Youth Justice Board, 2004).

Newburn et al. (2002) concluded from their research that the new orders were working well and many young people played an active role in their panel meetings. They found that 84 per cent of the young people felt they were treated with respect and 86 per cent said they were treated fairly. The research found that 75 per cent of the young people agreed that their plan or contract was 'useful' and 78 per cent agreed that it should help them stay out of trouble (Newburn et al., 2002). Parents also appeared to be positive about the orders, and compared to the experience of the youth court, parents appeared to understand the referral order process better and felt it easier to participate (Newburn et al., 2002).

Despite the rather positive evaluation findings, a number of concerns have been raised concerning referral orders (Goldson, 2000; Haines, 2000). Cullen (2001) argues that such orders raise questions about informed consent as some young people and parents may feel forced into agreeing plans. Children as young as 10 years, without legal representation, 'are being forced into what may be traumatic confrontations ... and in a roomful of adults [they] can be easily coerced into signing contracts involving serious deprivations of their liberty' (Cullen, 2001). Another concern is that the discretion of magistrates is greatly curtailed in the legislation whereby minor first-time offenders *have* to be referred to panels (Ball, 2002), effectively making them a mandatory sentence. The research by Newburn et al. (2002) confirms this, as 45 per cent of the magistrates interviewed felt that the lack of discretion in the legislation undermined their authority. Crawford and Newburn (2003) also found that some panels had difficulty devising suitable plans because of a lack of local resources and that panel members believed that adequate local facilities and resources were crucial to the success of panels.

More fundamental problems with the referral order, especially with regard to their potential to be restorative, centre around the low levels of victim involvement in the process. In their research, Newburn et al. (2002), note that victims attended in only 13 per cent of cases where at least an initial panel meeting was held. Such low levels of victim participation obviously greatly limit any chance of 'encounter, reparation, reintegration and participation' (Van Ness and Strong, 1997), supposedly essential for the restorative process. Furthermore, research has yet to establish whether such orders are having any net-widening effects, such as unnecessarily drawing minor offenders further into the criminal justice system; the extent to which such orders are truly proportionate to the offence committed; and their longer-term impact on recidivism, especially by comparison to other disposals (Mullan and O'Mahony, 2002).

Police-led restorative cautioning

In the UK restorative cautioning approaches have been used in a number of police forces, particularly by the Thames Valley police and more recently by the police in Northern Ireland. In essence this approach seeks to deal with crime and its aftermath by attempting to make offenders 'ashamed' of their behaviour, but in a way which aims to promote their reintegration into the community (Young and Hoyle, 2003).

The process of reintegrative shaming, which is central to restorative cautioning aims to deliver the police caution in a way that is not degrading – but rather is a 'reintegrative ceremony' (Braithwaite, 1989). This is addressed by attempting to get the young person to realise the harm caused by their actions to the victim, their family and themselves. The focus is placed on the wrongfulness of the action or behaviour rather than the wrongfulness of the individual. The process then attempts to reintegrate the young person, after they have admitted what they did was wrong, by focusing on how they can put the incident behind them, for example by repairing the harm caused through reparation and apology, and then it allows the young person to move forward and reintegrate back into their community and family. The whole process is usually facilitated by a trained police officer and often involves the use of a script or agenda that is followed in the conferencing process. The victim is encouraged to play a part in the process, particularly to reinforce upon the young person the impact of the offence on them, but as Dignan (2005) notes, restorative cautioning schemes have (at least initially) placed a greater emphasis on the offender and issues of crime control, than on their ability to meet the needs of victims.

Hoyle et al. (2002), researching the Thames Valley scheme (which included children and adults), have described the restorative approach as a significant improvement on the old-style and rather idiosyncratic methods of police cautioning. They found high levels of satisfaction with the process, both in terms of how conferences were facilitated and how fairly the participants were treated. Nearly all of the victims who attended the restorative cautions that were observed as part of the research expressed satisfaction with how their conference was managed and felt that it was a good idea, and some 71 per cent reported that they felt better following the conference. Hoyle et al. (2002) also found that most of the victims who attended meetings responded by saying that they felt differently about the offender as a result of the conference and just under 60 per cent reflected that the conference helped to put the offence behind them. However, levels of victim participation were very low, only 14 per cent of the cautioning sessions were attended by an actual victim (Hoyle et al., 2002).

In Northern Ireland, research on police-led restorative cautioning schemes for juveniles found them to be a significant improvement on previous cautioning practice (O'Mahony and Doak, 2004). The researchers noted that the schemes were successful in securing some of the traditional aims of restorative practice. In particular, reintegration was achieved through avoidance of prosecution and through a process which emphasised that the young person was not 'bad' whilst highlighting the impact of the young person's offending on the victim (O'Mahony and Doak, 2004). In common with research findings in respect of youth offender panels across England and Wales and restorative cautioning in the Thames Valley, the Northern Ireland research also found that levels of victim participation were relatively low, with an actual victim attending in only 20 per cent of the cases observed – limiting the restorative potential of such work. As such, the offender was often unable to directly experience the victim's perceptions first hand, whilst the victim too missed the opportunity to understand the incident from the offender's perspective and to see the person behind the crime. In effect, low victim participation detracted from the restorative goals of conferencing, where there should be a process of empowerment, dialogue, negotiation and agreement between all parties (O'Mahony and Doak, 2004).

A further concern to emerge from the research conducted in Northern Ireland was evidence of net-widening. The conferencing schemes were found to include very young and petty offenders in what was a demanding process of accountability resulting in a police caution – which was at times considered disproportionate to the harm done. There was little evidence that the restorative cautions were being used as an alternative to prosecution, rather it appeared they were often applied to cases that would have been previously dealt with informally. Indeed, the researchers noted that 80 per cent of the cases examined were for offences involving property worth less than £15 (O'Mahony and Doak, 2004). Despite such concerns, the research found the police to be enthusiastic and sincerely committed to the restorative process. They had been well trained and it was clear from the interviews with the young people and parents that they placed a high degree of confidence in and support for the scheme. There was also some evidence that it had other beneficial effects especially in terms of helping improve police/community relations, which have been considerably strained over the years of conflict (McEvoy and Mika, 2002).

Restorative conferencing

In the UK the only jurisdiction to adopt a mainstreamed statutory-based restorative conferencing model for young offenders has been Northern Ireland. Youth conferencing was introduced following recommendations from the Criminal Justice Review Group that: '... restorative justice should be integrated into the juvenile justice system in Northern Ireland' (2000: 205). In spite of the burgeoning development of community restorative justice schemes in Northern Ireland

(McEvoy and Mika, 2002), it was determined that for reasons of accountability, certainty and legitimacy, the mode of restorative justice implemented should be based in statute and fully integrated into the formal justice system (O'Mahony and Campbell, 2004). The new youth conferencing arrangements, therefore, have statutory footing in the Justice (Northern Ireland) Act 2002.

The format of the Youth Conference bears much similarity to the model used in New Zealand (Maxwell and Morris, 1993). It involves a meeting, chaired by an independent and trained youth conference facilitator (employed by the Youth Conferencing Service), where the young person is provided with the opportunity to reflect upon their actions and offer some form of reparation to the victim. The victim, who is encouraged to attend, is allowed to explain to the offender how the offence affected them, in theory giving the offender an understanding of the consequences of their actions whilst also allowing the victim an opportunity to separate the offender from the offence. Following dialogue, a 'youth conference plan' is devised which is intended to take account of the offence, the needs of the victim and the needs of the young person with the intention of achieving a 'restorative outcome' (O'Mahony and Campbell, 2004). The young person must consent to the plan, which can run for a period of no longer than one year.

The youth conferencing system in Northern Ireland is at an early stage of application and development but initial research findings (Beckett et al., 2005) have been generally positive, showing good levels of victim participation (62 per cent of conferences had a victim in attendance) and active engagement in the conferencing process. Nearly all conferences observed for the research, where a victim was present, resulted in the offender apologising to the victim as part of their plan and 78 per cent of plans contained some degree of reparation or restitution. All of the conferences observed resulted in an agreed plan and the vast majority of offenders (91 per cent) and victims (89 per cent) rated the plan as fair or very fair. Whilst victims participated well in the process, just under half (47 per cent) of offenders provided a full account of their offence. The failure of some offenders to engage in a full discussion of the offence was often related to their relative immaturity or nervousness at having to speak in a room full of adults, and for some it also appeared to be related to anger or defiance. However, the majority of participants interviewed for the research expressed positive feedback on their experience of conferencing, with all victims and all but two offenders stating that they would recommend the initiative to another person in their position.

Restorative justice and retributive/punitive youth justice

Developments in restorative justice policy and practice within contemporary youth justice contexts raise at least two fundamental questions. First, is restorative justice a separate and independent paradigm that stands alongside other approaches as an 'alternative', or is restorative justice simply a technique or method that can be subsumed within more traditional approaches to justice? Second, does punishment (retribution) have a place within restorative justice? Put more simply, are restorative and retributive approaches to justice compatible, or is there an inherent conflict between them? Perhaps surprisingly, these crucial questions have received scant attention in the restorative justice literature (although see von Hirsch et al., 2003).

The starting point for international proponents of restorative justice is that it stands in contrast to traditional approaches to justice – both retributive and rehabilitative (Bazemore and Umbreit, 1995; Walgrave, 1995). Indeed, Walgrave (1995) argues that the 'quest' to integrate restorative and traditional approaches is a 'mission impossible' – based on the inherent incompatibility of the two models. Walgrave's statement is based on three key propositions. First, traditional approaches rely on the *due process* which is a central principle of the classical 'justice' model. In contrast, restorative justice is not bound by due process. Second, retributive approaches primarily focus on past events (punishing for a wrong done), whereas treatment or rehabilitation is future oriented (achieving some change in future behaviour). Restorative justice aims to address past, present and future. Third, victims and their interests tend to be peripheral within traditional approaches, whereas restorative justice emphasises their centrality (Walgrave, 1995). Furthermore, it might be argued that traditional approaches (and particularly those embodying an element of punishment) often fail to achieve positive outcomes and may have additional unintended negative consequences, which restorative justice, implicitly, should not (Walgrave and Bazemore, 1999).

Daly (2000) contests the position that restorative justice offers a 'third way' and argues instead that it contains elements of both retributive and rehabilitative justice whilst contributing additional elements of its own which make it unique. She argues that restorative practices do indeed focus on the offence and the offender; that they are concerned with the censure of and sanctions for past behaviour – in ways which are proportionate to the seriousness of the offence; and that they are concerned with future outcomes, in particular those which 'make things right' (Daly, 2000). For Daly, as indeed for Walgrave, the additionality of restorative justice is found in the role of the victim, the objective of 'sentencing' (repairing the harm done), the involvement of non-juridical agents in decision-making and the extent of dialogue and negotiation in the process.

There is a sense, however, in which Walgrave and Daly are not arguing about the same thing. Walgrave is primarily concerned with restorative justice as a paradigm, so he is promoting the concept of restorative *justice* as opposed to traditional forms of justice. Daly, on the other hand, is primarily concerned with the question of whether punishment has a proper place within the administration of restorative *practices*. Daly is, therefore, focusing on a much more specific question that does not directly or adequately grapple with key differences in approach between the two systems of justice. Two such (potential) differences are particularly important. First, the emphasis on due process and the offence in justice-based models, which are at least de-emphasised or *ideally* not relevant in restorative justice (which is based on its own internal principles of process, see, for example, Braithwaite and Mugford, 1994). Second, albeit to a lesser extent, the fundamental purpose of 'sentencing' – the retributive and/or rehabilitative aims of traditional approaches vs. repairing the harm done and re-integrative objectives of restorative justice.

The arguments of Walgrave, and others who posit the distinctiveness of restorative justice, are convincing if the point of the argument is to establish whether *restorative justice* is different from *traditional justice*. A different conclusion is reached, however, if one is concerned to explore the applicability of restorative *approaches* within a traditional justice system. The theory-based distinctiveness of restorative vs. traditional justice is obviated once the objective of implementing a *wholly restorative justice-based system* is compromised by the enduring presence of retributive/punitive elements. From here on, it is no longer possible to talk about restorative *justice* as such. Restorative *approaches* on the other hand, can be implemented, in both theory and practice, amongst a range of other sentencing options (both as horizontal equivalents or alternatives and as vertical tariff-based options) within traditional justice models. In such cases where restorative approaches are implemented within traditional justice systems, the sentence to the restorative option is, paradoxically, retributive and, therefore, a *punishment* – and it is seen as/experienced by young people as a punishment. The content of such restorative sentences should approximate to the principles and practices of restorative justice/approaches (such as method, content, involvement, process) but the outcomes may include a punitive element alongside other measures. This possibility and the corresponding reality seem to be accepted by restorative justice theorists of international repute (such as Walgrave) and by those who carry out restorative interventions with young people.

The growth in popularity and spread of restorative justice precisely at a time when attitudes towards young people find expression in generally more controlling and/or punitive measures (especially in England and Wales) both rest in, and at the same time expose, the crucial tension within restorative justice to be simultaneously both positive and punitive. In practice, the positive elements are more rhetorical whilst the punitive expressions are more materially apparent.

Restorative approaches and children

How far and to what extent is restorative justice, or are restorative approaches, appropriate and applicable methods for working with children? What special considerations should apply to the treatment of children subjected to restorative interventions? The notion that children in trouble represent a special category of 'offenders' that merits distinct treatment from that afforded to adults dates back to the early 1800s (Gelsthorpe and Morris, 1994). Recognising that children are not yet adults both mitigates their degree of individual culpability (and in certain circumstances limits their legal ability to act with full adult responsibility) and provides for consideration of their cognitive and moral stage of development and hence for their developmental needs.

The principle that the criminal courts 'shall have regard to the welfare of the child or young person' appearing before it and 'shall take steps for securing that proper provision is made for his education and training' is well established in legislation in England and Wales (Children and Young Persons Act 1933 s 44(1) as amended by the Children and Young Persons Act 1969). This principle is further strengthened by Article 3 of the United Nations Convention on the Rights of the Child which places primary consideration on the best interests of the child in all actions concerning children (Haines, 2000). This special status means that young people should not and, indeed, cannot be held fully responsible for their actions and that in deciding on how they should be treated, following admission of guilt or conviction for a criminal offence, their best interests and future prospects should be given proper consideration. This principle has been taken to inform the contention that 'young offenders' should be treated as 'children' first and 'offenders' second (Haines and Drakeford 1998, Welsh Assembly Government and Youth Justice Board, 2004).

There is thus already an emergent tension between the principle of children first and the principles and practices of restorative approaches. 'Restorative justice practices assume mentally competent and hence morally culpable actors, who are expected to take responsibility for their actions' (Daly, 2000: 35). Indeed, one of the principal attractions of restorative approaches to the Home Office and Youth Justice Board for England and Wales is their utility in 'forcing' young people to take responsibility for their actions (Home Office, 2003). The requirement in restorative approaches for participants to be fully-functioning mental and moral actors and the capacity of restorative practices to inculcate individual responsibility are both muted and mitigated by the limited capacity of children in this respect.

The potential for coercion and even bullying of young people, outnumbered and outwitted by a 'room full of adults', none of which has the direct responsibility to safeguard and promote the best interests of the child and, moreover, where they may be a collusion of interests on the side of the victim, must be recognised and must be actively prevented by the 'good practice' of participants (as there are few built-in legal or procedural safeguards) (Braithwaite, 2002; Goldson, 2000; Haines, 1998). While there is substantial evidence of good practice in the 'process' of youth offender panels it is by no means universal (Newburn et al., 2002), but outcomes (*sentences*) of panels are equally important and here the evidence is less positive. In about 15 per cent of cases, questions could be raised about the quality of the process of panels (see Newburn et al., 2002). This may be interpreted as a good result given the experimental nature of panels but equivalent 'performance' would surely not be tolerated of the formal Youth Court. Furthermore, whilst 75 per cent of young people responded that they did not feel pushed into doing anything they disagreed with, 25 per cent clearly experienced some degree of coercion (see Newburn et al., 2002).

Results such as these lead to a fundamental questioning of restorative justice and practice within contemporary youth justice. Research consistently demonstrates that 'offenders' are also likely to be 'victims' themselves; both of direct criminal victimisation and, more widely, victims of social exclusion and discrimination (Smith and McAra, 2003). Any form of restorative *justice* that fails to take full account of these realities and which supplants the interests of adult victims over that of children and, moreover, which implicitly or explicitly justifies the use of controlling or punitive measures against offending children cannot lay any claim to be providing restorative justice in an individual or wider social sense. There are perhaps two key dynamics in evaluating the appropriateness of restorative approaches in youth justice practice. The first concerns the degree to which they promote the development of individual responsibility, and the second concerns their restorative utility and the extent to which they promote the best interests of the child.

The potential for restorative approaches to promote the development of 'taking responsibility for one's actions' on the part of a growing and maturing child is clearly important and relevant. Any approach, whether in a restorative or alternative milieu, that tries to force this development or which imposes sanctions with a supposed responsibilising effect may be doomed to failure. Sanctions which are explicitly punitive, or which are perceived to be punitive by the recipient, are at best ineffective in changing attitudes or future behaviour and, at worst, counter-productive. Indeed, the more punitive the sanction, the greater the likelihood of producing a deviancy amplificatory effect (Petrosino et al., 2003; MacKenzie et al., 1995). The inclusion of punitive sanctions within the panoply of 'restorative' outcomes and the potential for many non-deliberately punitive sanctions to be perceived by young people as a punishment flies in the face of what we know to be effective in reducing recidivism (Haines and Drakeford, 1998). Furthermore, this also undermines fundamentally any notion of restoration, compromises the best interests of the child and reduces any prospect of promoting individual responsibility.

The value and effectiveness of pro-social modelling as an important element in approaches to working with young people who have offended are well demonstrated (Bottoms et al., 1990). By promoting (and self-evidencing) desirable attitudes and behaviours, young people are much more likely to learn pro-social attitudes and develop pro-social behaviours. Implementing pro-social modelling, however, is a complex process. A restorative conference, for example, may constitute one instance of such a process, but if the learning opportunities for young people are to be meaningful and maximised, there must be continual evidence of the pro-social modelling process in the ongoing work that follows the restorative conference. In reality, there is scant evidence that anything like this is happening, rather there is some evidence in the outcomes from youth offender panels that negative criminogenically-focused interventions are occurring (Newburn et al., 2002).

Moreover, pro-social modelling is a key ingredient in the effectiveness of interventions with older and more serious offenders and there is much less evidence to support the importance of this element in interventions with younger, more minor, first-time offenders (Goldson, 2000). There is very limited, if any, evidence in the literature that youth justice-based restorative approaches pay due regard to the age of the offender or the level of seriousness of their offending in either the way in which processes are managed or the types of sanctions that are imposed upon young people. The lack of explicit and evident consideration of the age of the child, and their level of maturity, builds to form a picture of restorative interventions which fail to put children first. This basic omission raises questions as to whether such approaches possess even the possibility of promoting the development of individual responsibility or of promoting the best interests of the child. Further cause for concern, in this regard, is to be found in the perfunctory application of routine compulsory elements in youth offender contracts attached to the Referral Order (such as reparation) which few could even claim to be good restorative practice, let alone to be models of practice which promote individual responsibility or the best interests of the child.

The question of whether restorative approaches actually represent or achieve restorative aims is even more vexed. There is considerable disagreement in the literature of what it is that restorative practices are actually trying to restore (the harm caused by the offence, the victim, the offender). There is, additionally, considerable disagreement and debate about which practices are *de facto* restorative and, as noted, a lack of clarity of how restorative justice is defined. It is thus even more difficult to articulate what restorative practices, that are child-appropriate, might comprise. A primary requirement of any restorative approach or practice that aimed to be child-appropriate, however, would be that it put the child first. Such an approach would pay considerably less attention to the offence (at least to the extent that the offence is not allowed to determine the outcomes). Inevitably this raises tensions with the interests of victims but it might be argued that this should not form part of any mechanism designed to deal with the young person, unless it can be clearly demonstrated that to do so is in the best interests of the child.

We already know a great deal about the effectiveness of interventions with children and young people, specifically as they are related to future behaviour. Two fundamental principles can be discerned from the research. First, interventions with young people who have offended, that are designed to prevent further offending, are less effective if the focus of the intervention is solely criminogenic: effective interventions tend to be those which focus on promoting positive behaviour. Second, interventions that just focus on internal cognitive processes are less effective, while those which take account of the real lives and the social situations of young people and which focus on the linkages between the young person and their wider social situation are more effective (see Haines and Drakeford, 1998). A 'children first' restorative practice would, therefore, promote positive behaviour by focusing on the connections between the young person and their wider social situation – an approach that would hold out the possibility of being genuinely restorative and with real potential crime reduction gains. Such child-focused elements are evident in the outcomes of youth offender panels, but in small measure and swamped by compulsory reparation and offence-focused interventions (see Newburn et al., 2002). There is little or no evidence that such measures promote individual responsibility, scant evidence that they are in any way restorative and it is clearly difficult to sustain any kind of argument that they are in the best interests of the child.

Conclusion

Despite the enthusiasm with which many have embraced restorative justice, and despite the increasingly widespread introduction of restorative approaches into youth justice systems in the UK and elsewhere, there remains a lack of clarity and, indeed, some strong debate about the precise definition and nature of restorative justice. Moreover, issues concerning the processes of restorative justice, questions concerning who it is intended to 'restore', what makes these processes restorative and how they are supposed to work, remain contentious and contested.

While there is emerging evidence that some restorative approaches are being applied in practice effectively and many agencies and individual practitioners offer support for restorative practices, there remains serious questions about the extent to which these approaches are truly restorative or have properly taken central account of the child.

References

Audit Commission (1996) *Misspent Youth: Young People and Crime*. London: Audit Commission

Ball, C. McCormac, K. and Stone, N. (2001) *Young Offenders: Law, Policy and Practice*. London: Sweet and Maxwell.

Bazemore, G. and Umbreit, M. (1995) 'Rethinking the Sanctioning Function in Juvenile Court: Retributive or Restorative Responses to Youth Crime', *Crime and Delinquency*, 41: 296–316.

Beckett, H., Campbell, C., O'Mahony, D., Jackson, J. and Doak, J. (2005) *Interim Evaluation of the Northern Ireland Youth Conferencing Scheme*. Belfast: Northern Ireland Office, Statistics and Research Branch, Research and Statistical Bulletin 1/2005.

Bottoms, A., Brown, P., McWilliams, B., McWilliams, W., Nellis, M. with Pratt, J. (1990) *Intermediate Treatment and Juvenile Justice*. London: HMSO.

Braithwaite, J. (1989) *Crime, Shame and Reintegration*. Cambridge: Cambridge University Press.

Braithwaite, J. (2002) 'Setting Standards for Restorative Justice', *British Journal of Criminology*, 42(3): 563–77.

Braithwaite, J. and Mugford, S. (1994) 'Conditions of Successful Reintegration Ceremonies: Dealing with Juvenile Offenders', *British Journal of Criminology*, 33: 1–18.

Criminal Justice Review Group (2000) *Review of the Criminal Justice System in Northern Ireland.* Belfast: HMSO.

Claassen, R. (1996) *Restorative Justice: Primary Focus on People not Procedures* (available on-line at www.fresno.edu/deppacs/docs/rjprinc2.html).

Crawford, A. and Newburn, T. (2003) *Youth Offending and Restorative Justice: Implementing Reform in Youth Justice.* Cullompton: Willan.

Cullen, R. (2004) 'The Referral Order: The Main Issues Arising from its Evaluation and the Youth Justice Board's Efforts to Address Them', *Childright* 204: 8–9.

Daly, K. (2000) 'Revisiting the Relationship Between Retributive and Restorative Justice', in H. Strang and J. Braithwaite (eds) *Restorative Justice: Philosophy to Practice.* Aldershot: Ashgate.

Daly, K. (2002) 'Restorative Justice: The Real Story', *Punishment and Society*, 4: 55–79.

Dignan, J. (2005) *Understanding Victims and Restorative Justice.* Maidenhead: Open University Press.

Dignan, J. and Lowey, K. (2000) *Restorative Justice Options for Northern Ireland: A Comparative Overview.* Belfast: HMSO.

Goldson, B. (2000) 'Wither Diversion? Interventionism and the New Youth Justice', in B. Goldson (ed.) *The New Youth Justice.* Lyme Regis: Russell House Publishing.

Haines, K. (1998) 'Some Principled Objections to a Restorative Justice Approach to Working with Juvenile Offenders', in L. Walgrave (ed.) *Restorative Justice for Juveniles.* Leuven: University Press.

Haines, K. (2000) 'Referral Orders and Youth Offender Panels: Restorative Approaches and the New Youth Justice', in B. Goldson (ed.) *The New Youth Justice.* Lyme Regis: Russell House Publishing.

Haines, K. and Drakeford, M. (1998) *Young People and Youth Justice.* Basingstoke: Macmillan.

Home Office (2002) *Referral Order, Guidance for Courts.* London: Home Office.

Home Office (2003) *Restorative Justice: The Government's Strategy.* London: Home Office.

Hoyle, C., Young, R. and Hill, R. (2002) *Proceed with Caution: An Evaluation of the Thames Valley Police Initiative in Restorative Cautioning.* York: Joseph Rowntree Foundation.

MacKenzie, D., Brame, R., McDowall, D. and Souryal, C. (1995) 'Boot Camp Prisons and Recidivism in Eight States', *Criminology*, 33(3): 327–57.

Marshall, T. (1999) *Restorative Justice: An Overview.* London: Home Office Research Development and Statistics Directorate.

McCold, P. (1996) 'Restorative Justice: the Role of the Community', in B. Galaway and J. Hudson (eds), *Restorative Justice: International Perspectives,* Mosney, NY.: Criminal Justice Press.

McEvoy, K. and Mika, H. (2002) 'Restorative Justice and the Critique of Informalism in Northern Ireland', *British Journal of Criminology*, 43: 534–630.

Morris, A. and Maxwell, G. (1993) 'Juvenile Justice in New Zealand: A New Paradigm', *Australian and New Zealand Journal of Criminology*, 26: 72–90.

Mullan, S. and O'Mahony, D. (2002) *A Review of Recent Youth Justice Reforms in England and Wales.* Belfast: Northern Ireland Office, Research and Statistical Series Report, No. 8.

Newburn, T., Crawford, A., Earle, R., Goldie, S., Hale, C., Hallam, A., Masters, G., Netten, A., Saunders, R., Sharpe, K. and Uglow, S. (2002) *The Introduction of Referral Orders into the Youth Justice System: Final Report.* London: Home Office Research Study 242, Home Office Research, Development and Statistics Directorate.

O'Mahony, D. and Campbell, C. (2004) 'Mainstreaming Restorative Justice for Young Offenders through Youth Conferencing – the experience of Northern Ireland', European Society of Criminology – Thematic Working Group on Juvenile Justice (at http://www.esc-eurocrim.org/files/northern-ireland_report.doc)

O'Mahony, D. and Doak, J. (2004) 'Restorative Justice – Is More Better? The Experience of Police-led Restorative cautioning Pilots in Northern Ireland', *The Howard Journal*, 43: 484–505.

Petrosino, A., Turpin-Petrosino, C. and Buehler, J. (2003) 'Scared Straight and Other Juvenile Awareness Programs for Preventing Juvenile Delinquency: A Systematic Review of the Randomized Experimental Evidence', *The ANNALS of the American Academy of Political and Social Sciences*, 589: 41–62.

Roche, D. (2001) 'The Evolving Definition of Restorative Justice', *Contemporary Justice Review*, 4(3–4): 341–53.

Shapland, J., Willmore, J. and Duff, P. (1985) *Victims in the Criminal Justice System*. Aldershot: Gower.

Smith, D. and McAra, L. (2003) *The Edinburgh Study of Youth Transitions and Crime*, Report to the ESRC.

Umbreit, M. (1994) *Victim Meets Offender: The Impact of Restorative Justice and Mediation*. Monsey, New York: Criminal Justice Press.

Van Ness, D. and Strong, K. (1997) *Restoring Justice*. Cincinnati: Anderson.

Von Hirsch, A., Roberts, J., Bottoms, A., Roach, K. and Schiff, M. (2003) *Restorative Justice and Criminal Justice: Competing or Reconcilable Paradigms?*. Portland, OR: Hart Publishing.

Walgrave, L. (1995) 'Restorative Justice for Juveniles: Just a Technique or a Fully Fledged Alternative?', *The Howard Journal*, 34: 228–49.

Walgrave, L. and Bazemore, G. (1999) 'Reflections on the Future of Restorative Justice for Juveniles', in G. Bazemore and L. Walgrave (eds) *Restorative Juvenile Justice: Repairing the Harm of Youth Crime*, Monsey, NY: Criminal Justice Press.

Welsh Assembly Government and Youth Justice Board (2004) *All Wales Youth Offending Strategy*. Cardiff: Welsh Assembly Government.

Young, R. and Hoyle, C. (2003) 'New, improved police-led restorative justice? Action research and the Thames Valley Police initiative', in A. von Hirsch, et al. *Restorative Justice and Penal Justice: Competing or Reconcilable Paradigms?* Oxford: Hart.

Youth Justice Board (2004) *Youth Justice Annual Statistics 2003/04*, London: Youth Justice Board.

Zehr, H. and Mika, H. (2003) 'Fundamental Concepts of Restorative Justice', in E. McLaughlin, R. Furgusson, G. Hughes and L. Westmarland (eds) *Restorative Justice Critical Issues*. Milton Keynes: Open University Press.

Community Supervision: Context and Relationships Matter

Fergus McNeill

Introduction

This chapter explores the relationships between evidence, policy and practice in community-based interventions with young offenders. The debates and controversies about the effectiveness of community supervision are considered alongside an analysis of the emergence of correctionalism in contemporary youth justice. Furthermore, desistance from offending is discussed and, on the basis of evidence, the means by which community supervision might be reconstructed are explored. The central argument is that a critical reading of research evidence suggests that correctionalist discourses, policies and practices serve to inhibit and frustrate the achievement of their expressed purpose – the prevention of youth offending and re-offending. Given that such an outcome is likely to result in further use of custodial detention – a less effective, more expensive and more damaging sanction – a critical reconstruction of community supervision is urgently required.

Community supervision and its effectiveness

In England and Wales, a variety of orders are available to the courts that provide for some element of community supervision of young people who have offended including: action plan orders; reparation orders; and drug treatment and testing orders. The supervision order itself, however, is of most relevance here. Under sections 63–68 of the Powers of Criminal Courts (Sentencing) Act 2000, supervision orders can be imposed on children and young people at the point of conviction; the orders have no minimum length but the maximum is three years. Since the order is a community sentence, it can only be imposed where the offending is 'serious enough' to require such a measure; the restriction of liberty involved must be commensurate with the seriousness of the offence and the order must be the most suitable method available for the young person. The main effect of the order is to place the child or young person under supervision (provided by a local authority, a probation officer or a member of a multi-agency youth offending team) in respect of which the supervisor is obliged to 'advise, assist and befriend' the supervisee. In addition to the standard conditions of supervision orders (retaining contact with the supervising officer and complying with instructions), in certain circumstances a wide range of additional conditions can also be imposed by the courts, including: requirements to undertake 'intermediate treatment' and/or 'specified activities'; to make reparation either to the community or to specific individuals; to submit to 'night restriction' conditions (curfews); to refrain from particular activities; to reside in local authority accommodation; to receive treatment for a 'mental condition'; and to comply with educational arrangements (Nacro, 2002).

Perhaps most significantly, intensive supervision and surveillance programmes (ISSPs) can now be deployed as part of a supervision order where a young person meets the (non-statutory) eligibility criteria; these include having been charged, warned or convicted of offences committed on four or more separate occasions in the preceding 12 months and having received at least one previous community sentence or custodial penalty; or being at risk of custody because the current charge is so serious that an adult could be sentenced to 14 years prisonment or more. As the name suggests, such programmes combine intensive supervision and *surveillance* either by tracking, tagging, voice verification or intelligence-led policing (Moore, 2005; Nellis, 2004).

The most recent study of the effectiveness of community interventions with young people in England and Wales (Jennings, 2003) concluded that such measures had delivered a fall of 22 per cent in predicted reconvictions within 12 months of reprimand, warning or conviction when measured against an 'adjusted predicted' rate. However, leaving aside the methodological limitations of this study noted by some commentators (Bateman and Pitts, 2005; Bottoms and Dignan, 2004), the largest improvements were associated with reprimands and final warnings. By contrast, orders (primarily supervision orders) aimed at young people involved in more persistent offending achieved at best marginal effects in terms of reconviction; a finding that the Audit Commission (2004) has recently underlined. A similar problem in tackling persistent offending was apparent in Feilzer et al.'s (2004) evaluation of 23 cognitive behavioural programmes in youth justice. Only 47 per cent of children and young people referred completed the programmes and 71 per cent of 'completers' re-offended within 12 months. Feilzer et al. (2004) concluded that 'methodological shortcomings' made it impossible to assess the independent effectiveness of the programmes in reducing offending. While the detailed conclusions from the ongoing evaluations of ISSPs are not yet available, Moore's (2004) optimistic review of related research is ultimately equivocal in terms of the prospects for reducing both reconviction and the use of custody.

In Scotland, supervision orders may involve similar conditions and forms of intervention to those applied in England and Wales. The principal difference, however, is that they are located within a Children's Hearings system in which, in theory at least, the welfare of the child is paramount and no non-beneficial orders should be imposed (Children (Scotland) Act 1995, section 16).[1] Crucially, the latter principle requires a parsimonious approach to regulatory/correctional intervention. Although the relative dearth of evaluative studies makes it difficult to reach reliable conclusions about the effectiveness of the Children's Hearings System in tackling youth offending, some studies undertaken in the late 1990s exposed certain problems, including: a lack of clarity about decision-making; substantial 'drift'; and a failure to prevent escalation in the offending of a small group of typically older boys and young men at high risk of progression to the adult courts and thence to custody (often at the age of 16 in Scotland) (Hallett et al., 1998; Waterhouse et al., 2000). Despite such problems, however, there is some emerging evidence that the Hearings system can, in some circumstances at least, deliver encouraging reductions in youth offending. For example, 'Fast Track Hearings', targeted at young people involved in persistent offending, and aimed at reducing 'drift', were set up on a pilot basis in 2003, operating within the principles of the Hearings system but at greater speed and with additional resources. The interim evaluation report suggests that the measures are producing reductions in levels of offending and re-referrals to the Hearings (Hill et al., 2004). To some extent, the positive evaluation of the Freagarrach Project (which provides intensive supervision for young people involved in persistent offending) had already implied that such success could be achieved within the Hearings system, where the right kind of services were provided for children and young people (Lobley et al., 2001).

Despite predictable (if under-recognised) difficulties in addressing the complexities of the needs of children and young people involved in persistent offending (Liddle and Solanki, 2002; McNeill and Batchelor, 2002), there is reason to be optimistic about the potential of properly targeted, resourced and constructed community supervision. That said, the strongest case for increasing (and crucially, repeating) the use of community supervision with those involved in persistent offending rests on the compelling evidence about the ineffectiveness of custody, particularly in the light of its high fiscal and human costs (Goldson,

---

1. Children's Hearings are welfare tribunals headed by lay people from the local community. Children can be brought before a Hearing because they: are beyond the control of parents; are being exposed to moral danger; are likely to suffer unnecessarily or suffer serious impairment to health or development through lack of parental care; are the victim of a sex or cruelty offence; are failing to attend school regularly; are misusing drugs, alcohol or solvents; or have committed an offence. If the Hearing thinks compulsory measures of supervision are appropriate, it will impose a supervision requirement, which may be renewed until the child becomes 18.

2002; Hagell, 2005). No youth justice system that is serious about reducing youth crime has any option other than to look towards developing the effectiveness of community supervision.

Correctionalism and community supervision

The focus and nature of supervision are inevitably shaped by political discourses about youth crime and 'young offenders'. In this regard, some commentators have argued that a kind of authoritarian corporate correctionalism has recently emerged in youth justice, particularly in England and Wales (Goldson, 2001; Muncie, 2002; Pitts, 2001). This correctionalism, it is argued, narrowly emphasises constructions of individual responsibility and parental accountability for the behaviour of children and young people, entailing a concomitant policy and practice focus on correcting personal and/or parental 'deficits' (Goldson and Jamieson, 2002). Equally, the wider social and structural contexts within which youth crime is located are essentially overlooked.

Some similar conceptual trends are apparent in Scotland. Although the very different systemic context provided by the system of Children's Hearings might be seen to comprise a barrier to the imposition of crudely correctionalist approaches, hopes that these arrangements will continue to facilitate a significantly different policy and practice line from that in England and Wales (Allen, 2002; Smith, 2000) are beginning to seem unduly optimistic (McAra, 2004). Just as populist discourse in England and Wales has vilified 'yobs' and 'yob culture', so in Scotland, coverage of 'ned crime'[2] was prominent during the Scottish Parliamentary election campaign of 2003. Hard on the heels of similar developments in England and Wales, therefore, the Labour-Liberal Democrat Executive has, since the 2003 election, delivered 'tough' measures including: the tagging of young people involved in offending; an expansion of the secure estate; parenting orders (underwritten by the threat of imprisonment for parents who failed to control their children); and anti-social behaviour orders for the under-16s.[3] Thus, at the level of policy there is significant evidence of a much stronger focus neither on children and young people's needs nor on their rights, but on their deeds and risks, particularly in relation to persistent and prolific offending. Young people who offend persistently are increasingly cast in both jurisdictions not as vulnerable subjects of risks to their welfare but as dangerous or anti-social bearers of risks to the welfare of 'the community'.

Paradoxically perhaps, given this increasingly populist and correctionalist context, the question of 'what works?' and the promise that research might constructively inform policy formation and practice development have gathered momentum. A decade ago, McGuire and Priestley (1995) produced a highly

2. A 'ned' is the Scottish colloquial equivalent to 'yob'.
3. The Anti-social Behaviour (Scotland) Act 2004 contains these and other measures.

influential summary of six key principles for the design and delivery of effective supervision programmes to reduce re-offending, drawn from meta-analyses of programme evaluations. First, the level of service provided should match the level of 'risk' assessed; where the risk of re-offending is high, more intensive programmes are required. Second, only some factors contribute to, or are supportive of, offending; the focus of intervention should be on addressing offending by alleviating those factors that are 'criminogenic'. Third, the learning styles of people involved in offending vary but in general they require active rather than didactic 'programmes'. Fourth, programmes in the community fare better than those in institutions. Fifth, effective interventions recognise the variety of problems experienced by people who offend and, therefore, they employ a skills-oriented approach, using methods drawn from behavioural, cognitive, or cognitive-behavioural sources. Sixth, effective interventions connect the methods used to the aims stated, are carried out by appropriately trained and supported staff, are adequately resourced, and plan monitoring and evaluation from the outset.

Whereas McGuire and Priestley's principles derived from 'treatment' studies not limited specifically to juveniles, Lipsey's (1995) meta-analysis was concerned exclusively with the effectiveness of 'programmes' for young people. Notably, Lipsey (1995: 77) reached more circumspect conclusions, suggesting that 'the best general practical advice' was threefold. First, 'treatment' should be focused on behavioural, training or skills issues appropriate to the young people, using concrete, structured approaches as far as possible. Second, 'treatment' should be monitored, supervised and implemented well. 'Fidelity' to the 'treatment' plan should be maintained so that the 'treatment' is delivered as intended. Third, enough service should be provided. Lipsey recognised that such advice was necessarily 'general and broadbrush', adding the proviso that all 'treatment' must be 'carefully tailored in its details to the pertinent clientele and circumstances' (ibid.: 78).

In some respects, these principles of effective community-based intervention and supervision seem uncontroversial. More often than not, the principal contention/conclusion might be summarised thus: to say that 'nothing works' is erroneous given that the evidence suggests that some things 'work' with some people some of the time, but more research is required with regard to the specific details. However, such a considered (even cautious) approach, has been less evident in the drive of the Youth Justice Board for England and Wales to engineer 'what works' principles into youth justice practice (Bateman and Pitts, 2005). Critical commentators have argued that the resultant pre-occupation with standardised risk/needs assessments and targeted programmes in delivering effective practice has led to a managerialised and homogenising approach to assessment and intervention that has predictably struggled to cope with the heterogeneity of children and young people and the complexities of their circumstances (Eadie and Canton, 2002). Indeed some critics have argued that the current approach is more about the micro-management of the system than its likely impact on offending (Pitts, 2001).

The fundamentally flawed assumption underlying the managerialisation of practice through structured assessments and targeted programmes is, of course, that it is the standardised and quality assured application of 'assessment tools' and 'programmes' ('treatment') that lies at the heart of effective practice. Even within the 'treatment' literature, however, it is possible to find strong evidence that challenges this assumption. One authoritative recent review, for example, highlights the increasing attention that is being paid to the need for professional staff to use interpersonal skills, to exercise some discretion in their interventions, to take diversity amongst participants into account, and to look at how the broader service context can best support effective practice (Raynor, 2004: 201). Still stronger evidence is found in the broader literature exploring the effectiveness of psychological interventions more generally (that is, beyond criminal and youth justice contexts). Here, it is a recurring finding that no method of intervention is, in and of itself, any more 'effective' than any other; rather, there are common features of each intervention that are most likely to bring about positive change (Hubble et al., 1999; Bozarth, 2000). These 'core conditions' of effectiveness include: empathy and genuineness; the establishment of a working alliance; and the adoption of person-centred, collaborative and 'client-driven' approaches. Perhaps even more significantly, the most crucial variables of all – chance factors, external factors and 'client' factors – are derived from the personal and social contexts of the interventions as distinct from 'programme' content. For example, the extent to which a young person is prepared to change and prepared for change, the extent to which his or her significant others support or subvert change, and the extent to which his or her social networks create or constrain opportunities for change, are all factors beyond the reach of 'programmes' but critical to the success or failure of the change effort. Such findings, despite their disciplinary affiliation with 'treatment', in fact attest to the importance of relationships, social and material contexts above programmes. With regard to the policy and practice of community supervision, this 'scientific' evidence seems to counter the prevailing tendency of narrowing the gaze to responsibilising correctionalism and to challenge its more authoritarian and coercive imperatives.

Beyond correctionalism

Leaving aside the contested evidence about what matters most in 'treatment' effectiveness, critical commentators have raised more fundamental concerns about the assumptions underlying 'what works?' research, questioning whether its methodologies can adequately capture the nature of the human change processes involved in desistance from offending (for example, Farrall, 2002). The alternative methodologies involved in 'desistance' research explore how 'criminal careers' come to be truncated and terminated. Given that this is a principal purpose of tertiary crime reduction (and community supervision), the fact that desistance research has had, until recently, a muted impact on policy and practice is somewhat surprising. Building an understanding of the human processes and social contexts within which desistance occurs should be a necessary precursor to developing effective community supervision; put another way, constructions of policy and practice should be 'embedded' in understandings of desistance. More bluntly, thinking about 'treatment' efficacy is the wrong starting point for evidence-based practice.

Explanations for desistance from offending tend to stress ageing and developing maturity (the 'growing out of crime' thesis – see Rutherford, 1992), the development of positive social bonds and changes in the way that 'desisters' construct their personal and social identities (McNeill, 2003). A study of young people in Scotland (Jamieson et al., 1999), for example, demonstrated age and gender-related differences in desistance from offending, suggesting that both offending and desistance are affected by the complex and gendered transitions from childhood through youth to adulthood. Earlier research by Graham and Bowling (1995) had found that young women tended to stop offending quite abruptly as they left home, formed partnerships and had children,[4] but that the process for young men was much more elongated, gradual and intermittent. Young men were less likely to achieve independence and those that did leave home, formed partnerships and had children, were no more likely to desist than those that did not. More recent studies have revised Graham and Bowling's (1995) conclusions, suggesting that similar processes of change do indeed occur for (some) young men but that they seem to take longer to 'kick-in'; in other words, the assumption of responsibilities in and through intimate relationships and employment does make a difference but this difference is more notable in men aged 25 and over (Farrall and Bowling, 1999; Flood-Page et al., 2000; Uggen and Kruttschnitt, 1998).

Farrall stresses the significance of the relationships between what we might term 'objective' changes in each person's life and his or her 'subjective' assessment of the value or significance of these changes:

> ... the desistance literature has pointed to a range of factors associated with the ending of active involvement in offending. Most of these factors are related to acquiring 'something' (most commonly employment, a life partner or a family) which the desister values in some way and which initiates a re-evaluation of his or her own life ... (2002: 11)

Desistance, therefore, seems to reside somewhere in the interface between developing personal maturity, the changing social bonds associated with certain life transitions, and the individual subjective narrative constructions which people

---

4. In a more recent article, Rumgay (2004) has suggested that women's desistance from crime is best understood as a process initiated by the *perception of an opportunity* to claim a pro-social identity during a period of *readiness to reform*, which is subsequently sustained by the deployment of strategies of resilience and survival in conditions of adversity.

who have been involved in offending build around these key events and changes. It is not just the events and changes that matter; it is what these events and changes mean to those involved. We might add to Farrall's (2002) summary a more structural perspective; it seems obvious that for young people both access to opportunities to desist and positive reasons to attempt desistance, have been structurally constrained in recent decades by the increasingly problematic nature of youth transitions to adult status, most notably in the labour market (Newburn and Shiner, 2005).[5]

Indeed, desistance itself is perhaps best understood as a process of transition. Maruna et al. (2004) suggest that it is helpful to distinguish primary desistance (the achievement of an offence-free period) from secondary desistance (an underlying change in self-identity). Though the desistance research has little to tell us, as yet, about how young people who have been involved in persistent offending navigate secondary desistance, and how youth justice interventions might contribute to this process, research studies involving adult desisters do offer some significant insights. For example, Burnett's (1992; 2000) research revealed that released prisoners who were most confident and optimistic about desisting had greatest success in doing so. This implies that nurturing and sustaining hope is a key task in community supervision but that, particularly in respect of desisting from persistent offending, youth justice workers and sentencers should expect the process of desistance to be neither linear nor straightforward nor swift. Establishing a desisting 'identity' will take time, effort and patience; moreover, the emergence of such identities is likely to be delayed or prevented by the imposition of punitive sanctions for any re-offending.

Maruna's more recent study (2001) offers a particularly important contribution to understanding the achievement of secondary desistance. Comparing the narrative 'scripts' of 20 adult 'persisters' and 30 adult 'desisters' who shared similar 'criminogenic traits' and backgrounds and who lived in similarly 'criminogenic environments', Maruna discerned a 'condemnation script' that emerged from the 'persisters'. Their stories echo the fatalism that previous studies of young people involved in persistent offending have revealed (Smith and Stewart, 1998). Though the desisters' 'redemption script' contains a similarly fatalistic account of their pasts, in their accounts of achieving change there is evidence that desisters have to 'discover' agency in order to resist and overcome the criminogenic structural pressures that play upon them. This 'discovery of agency' seems to relate to the role of significant 'others' in envisioning an alternative identity and an alternative future for the would-be desister even through periods when they cannot see these possibilities for themselves.

Although this research primarily relates to adult 'persisters' and 'desisters', it has particular resonance for those involved in supervising young people

---

5. That it is desistance from property offending that is, in general, significantly slower for young men may tend to support this suggestion (Flood-Page et al., 2000).

involved in offending during adolescence; a period of malleability during which there may be the opportunity to enable the development of positive identities before negative messages are internalised. However, this very malleability also carries with it the danger that correctionalist approaches, through their implicit focus on negative behaviours, risks and deficits, may frustrate the very change process that they purport to support.

Reconstructing community supervision

Some recent studies have began to explore critical questions around the role that community supervision might play in supporting processes of desistance (for example, Farrall, 2002; McCulloch, 2005; Rex, 1999). Again, to date, this evidence primarily relates to interventions involving adults subject to probation orders. However, such studies can be read and interpreted in the light of other research on young people. For example, in one study of 'assisted desistance', Rex (1999) explored the experiences of 60 probationers, 11 of whom were aged 20 or under, and found that those who attributed changes in their behaviour to community supervision described it as active and participatory. Probationers' commitments to desist appeared to be generated by the personal and professional commitment shown by their probation officers, whose reasonableness, fairness, and encouragement seemed to engender a sense of personal respect and accountability. Probationers interpreted advice about their behaviours and underlying problems as evidence of concern for them as people, and 'were motivated by what they saw as a display of interest in their well-being' (1999: 375). Such encouragement seemed especially important for younger probationers involved in recidivist offending. These findings accord with other studies which suggest that it is vitally important to young people that they are treated as 'ordinary human beings', not just as 'a client' (de Winter and Noom, 2003), and as whole people rather than as instances of some 'problem' or 'disorder' (Hill, 1999).

The evidence suggests, therefore, that relationships matter a great deal in promoting and sustaining desistance (Batchelor and McNeill, 2005; Burnett and McNeill, 2005; McNeill et al., 2005). Given that young people, in particular, often conceptualise relationships both as a primary source of the distress they experience (Armstrong et al., 1998), and as a key resource in the alleviation of their difficulties (Hill, 1999), the role of relationships in youthful desistance is likely to be particularly significant, not least because the relational experiences of most young people involving in offending are characterised by disconnection and violation (Liddle and Solanki, 2002; McNeill and Batchelor, 2002). If, as has been argued above, secondary desistance (for those involved in persistent offending at least) requires a narrative reconstruction of identity, then it becomes obvious why the relational aspects of community supervision are so significant.

However, youth justice workers and working relationships are neither the only nor the most important resources in promoting desistance. Young people's own resources and social networks are often better at resolving their difficulties than social services' personnel (Hill, 1999). The potential of social networks is highlighted by 'resilience perspectives' which – in contrast to 'risk factor' models of offending that focus primarily on young people's 'deficits' and problems – consider the 'protective factors and processes' involved in positive adaptation in spite of adversity. In terms of practice with young people, such perspectives entail an emphasis on the recognition, exploitation and development of their competences, resources, skills and assets (Schoon and Bynner, 2003). Thus promoting desistance also means striving to develop the young person's strengths – at both an individual and a social network level – in order to build and sustain momentum for change.

Barry's recent study (2004) provides another key reference point for exploring how themes of agency, identity and transition play out specifically for younger people desisting from offending. Through in-depth interviews with 20 young women and 20 young men, Barry explored why they started and stopped offending and what influenced or inhibited them as they grew older. The young people revealed that their decisions about offending and desisting were related to their need to feel included in their social world, through friendships in childhood and through wider commitments in adulthood. The resolve displayed by the young people in desisting from offending seemed remarkable to Barry, particularly given that they were from disadvantaged backgrounds and were limited in their access to mainstream opportunities (employment, housing and social status) because of their age as well as their social class. Barry recognises crucially that:

> Because of their transitional situation, many young people lack the status and opportunities of full citizens and thus have limited capacity for social recognition in terms of durable and legitimate means of both accumulating and expending [social] capital through taking on responsibility and generativity ... Accumulation of capital requires, to a certain extent, both responsibilities and access to opportunities; however, children and young people rarely have such opportunities because of their status as 'liminal entities' not least those from a working class background. (2004: 328–9)

To facilitate desistance then, practitioners may need to assist young people in navigating transitions; both by acting as a conduit to 'social capital' and by seeking to build it. This implies, amongst other things, a re-assertion of the centrality of advocacy as a core task for youth justice staff. While this focus is justified normatively by recognition of the disempowered and disaffected social position of those young people whose behaviours are most commonly criminalised, the evidence from desistance studies suggests a strong empirical case for the necessity of social advocacy in the prevention of offending. Help in developing or sustaining social bonds is doubly significant in the promotion of desistance. Whereas Farrall (2002) underlines its importance in overcoming practical obstacles to desistance, Rex (1999) suggests that this kind of assistance is also critical in establishing the loyalty and trust that people value in supporting their efforts to change. There is a synergy between acts of practical assistance and their subjective impact on the working relationship; the worker's actions confirm his or her compassion and trustworthiness, increasing the preparedness of the young person to take steps towards desistance. In terms of the worker's contribution to change, success may depend at least as much on her or his ability to access opportunities to reinforce positive identities as it does on her or his ability to foster individual motivation and build individual capacities or skills. In other words, effective youth justice is likely to be at least as much about addressing social–structural disadvantage as it is about 'correcting deficits'.

Conclusions

This chapter has attempted to show that while community supervision in certain forms can be effective in reducing offending, its effectiveness is likely to be diminished rather than enhanced by the increasingly correctionalist discursive context of practice. While other commentators have made this case on the basis of critiques of 'what works?' as implemented in youth justice practice in England and Wales (Bateman and Pitts, 2005), here the argument has focused on recent revisions to 'what works' principles in the context of the wider literature about 'treatment efficacy' and, in greater detail, on the evidence from desistance studies. As well as suggesting fundamentally that the construction of community supervision should begin not with evaluations of 'tools' and 'programmes' (belonging to 'experts' and 'professionals') but with understandings of processes and transitions (belonging to young people), the evidence that has been reviewed conveys three key messages. First, relationships matter at least as much as 'tools' and 'programmes' in influencing the outcomes of supervision. Second, social contexts are at least as significant to offending and desistance as individual problems and resources. Third, in supporting desistance, social advocacy is at least as necessary as individualised responsibilisation.

Neglecting these messages will limit the effectiveness of community supervision, especially with young people involved in repeat and persistent offending. That such young people should be the primary 'target group' for such supervision is justified both by the principles of proportionality (in England and Wales) and parsimony (in Scotland), and by the empirical evidence about the proper role that informal and diversionary work should play in any effective youth justice system (Goldson, 2000). Ultimately, developing properly targeted and effective community supervision matters as much as it does because, in a punitive climate, any perceived failure of community supervision may unleash ever more coercive modes of correction and control. Though technological innovations may bring with them possibilities of increasingly coercive control in the community, ultimately the most likely consequence is an accelerated 'rush to youth custody' (Rutherford, 2002). Regrettably, the negative outcomes of that particular sanction, with its perverse and destructive impacts on the personal and social resources required to enable desistance, seem much more easily ignored than any limitations in the successes that may be achieved by community supervision. Thus, even without questioning the privileging of the 'prevention of offending' as the governing aim of youth *justice* in England and Wales, there are compelling ethical and empirical reasons for critiquing and resisting correctionalism, and for seeking to build other models and modes of practice in community supervision in the common interests of young people and of their communities.

References

Allen, R. (2002) '"There Must be Some Way of Dealing with Kids": Young Offenders, Public Attitudes and Policy Change', *Youth Justice*, 2(1): 3–13.

Armstrong, C., Hill, M. and Secker, J. (1998) *Listening to Children*. London: Mental Health Foundation.

Audit Commission (2004) *Youth Justice 2004: A Review of the Reformed Youth Justice System*. London: Audit Commission.

Barry, M.A. (2004) 'Understanding Youth Offending: In search of "Social Recognition"'. PhD dissertation, University of Stirling.

Batchelor, S. and McNeill, F. (2005) 'The Young Person-Worker Relationship', in T. Bateman and J. Pitts (eds) *The RHP Companion to Youth Justice*. Lyme Regis: Russell House Publishing. pp. 166–71.

Bateman, T. and Pitts, J. (2005) 'Conclusion: What the Evidence Tells Us', in T. Bateman and J. Pitts (eds) *The RHP Companion to Youth Justice*. Lyme Regis: Russell House Publishing. pp. 248–58.

Bottoms, A. and Dignan, J. (2004) *Youth Crime and Youth Justice: Comparative and Cross-national Perspectives*. Chicago, University of Chicago Press.

Bozarth, J. (2000) 'The Specificity Myth: the Fallacious Premise of Mental Health Treatment', paper presented to the American Psychological Association, Washington, DC.

Burnett, R. (1992) *The Dynamics of Recidivism*. Oxford: University of Oxford Centre for Criminological Research.

Burnett, R. (2000) 'Understanding Criminal Careers Through a Series of In-Depth Interviews', *Offender Programs Report*, 4(1): 1–16.

Burnett, R. and McNeill, F. (2005) 'The Place of the Officer–Offender Relationship in Assisting Offenders to Desist From Crime', *Probation Journal*, 52(3): 247–68.

de Winter, M. and Noom, M. (2003) 'Someone Who Treats You as an Ordinary Human Being', *British Journal of Social Work*, 33: 325–37.

Eadie, T. and Canton, R. (2002) 'Practising in a Context of Ambivalence: The Challenge for Youth Justice Workers', *Youth Justice*, 2(1): 14–26.

Farrall, S. (2002), *Rethinking What Works with Offenders: Probation, Social Context and Desistance from Crime*. Cullompton: Willan Publishing.

Farrall, S. and Bowling, B. (1999) 'Structuration, Human Development and Desistance from Crime', *British Journal of Criminology*, 17(2): 252–67.

Feilzer, M. with Appleton, C., Roberts, C. and Hoyle, C. (2004) *The National Evaluation of the Youth Justice Board's Cognitive Behaviour Projects*. London: Youth Justice Board.

Flood-Page, C., Campbell, S., Harrington, V. and Miller, J. (2000) *Youth Crime: Findings from the 1998/99 Youth Lifestyles Survey*. Home Office Research Study 209. London: The Home Office.

Goldson, B. (2000) 'Wither Diversion? Interventionism and the New Youth Justice', in B. Goldson (ed.) *The New Youth Justice*. London: Russell House Publishing.

Goldson, B. (2001) 'A Rational Youth Justice? Some Critical Reflections on The Research, Policy and Practice Relation', *Probation Journal,* 48(2): 76–85.

Goldson, B. (2002) 'New Punitiveness: The Politics of Child Incarceration', in J. Muncie, G. Hughes and E. McLaughlin (eds) *Youth Justice: Critical Readings*. London: Sage. pp. 386–400.

Goldson, B. and Jamieson, J. (2002) 'Youth Crime, the "Parenting Deficit" and State Intervention: A contextual critique'. *Youth Justice*, 2(2): 82–99.

Graham, J. and Bowling, B. (1995) *Young People and Crime*. Home Office Research Study 145. London: Home Office.

Hagell, A. (2005) 'The Use of Custody for Children and Young People', in T. Bateman and J. Pitts (eds) *The RHP Companion to Youth Justice*. Lyme Regis: Russell House Publishing. pp. 151–7.

Hallett, C. and Murray, C. with Jamieson, J. and Veitch B. (1998) *The Evaluation of Children's Hearings in Scotland. Volume 1: Deciding in Children's Interests*. Edinburgh: Scottish Office Central Research Unit.

Hill, M. (1999) 'What's the Problem? Who can Help? The Perspectives of Children and Young People on their Well-Being and on Helping Professionals', *Journal of Social Work Practice*, 13(2): 135–45.

Hill, M., Walker, M., Khan, F. and Moodie, K. (2004) *Fast Track Hearings Research: Interim Report November 2003*. Edinburgh: The Scottish Executive.

Hubble, M.A., Duncan B.L. and Miller S.D. (eds) (1999) *The Heart and Soul of Change: What Works in Therapy*. Washington, D.C.: American Psychological Association.

Jamieson, J., McIvor, G. and Murray, C. (1999) *Understanding Offending Among Young People*. Edinburgh: The Scottish Executive.

Jennings, D. (2003) *One Year Juvenile Reconviction Rates: First Quarter of 2001 Cohort*. On Line Report 18/3. London: Home Office.

Liddle, M. and Solanki, A.-R. (2002) *Persistent Young Offenders*. London: Nacro.

Lipsey, M. W. (1995) 'What Do We Learn From 400 Research Studies on the Effectiveness of Treatment with Juvenile Delinquents?', in J. McGuire and P. Priestley (eds) *What Works: Reducing Reoffending. Guidelines from Research and Practice*. Chichester: Wiley. pp. 63–78.

Lobley, D., Smith, D. and Stern, C. (2001) *Freagarrach: An Evaluation of a Project for Persistent Juvenile Offenders*. Edinburgh: The Scottish Executive.

Maruna, S. (2001) *Making Good*. Washington, D.C.: American Psychological Association.

Maruna, S., Immarigeon, R. and LeBel, T. (2004) 'Ex-Offender Reintegration: Theory and Practice', in S. Maruna and R. Immarigeon (eds) *After Crime and Punishment: Pathways to Offender Reintegration*. Cullompton: Willan, pp. 3–26.

McAra, L. (2004) 'The Cultural and Institutional Dynamics of Transformation: Youth Justice in Scotland, England and Wales', *The Cambrian Law Review,* 35: 23–54.

McCulloch, P. (2005) 'Probation, Social Context and Desistance: Retracing the Relationship', *Probation Journal*, 52(1): 8–22.

McGuire, J. and Priestley, P. (1995) 'Reviewing "What Works": Past, Present and Future', in J. McGuire and P. Priestley (eds) *What Works: Reducing Reoffending. Guidelines from Research and Practice*. Chichester: Wiley, pp. 3–34.

McNeill, F. (2003) 'Desistance-Focused Probation Practice', in W-H Chui and M. Nellis (eds) *Moving Probation Forward: Evidence, Arguments and Practice*. Harlow: Pearson Longman. pp. 146–62.

McNeill, F. and Batchelor, S. (2002) 'Chaos, Containment and Change: Responding to Persistent Offending by Young People', *Youth Justice*, Vol. 2, No. 1, pp. 27–43.

McNeill, F., Batchelor, S., Burnett, R. and Knox, J. (2005) *21st Century Social Work. Reducing Re-offending: Key Practice Skills*. Edinburgh: The Scottish Executive.

Moore, R. (2004) 'Intensive Supervison and Surveillance Programmes for Young Offenders: the Evidence Base So Far', in R. Burnett and C. Roberts (eds) *What Works in Probation and Youth Justice: Developing Evidence-based Practice*. Cullompton: Willan pp. 159–79.

Moore, R. (2005) 'The Use of Electronic and Human Surveillance in a Multi-Modal Programme'. *Youth Justice*, 5(1): 17–32.

Muncie, J. (2002) 'Policy Transfers and "What Works": Some Reflections on Comparative Youth Justice', *Youth Justice*, 1(3): 27–35.

Nacro (2002) *Youth Crime Briefing: Supervision Orders – An Overview*. London: Nacro.

Nellis, M. (2004) 'The "Tracking" Controversy: The Roots of Mentoring and Electronic Monitoring'. *Youth Justice*, 4(2): 77–99.

Newburn, T. and Shiner, M. (2005) *Dealing with Disaffection: Young People, Mentoring and Social inclusion*. Cullompton: Willan.

Pitts, J. (2001) 'The New Correctionalism: Young People, Youth Justice and New Labour', in R. Matthews and J. Pitts (eds) *Crime, Disorder and Community Safety*. London: Routledge. pp. 167–92.

Raynor, P. (2004) 'Rehabilitative and Reintegrative Approaches', in A. Bottoms, S. Rex and G. Robinson (eds) *Alternatives to Prison: Options for an Insecure Society*. Cullompton: Willan, pp. 195–223.

Rex, S. (1999) 'Desistance from Offending: Experiences of Probation', *Howard Journal of Criminal Justice,* 36(4): 366–83.

Rumgay, J. (2004) 'Scripts for Safer Survival: Pathways out of Female Crime', *Howard Journal of Criminal Justice,* 43(4): 405–19.

Rutherford, A. (1992) *Growing out of Crime: the New Era*. Winchester: Waterside Press.

Rutherford, A. (2002) 'Youth Justice and Social Inclusion', *Youth Justice*, 2(2): 100–7.

Schoon, I.J. and Bynner, H. (2003) 'Risk and Resilience in the Life Course: Implications for Interventions and Social Policies', *Journal of Youth Studies*, 6(1): 21–31.

Smith, D. (2000) 'The Limits of Positivism Revisited', paper presented at 'Theorising Social Work Research Seminar 4: What Works as Evidence for Practice? The Methodological Repertoire in an Applied Discipline', Cardiff.

Smith, D. and Stewart, J. (1998) 'Probation and Social Exclusion', in C. Jones Finer and M. Nellis (eds) *Crime and Social Exclusion*. Oxford: Blackwell, pp. 96–115.

Uggen, C. and Kruttschnitt, K. (1998) 'Crime in the Breaking: Gender Differences in Desistance', *Law and Society Review*, 32(2): 339–66.

Waterhouse, L., McGhee, J., Whyte, B., Loucks, N., Kay, H. and Stewart, R. (2000) *The Evaluation of Children's Hearings in Scotland. Volume 3 – Children in Focus*. Edinburgh: Scottish Office Central Research Unit.

Penal Custody: Intolerance, Irrationality and Indifference

10

Barry Goldson

Introduction

Mapping the historical trajectory of youth justice policy and practice in England and Wales exposes a conspicuous affinity with custodial institutions (Hagell and Hazel, 2001). Following the separation of child from adult prisoners in the hulks of ships in the early nineteenth century, and the establishment of the first land-based penal institution exclusively for children at Parkhurst Prison in 1838, an array of policy initiatives, statutory reforms and carceral experiments have created and sustained a panoply of institutional forms. The Youthful Offenders Act 1854 provided the *Reformatory*; the Prevention of Crime Act 1908 ushered in *Borstals*; the Children and Young Persons Act 1933 replaced the Reformatories with *Approved Schools*; the Criminal Justice Act 1948 established *Remand Centres* and *Detention Centres*; the Criminal Justice Act 1982 set up *Youth Custody Centres*; the Criminal Justice Act 1988 replaced both the Detention and Youth Custody Centres with *Young Offender Institutions*; the Criminal Justice and Public Order Act 1994 prefaced the opening of *Secure Training Centres* and, most recently, the Crime and Disorder Act 1998 has served to 'modernise' the 'juvenile secure estate' (Goldson, 2002a). In other words, penal custody, in its various forms, has retained a foothold in the youth justice system since the 'invention' of 'juvenile delinquency' in the early nineteenth century (Magarey, 1978) and the subsequent inception of a specific corpus of legislation, court structures, policies, procedures and practices for the processing of 'juvenile offenders' at the beginning of the twentieth.

Despite the permanent presence of penal institutions, however, the extent to which custodial remands and sentences have been employed, and the actual size of the child prisoner population at any given time, have fluctuated across history. The related claims that such fluctuations are symptomatic of changes in the volume and/or seriousness of crime, and that penal custody represents the most effective means of limiting crime, are not uncommon. Both claims are fallacious, however. As Hagell (2005: 157) has observed: 'it is clear from a range of statistics and research that levels of custody ... do not necessarily reflect levels of juvenile crime nor do they particularly reflect evidence on its effectiveness'. In this sense, patterns in the use of penal custody are determined *independently*; they have little or no direct relation either to the actual volume and/or seriousness of youth crime on the one hand, or the outcomes of incarcerative interventions on the other. Rather the ebbs and flows of custodial sanctions are more readily explained by reference to the vagaries of political imperatives and policy contingencies.

From the early 1990s to the present time a 'new punitiveness' (Goldson, 2002a) has consolidated within the youth justice system in England and Wales, most graphically illustrated by a sharp rise in the numbers of child prisoners. This chapter specifically engages with the contemporary politics of penal custody derived from what Muncie (1999) has termed 'institutionalised *intolerance*'. It is argued that developments in law and policy, serving to detain increasing numbers of children in custodial institutions, negate a wealth of research evidence and practice experience – illuminating the counter-productive 'outcomes' of penal custody as a measure of youth crime prevention – and, in this sense, the 'new punitiveness' represents penological *irrationality*. Furthermore, deliberate penal expansion is not only inattentive to 'outcome' evidence; it also disregards the harm and damage that is routinely encountered by children in custodial institutions, it displays a curious *indifference*.

The contemporary politics of penal custody: From the 'reductionist agenda' to 'the rush to custody'

Newburn (1997: 642) described the 1979 Conservative Manifesto as 'the most avowedly "law and order" manifesto in British political history': it 'promised, among many other measures, to strengthen sentencing powers with respect to juveniles'. Indeed, the 1980 White Paper *Young Offenders* proposed the re-introduction of Detention Centres with tough regimes designed to deliver a 'short, sharp, shock' and William Whitelaw, the Home Secretary, warned that the children and young people 'who attend them will not ever want to go back' (cited in Newburn, 1997: 642; see also Muncie, 1990). Paradoxically, however, the decade that followed comprised 'one of the most remarkably progressive periods of juvenile justice policy' (Rutherford, 1995: 57) within which a 'reductionist agenda' (Rutherford, 1984) in respect of penal custody consolidated. A coincidence of four otherwise disparate (even contradictory) concerns combined to legitimise penal reduction. First, elements of academic research demonstrated the counter-productive consequences of disproportionate forms of criminal justice intervention generally, and custodial sanctions in particular (Goldson, 1997a). Second, developments in juvenile/youth justice practice, especially imaginative community-based 'alternative to custody' schemes (Haines and Drakeford, 1998). Third, specific policy objectives of Thatcherite Conservatism; as Pratt (1987: 429) observed: 'to reduce the custodial population on the grounds of cost effectiveness ... led to a general support for alternatives to custody initiatives'. Fourth, the stated imperatives of the police and the courts to reduce the incidence of juvenile crime; whilst some reservations remained, many senior police officers and court officials positively embraced the reductionist agenda (Gibson, 1995) in the light of 'the plethora of Home Office research ... that evidenced the discernible success of such policies' (Goldson, 1994: 5).

The combination of permissive statute[1] and innovatory 'alternative to custody' practice, was not insignificant. The number of custodial sentences imposed on children fell from 7,900 in 1981 to 1,700 in 1990 (Allen, 1991). Furthermore, the 'reductionist agenda' was effective not only in terms of substantially moderating the practice of child imprisonment but also, according to David Faulkner the Head of the Home Office Crime Department between 1982 and 1990, it was 'successful in the visible reduction of known juvenile offending' (cited in Goldson, 1997b: 79). Indeed, faith in the effectiveness and rationality of decarceration was such that penal reform organisations confidently advocated 'phasing out prison department custody for juvenile offenders' and 'replacing custody' (Nacro, 1989a and 1989b). Government support for the 'reductionist agenda' was always contingent, however, and its fortunes ultimately depended upon the extent to which it continued to suit wider political priorities.

The size of the Conservatives' parliamentary majority and the strength of its electoral mandate throughout the 1980s, were such that the Party was both able and prepared to relax its long-established attachment to a punitive 'law and order' politics. Between 1989 and 1992, however, Britain experienced a major economic recession which indirectly, but no less dramatically, served to subvert political support for the 'reductionist agenda'. The opinion polls started to signal that public confidence in the Conservatives was abating and, as a consequence, the triumphalism of Thatcherism finally looked vulnerable. Downes (2001: 69) observed that: 'with ... a prison population falling from 50,000 to 42,000 ... the Conservative lead over Labour as the party best able to guarantee law and order' [was seriously threatened] for the first time in over 30 years'. The Conservative Party reacted by deposing Margaret Thatcher and installing John Major as leader, and Prime Minister. Along with senior colleagues, Major set about restoring the Party's more traditional 'law and order' mantle.

---

1. For example: the Criminal Justice Act 1982 imposed tighter criteria for custodial sentencing and introduced the 'Specified Activities Order' as a direct alternative to custodial detention; the Criminal Justice Act 1988 tightened the criteria for custodial sentencing further; the Children Act 1989 abolished the Criminal Care Order and the Criminal Justice Act 1991 abolished prison custody for 14-year-old boys and provided for the similar abolition of penal remands for 15–17-year-olds (although this provision has never been implemented). For a fuller discussion, see Goldson (2002b) and Goldson and Coles (2005).

By early 1993 juvenile crime came into sharp focus. In particular, the media drew attention to car crime, youth disorder, children and young people offending whilst on court bail, and those whom they described as 'persistent young offenders', with increasing regularity and developing force. Such phenomena were shrouded in vagueness and there was minimal effort to distinguish, and thus account for, the specificities of the various forms of 'anti-social behaviour', youth 'disorder' and/or the different 'types' of child 'offender'. Rather every troublesome child was portrayed as 'out of control' and a 'menace to society'. There was a developing sense that 'childhood' was in 'crisis' (Scraton, 1997) and any lingering doubts were seemingly extinguished by a single case in February 1993, in which two children aged ten were charged with the murder of two-year-old James Bulger. This imposed enormous symbolic purchase over the public imagination and activated processes of demonisation (Davis and Bourhill, 1997; Goldson 1997a), as 'myth and fantasy [began] to replace objectivity and detachment and conjure monsters that seem to lurk behind the gloss and glitter of everyday life' (Pratt, 2000: 431). Troublesome children were 'essentialised as other' (Young, 1999) and an 'ecology of fear' (Davis, 1998) was awakened and mobilised. The reaction from a government intent on re-establishing its traditional credentials with regard to law and order was predictable. The Prime Minister, John Major, argued that the time had come for society 'to condemn a little more and understand a little less' and the Home Secretary, Michael Howard, proclaimed that 'prison works' (cited in Goldson, 1997a: 130–1).

For its part, the re-styled New Labour project – emerging under the steadily increasing influence of Tony Blair – broke with its conventionally moderate position on questions of penal policy and 'pressed home (its) advantage ... by emphasising the ... leniency of sentencing' (Downes, 2001: 69). In January 1993, three days after returning from a visit to the USA, Tony Blair – as Opposition Home Secretary – coined what was to become a famous New Labour sound-bite in declaring his intention to be 'tough on crime, tough on the causes of crime'. Blair had been persuaded – by what he had seen and learnt in the US – to exploit the political vulnerabilities of the Major administration by following the example set by Bill Clinton's New Democratic Coalition. Clinton had repoliticised crime to positive electoral effect in the USA and Blair intended to do likewise in Britain (Tonry, 2004). The 'Americanisation' of criminal justice in general, and youth justice in particular, operated *both* at the symbolic level of political rhetoric *and* more significantly, at the material level of policy development (Jones and Newburn, 2004; Muncie, 2002; Pitts, 2000 and 2001).

Throughout the period 1993–97, New Labour policy-makers published a wide range of policy documents focusing on youth justice and related matters, within which a creeping punitivity was increasingly evident (Jones, 2002). It was not until the election of the first New Labour Government in May 1997, however, that the full weight of its 'toughness' agenda was felt. Within months of coming to office, the newly elected government produced a raft of consultative documentation in relation to youth justice (Home Office, 1997a; 1997b; 1997c), followed by a White Paper, ominously entitled *No More Excuses: A New Approach to Tackling Youth Crime in England and Wales* (Home Office, 1997d). Clinton adopted and applied the notion of 'zero tolerance' in the USA. Blair settled for 'no more excuses' in England and Wales. The 'reductionist agenda' had been abandoned and, instead, the 'rush to custody' (Rutherford, 2002: 102) was concretised. Political calculations and electoral ambitions served to usurp penological rationality.

Intolerance: Enacting custodial punishment

From the early-1990s, both Conservative and New Labour governments translated 'tough' political rhetoric and symbolic posturing into legislation and youth justice policy. It is not practical in a chapter such as this to analyse the provisions of statute in detail, but there is value in sketching some of their defining characteristics with regard to the question of penal custody.

The Criminal Justice and Public Order Act 1994 ushered in new punitive powers in three particularly significant ways. First, the Act lowered the age threshold – from 14 to 10 – for the imposition of indeterminate sentences (14 years or more) in cases where children are convicted of 'grave crimes' in the Crown Court. Second, it doubled the length of the maximum determinate sentence of detention in a Young Offender Institution – for 15–17-year-old children – from 12 to 24 months. Third, and perhaps most significant of all, section 1 of the 1994 Act created a new custodial sentence for 12–14-year-old children – the Secure Training Order – to be served in a private jail (a Secure Training Centre) for terms of up to 24 months. The legislation was implemented by a Conservative government with little tangible opposition from Labour. Although Labour opposed various aspects of the Bill at Parliamentary Committee stages, it abstained during the final vote (Howard League, 1995: 3). The significance of this should not be under-estimated; the Criminal Justice and Public Order Act 1994 effectively reversed the decarcerative provisions of youth justice law and policy – in respect of children aged 12–14 years – that dated back to the Children Act 1908 (Rutherford, 1995).

The Crime and Disorder Act 1998 (implemented by the first New Labour administration) is an extraordinarily wide-ranging piece of legislation. Whilst it served to abolish the Secure Training Order (for 12–14-year-old children) it substituted it with the Detention and Training Order (which also replaced the sentence of detention in a Young Offender Institution for children aged 15–17 years). The new custodial sentence became operational in April 2000 and the length of a Detention and Training Order is set at 4, 6, 8, 10, 12, 18 or 24 months. It is served half in penal custody and half in the community, although the Act allows for varying the balance of the sentence (including extending the custodial element) depending upon 'assessments' of the child's progress. Thus the courts' power to lock up children between the ages of 12 and 17 years for non-grave offences is now provided within the remit of a single custodial sentence, and there is provision in the Crime and Disorder Act 1998 to allow the Home Secretary to further extend the powers of the court to encompass children aged 10 and 11 years.

The Powers of the Criminal Courts (Sentencing) Act 2000 contained provisions (at sections 90–92) for the custodial sentencing of children convicted of 'grave crimes' and, according to Bateman (2002), when combined with the Detention and Training Order powers contained within the Crime and Disorder Act 1998, the legislation comprises a 'recipe for injustice'.

Finally, for the purposes here, section 130 of the Criminal Justice and Police Act 2001 significantly relaxes the penal remand criteria in respect of children. The Act empowers the courts to remand children to custodial institutions in cases where they have 'repeatedly' committed offences whilst on bail (including shoplifting, petty theft and criminal damage), irrespective of whether or not such offences are adjudged to expose the public to 'serious harm'. The term 'repeatedly' has been defined in case law as meaning 'on more than one occasion' (Monaghan et al., 2003: 31). Thus, section 130 of the Criminal Justice and Police Act 2001 effectively replaced the long-established 'seriousness' threshold with a 'nuisance' test: a perfect exemplar of 'institutionalised intolerance'. Bearing in mind that in practice many penal remands are imposed upon children awaiting trial or sentence in respect of *non-serious* offences (Goldson and Peters, 2002), together with all that is known about the particular vulnerabilities of child remand prisoners (Goldson, 2002b), the provisions of the Criminal Justice and Police Act 2001 also convey penological irrationality and indifference to the welfare of child remand prisoners.

Hough et al. (2003) have noted that the combined practical effect of the above – together with similar developments in law and policy – has precipitated significant penal expansion:

> The increases in custody rates and sentence length strongly suggest that sentencers have become more severe. This greater severity undoubtedly reflects, in part, a more punitive legislative and legal framework of sentencing. Legislation, guideline judgements and sentence guidelines have all had an inflationary effect on sentences passed. At the same time, the climate of political and media debate about crime and sentencing has become more punitive, and is also likely to have influenced sentencing practice. (ibid.: 2)

Indeed, *total rates* of imprisonment in England and Wales have escalated significantly during the last decade or more. In 1994 the average prison population was 48,631 but by 1997 it had risen to 60,131 (Prison Reform Trust, 2004: 3). This 'inflationary effect' has continued since the first New Labour administration took office in 1997. In 2002, for example, the *average* prison population, at 70,860, was higher than in any previous year (Councell, 2003: 1; Home Office 2003a: 3), by March 2004, however, the *total* prison population exceeded 75,000

(Howard League for Penal Reform, 2004a) and, by May 2005, it had reached more than 76,000 for the first time in penal history (British Broadcasting Corporation, 2005). Between 1997 and 2005 there was 'an increase in prison numbers of 25 per cent' (Stern, 2005: 81). Expressed as a rate per 100,000 of the national population, the prison population in England and Wales is now the highest among countries of the European Union (Home Office, 2003b).

Contemporary statistical trends in relation to child prisoners follow similar contours. The *total number* of custodial sentences imposed upon children rose from approximately 4,000 per annum in 1992 to 7,600 in 2001, a 90 per cent increase (Nacro, 2003 and 2005). During the same period the child remand population grew by 142 per cent (Goldson, 2002b). Whilst it is true to say that such trends were initiated prior to the election of the first New Labour government in 1997, they have simply consolidated since that time (Hagell, 2005). In March 2004 alone, there were 3,251 children and young people (10–17 years inclusive) in penal custody in England and Wales: 2,772 in Prison Service Young Offender Institutions; 290 in Local Authority Secure Children's Homes and 189 in privately managed Secure Training Centres (Youth Justice Board, 2005a: 78). Moreover, such trends appear to be unrelenting. The 'number of young people in custody rose in June and July [2005] causing concern [because] the secure estate is under severe pressure' (Youth Justice Board, 2005b: 8), and 'in August the overall under-18 population rose ... during a month when we would normally expect the custody level to fall slightly ... the increase is due to a surge in the remand population' (Youth Justice Board, 2005c: 5).

Furthermore, within the general trend of penal expansion in respect of child prisoners in England and Wales, a range of additional observations might be made. First, whilst comparative analyses of youth justice systems in general, and rates of child imprisonment in particular, are extraordinarily difficult (Muncie, 2003 and 2005; Muncie and Goldson, 2006), it appears that greater use of penal custody for children is now made in England and Wales than in most other industrialised democratic countries in the world (Youth Justice Board for England and Wales, 2004). Second, in addition to substantial increases in the numbers of children sent to custody, sentences have also increased in length (Home Office, 2003b), and proportionately more children are sentenced to long-term detention (Graham and Moore, 2004). Third, law and policy have provided for the detention of younger children and Nacro (2003: 12) has observed that: 'as a consequence the detention of children under the age of 15 years has become routine'. Fourth, the expansionist drift has been disproportionately applied in terms of gender and the rate of growth is higher for girls than boys (Nacro, 2003). Furthermore, girls are regularly detained alongside adult prisoners, a practice that has been seriously questioned by penal reform organisations (Howard League for Penal Reform, 2004b) and Her Majesty's Chief Inspector of Prisons (2004) alike. Fifth, racism continues to pervade youth justice sentencing processes and custodial regimes. For example, black boys are 6.7 times more likely than their white counterparts to have custodial sentences in excess of

12 months imposed upon them in the Crown Court (Feilzer and Hood, 2004), and black child prisoners are more likely than white detainees to encounter additional adversity within custodial institutions owing to racist practices (Cowan, 2005). Sixth, the expansionist drive bears virtually no relation to either the incidence or the seriousness of youth crime (Goldson and Coles, 2005; Nacro, 2005); it is purely an artefact of the 'new punitiveness'.

Irrationality and indifference: Negating the evidence

Substantial penal expansion within the youth justice system in England and Wales, triggered by the Conservative government during the period between 1993 and 1997, and consolidated by three successive New Labour administrations thereafter, pays scant regard to the imperatives of 'evidenced-based policy' and 'what works' priorities. Indeed, the penological irrationality of the 'new punitiveness' is expressed via its indifference to a wealth of evidence in at least three key respects: the corrosive nature of custodial regimes for children and young people; the failure of penal custody to prevent youth offending (the 'principal aim' of the youth justice system as provided by section 37 of the Crime and Disorder Act 1998); and the enormous financial burden that penal expansion imposes on the public purse.

Child imprisonment: Conditions and treatment

Child prisoners are routinely drawn from some of the most structurally disadvantaged and impoverished families, neighbourhoods and communities in England and Wales (Goldson, 2002b; Goldson and Coles, 2005). Her Majesty's Chief Inspector of Prisons (1999: 3) has noted that penal custody often marks 'just one further stage in the exclusion of a group of children who between them, have already experienced almost every form of social exclusion on offer', later adding that:

> Before any work can be done to sensitise [child prisoners] to the needs of others and the impact of their offending on victims, their own needs as maturing adolescents for care, support and direction have to be met. (Her Majesty's Chief Inspector of Prisons, 2000: 25)

Approximately half of the children held in penal custody at any one time will be, or will have been, 'open cases' to statutory child welfare agencies as a result of neglect and/or other child protection concerns; a significant proportion will have biographies scarred by adult abuse and violation (Association of Directors of Social Services et al., 2003; Challen and Walton, 2004; Holmes and Gibbs, 2004; Prison Reform Trust, 2004; Social Exclusion Unit, 2002; Social Services Inspectorate et al., 2002). In a major review of the educational needs of children in penal custody, Her Majesty's Chief Inspector of Prisons and the Office for Standards in Education (2001: 10) found that: 84 per cent of child prisoners had been excluded from school; 86 per cent had regularly not attended school; 52 per cent had left school aged 14 years or younger; 29 per cent had left school aged 13 years or younger and 73 per cent described their educational achievement as 'nil'. Over 25 per cent of child prisoners have literacy and numeracy skills equivalent to a 7-year-old (Social Exclusion Unit, 2002) and 'most' have 'very significant learning needs and problems' (Social Services Inspectorate et al., 2002: 70). The British Medical Association, commenting upon the relationship between poverty, disadvantage and poor health, observed:

> ... patients within prison are amongst the most needy in the country in relation to their health care needs. Over 90 per cent of patients who reside in our jails come from deprived backgrounds ... 17 per cent of young offenders were not registered with a general practitioner and generally the young people had a low level of contact with primary health care. (2001: 1 and 5)

Moreover, and not surprisingly, the experience of imprisonment itself has been identified as having a deleterious effect on the physical and mental well-being of children (Farrant, 2001; Goldson, 2002b; Goldson and Coles, 2005; Leech and Cheney, 2001; Mental Health Foundation, 1999). In sum, when taking account of the backgrounds and personal circumstances of child prisoners: 'it is evident that on any count this is a significantly deprived, excluded, and abused population of children, who are in serious need of a variety of services' (Association of Directors of Social Services et al., 2003: 6) and the 'Juvenile Secure Estate' is 'not equipped to meet their needs' (Her Majesty's Chief Inspector of Prisons, 2000: 69–70).

In England and Wales, more than 80 per cent of child prisoners are detained in Young Offender Institutions (managed by the Prison Service)[2] and this raises important issues with regard to conditions and treatment:

> One of the most important factors in creating a safe environment is size. The other places where children are held – Secure Units and Secure Training Centres – are small, with a high staff–child ratio. The Prison Service, however, may hold children in what we regard as unacceptably high numbers and units. Units of 60 disturbed and damaged adolescent boys are unlikely to be safe ... There are therefore already significant barriers to the Prison Service being able to provide a safe and positive environment for children; and the question whether it should continue to do so is a live one. Yet during the year the number of children has risen, to close to 3,000, and looks set to rise further. Promises to reduce unit size ... are further than ever from being delivered. (Her Majesty's Chief Inspector of Prisons, 2002: 36–7)

---

2. The remaining number are held in private jails (Secure Training Centres) or Local Authority Secure Children's Homes (see Goldson and Coles, 2005: 25–6).

The Children's Rights Alliance for England (2002: 49–137) undertook a detailed analysis of the conditions and treatment experienced by children in Young Offender Institutions, drawing on reports prepared by Her Majesty's Inspectorate of Prisons. The results were illuminating: widespread neglect in relation to physical and mental health; endemic bullying, humiliation and ill-treatment (staff-on-child and child-on-child); racism and other forms of discrimination; systemic invasion of privacy; long and uninterrupted periods of cell-based confinement; deprivation of fresh air and exercise; inadequate educational and rehabilitative provision; insufficient opportunities to maintain contact with family; poor diet; ill-fitting clothing in poor state of repair; a shabby physical environment; and, in reality, virtually no opportunity to complain and/or make representations. All of these negative and neglectful processes define the conditions within which children are routinely held in penal custody leading Mr Justice Munby, a High Court Judge, to conclude that:

> They ought to be – I hope they are – matters of the very greatest concern to the Prison Service, to the Secretary of State for the Home Department and, indeed, to society at large. For these are things being done to children by the State – by all of us – in circumstances where the State appears to be failing, and in some instances failing very badly, in its duties to vulnerable and damaged children ... [these are] matters which, on the face of it, ought to shock the conscience of every citizen. (Munby, 2002: paras. 172 and 175)

Penal custody for children, therefore, can never be a neutral experience. Bullying, in all of its forms, is a particular problem that exerts substantial human costs for child prisoners. Her Majesty's Chief Inspector of Prisons (2005: 56) surveyed children in one Young Offender Institution and found that: 56 per cent reported that they had felt 'unsafe'; 'nearly a quarter said they had been hit, kicked or assaulted' and there 'had been 150 proven assaults in eight months'. Physical assault – or physical abuse – is clearly commonplace in penal custody. Furthermore, children are also exposed to other forms of 'bullying' including sexual assault; verbal abuse (including name-calling; threats; racist, sexist and homophobic taunting); extortion and theft; and lending and trading cultures – particularly in relation to tobacco – involving exorbitant rates of interest that accumulate on a daily basis (Goldson, 2002b). Staff–child ratios are so stretched within penal custody that levels of supervision inevitably are strained. Bullying is insufficiently 'managed': it is entrenched within the very fabric of prison life.

For all child prisoners, such harsh conditions and treatment perpetuate misery and/or fear and thousands are emotionally and psychologically damaged. For some, it is literally too much to bear. Between 1998 and 2002, for example, there were 1,659 reported incidents of self-injury or attempted suicide by child prisoners in England and Wales (Howard League for Penal Reform, 2005). At the sharpest extremes, 29 children died in penal custody in England and Wales between July 1990 and September 2005 (27 in state prisons and 2 in private jails), all but two of the deaths were apparently self-inflicted (Goldson and Coles, 2005).

The paradoxical fact about the corrosive effect of penal custody on children, is that it is recognised comprehensively by government ministers and major state agencies alike. In answer to a Parliamentary question on 7 June 2004, for example, Paul Goggins, Home Office Minister, confirmed that the numbers of *vulnerable* children placed in Young Offender Institutions have followed upward trajectories each year since 2000. The figures given for children officially assessed as 'vulnerable' and yet still 'placed' in Prison Service establishments by the Youth Justice Board for England and Wales were: 432 for 2000–01; 1,875 for 2001–02; 2,903 for 2002–03 and 3,337 for 2003–04 (cited in Bateman, 2004). Furthermore, the most senior personnel from eight major statutory inspectorates have concluded that 'young people in YOIs still face the gravest risks to their welfare' (Social Services Inspectorate et al., 2002: 72), and Her Majesty's Chief Inspector of Prisons (2005: 57) has observed that 'some young people are not safe ... simply because they should not be there'. In October 2002, the United Nations Committee on the Rights of the Child (2002: para. 57) formally reported its 'deep concern' at 'the high increasing numbers of children in custody' in England and Wales and its 'extreme concern' regarding 'the conditions that children experience in detention', including the 'high levels of violence, bullying, self-harm and suicide'. Three years later, the Council of Europe's Commissioner for Human Rights noted that: 'one can only conclude that the prison service is failing in its duty of care towards juvenile inmates' (Office for the Commissioner for Human Rights, 2005: para 93).

Despite all of the evidence in respect of the damaging and harmful impositions of penal custody on children, excessive practices of child imprisonment in England and Wales continue. Such indifference towards evidence is curious. It implies, to paraphrase Cohen (2001: 1), that human suffering is being 'denied', 'evaded', 'neutralised' or 'rationalised away'.

Child imprisonment: The prevention of offending?

Jerome Miller noted:

> The hard truth is that ... juvenile penal institutions have minimal impact on crime. If most prisons were closed tomorrow, the rise in crime would be negligible ... incapacitation as the major tenet of crime control is a questionable social policy. (1991: 181–2)

Similarly, Hagell and Hazel (2001) have reflected that concern with 'poor performance' (primarily measured in terms of re-conviction rates) has been a recurrent theme throughout the history of child imprisonment. The continuing failure of penal custody to prevent children from offending is clearly illustrated by reconviction analyses that relate to: 'the proportion of prisoners discharged from prison [who] are convicted on a further occasion within a given period (usually two years)' (Home Office, 2003a: 150). Whilst it is important to acknowledge that there are variations in reconviction data and comparative analyses over time are extraordinarily complex, one reading of the evidence suggests that re-conviction rates have heightened in recent years: 'the reconviction rate for males has risen by 8 percentage points since its lowest level in 1992 [and] the reconviction rate for females has increased by 17 percentage points' (Home Office, 2003a: 153). Furthermore, in October 2004, a Parliamentary Select Committee reported that re-conviction rates stand at 80 per cent with regard to released child prisoners (House of Commons Committee of Public Accounts, 2004).

The Detention and Training Order, as discussed above, is the latest custodial sentence relating to children. Although an evaluation of nearly 6,000 children subject to a Detention and Training Order identified elements described as 'good practice', it also reported high rates of re-offending, particularly in the first few weeks following release (Hazel et al., 2002). Similarly, recent experiments relating to 'intensive' custodial regimes do not appear to yield positive lasting results in respect of children: 'preliminary findings' suggest that initial 'improvements' in reconviction patterns are unlikely to endure over time (Farrington et al., 2000). Equally, the results from research into the 'new wave' of private children's jails (Secure Training Centres) in England and Wales, revealed that 11 per cent of children were arrested for a further offence within seven days of their discharge, 52 per cent were similarly arrested within seven weeks and 67 per cent were arrested within 20 weeks of release (Hagell et al., 2000).

Such consistent failure is inconsistent with the statutory 'principal aim' of the youth justice system in England and Wales – to 'prevent offending' (and re-offending) – as provided by section 37 of the Crime and Disorder Act 1998. To put it another way, processes of penal expansion are irrational when set against the failure of custodial institutions to deliver in accordance with the provisions of statute.

Child imprisonment: Value for money?

Although estimates vary, an enormous amount of public money is spent on imprisoning children in England and Wales. The Audit Commission (2004: 2) reported that to 'place' a single child in a young offender institution costs £977.00 per week or £50,800 per year. The costs of a similar 'placement' in a private jail for children (a Secure Training Centre) are substantially higher standing at £3,168 per week or £164,750 per year (House of Commons Committee of Public Accounts, 2004: 4). According to the Chairperson of the Youth Justice Board for England and Wales, the gross costs of imprisoning children amounted to £293.5 million in the financial year 2003–04 alone (Morgan, 2004). Such figures tell only part of the fiscal story. They exclude the considerable public expense incurred in processing children through the courts and imposing penal remands and/or custodial sentences. The Social Exclusion Unit (2002: 2) has reported that: 'the average cost of a prison sentence imposed at a crown court is roughly £30,500, made up of court and other legal costs'. When the real and absolute annual costs of child imprisonment are calculated, therefore, the £293 million plus of public money spent by the Youth Justice Board for England and Wales pays only part of the bill.

Stern describes her experience of a conference in Brooklyn, New York, attended by people living in disadvantaged neighbourhoods:

> They were talking about housing, employment, health and education and they were adding up dollars. They had done some geographical plotting. They had analysed where the prisoners lived, where the poor people lived, where the victims lived, where the most social services were needed and were not available in sufficient quantity. They found, not surprisingly, that where the poor people lived and where the services are needed is also where the prison population comes from. Some blocks, single streets, consume one million dollars worth of imprisonment in a year ... Now those people in Brooklyn were asking, 'Can we have that money and spend it on the people here ... instead of sending them to prison?'. (2005: 83)

Bearing in mind all that is known about the adverse social circumstances from which child prisoners are routinely drafted; the damaging conditions and treatment to which they are exposed; and the failings of penal institutions to deliver in terms of crime prevention and community safety, serious questions have to be asked. There is a persuasive rationality and logic in Stern's account of her conference experience that is missing in youth justice laws, policies and practices serving to swell the ranks of child prisoners in England and Wales.

Conclusion

The central line of argument and analysis within this chapter is that penal expansion is derived from a politics of intolerance and punitiveness that has come to frame contemporary youth justice policy in England and Wales. Custodial institutions for children are 'socially unproductive' (Stern, 2005: 82) and such expansion has no claim to penological rationality and legitimacy: it is actually indifferent to evidence.

Bateman (2005) detects an 'emerging consensus that the current number of children within penal establishments needs to be addressed as a matter of urgency'. He suggests that the Youth Justice Board for England and Wales and the Home Office appear to share this consensus. The fact that every Youth Offending Team has been issued with specific 'targets' to reduce the use of penal custody, and the Youth Justice Board is looking towards a 10 per cent reduction in the number of child prisoners by 2007 (Youth Justice Board, 2004), might be taken to indicate that such 'consensus' is consolidating. Indeed, within the 'professional' youth justice community there are few, if any people, who would choose to quarrel with this. Perhaps the conditions are emerging within which tolerance, penological rationality and responsible concern (for child 'offenders' in particular, and the interests of the 'community' more generally) might impact more positively upon youth justice policy and practice in coming years.

Such optimism has to be historically contextualised, however. A key lesson from history with regard to penal policy provides that, in itself, 'failure never matters' (Muncie, 1990). For penal reduction – if not abolition – to be realised, therefore, it will require more than legitimising evidence. Ultimately, it is precisely because the 'new punitiveness' is derived from political calculations, that the enduring imperative to be seen to be 'tough' always outweighs penological rationality. In this respect, Prime Minister Tony Blair's reported concerns that Charles Clarke, the current Home Secretary, is 'going soft in the fight against crime' (Hennessey, 2005), together with punitive posturing from each of the major political parties leading up to the General Election in 2005 (Conservative Party, 2005; Labour Party, 2005; Liberal Democratic Party, 2004), implies a rather different, less optimistic and almost certainly more powerful, 'consensus'.

References

Allen, R. (1991) 'Out of Jail: The Reduction in the Use of Penal Custody for Male Juveniles 1981–1988', *The Howard Journal of Criminal Justice*, 30(1): 30–52.

Association of Directors of Social Services, Local Government Association, Youth Justice Board for England and Wales (2003) *The Application of the Children Act (1989) to Children in Young Offender Institutions*. London: ADSS, LGA and YJB.

Audit Commission (2004) 'Youth Justice 2004: A Review of the Reformed Youth Justice System', *Criminal Justice Briefing*. London: Audit Commission.

Bateman, T. (2002) 'A Note on the Relationship between the Detention and Training Order and Section 91 of the Powers of the Criminal Courts (Sentencing) Act 2000: A Recipe for Injustice', *Youth Justice*, 1(3): 36–41.

Bateman, T. (2004) 'Vulnerable Children Routinely Held in Prison Service Custody', Youth Justice News, *Youth Justice*, 4(2): 144–45.

Bateman, T. (2005) 'Reducing Child Imprisonment: a Systemic Challenge', *Youth Justice*, 5(2): 91–105.

British Broadcasting Corporation (2005) 'Prison Numbers Continue to Climb', *BBC News* Friday 27 May, http://news.bbc.co.uk/1/hi/uk/4586949.stm

British Medical Association (2001) *Prison Medicine: A Crisis Waiting to Break*. London: British Medical Association.

Challen, M. and Walton, T. (2004) *Juveniles in Custody*. London: Her Majesty's Inspectorate of Prisons.

Children's Rights Alliance for England (2002) *Rethinking Child Imprisonment: A Report on Young Offender Institutions*. London: Children's Rights Alliance for England.

Cohen, S. (2001) *States of Denial: Knowing about Atcocities and Suffering*. Cambridge: Polity Press.

Conservative Party (2005) 'Are you Thinking What We're Thinking? It's Time for Action', *Conservative Election Manifesto*, London: Conservative Party.

Councell, R. (2003) *The Prison Population in 2002: A Statistical Review*, Findings 228. London: Home Office.

Cowan, R. (2005) 'Juvenile Jail Staff Accused of Racism'. *The Guardian*, 14 June.

Davis, H. and Bourhill, M. (1997) '"Crisis": The Demonization of Children and Young People', in P. Scraton (ed.) *'Childhood' in 'Crisis'?* London: UCL Press.

Davis, M. (1998) *Ecology of Fear: Los Angeles and the Imagination of Disaster*. New York: Metropolitan Press.

Downes, D. (2001) 'The *Macho* Penal Economy: Mass incarceration in the United States – a European Perspective', *Punishment and Society*, 3(1): 61–80.

Farrant, F. (2001) *Troubled Inside: Responding to the Mental Health Needs of Children and Young People in Prison*. London: Prison Reform Trust.

Farrington, D., Hancock, G., Livingston, M., Painter, K. and Towl, G. (2000) *Evaluation of Intensive Regimes for Young Offenders*, Research Findings No. 21. London: Home Office.

Feilzer, M. and Hood, R. (2004) *Differences or Discrimination?* London: Youth Justice Board for England and Wales.

Gibson, B. (1995) 'Young People, Bad News, Enduring Principles', *Youth and Policy*, 48: 64–70.

Goldson, B. (1994) 'The changing face of youth justice', *Childright*, 105: 5–6.

Goldson, B. (1997a) 'Children in Trouble: State Responses to Juvenile Crime', in P. Scraton (ed.) *'Childhood' in 'Crisis'?* London: UCL Press.

Goldson, B. (1997b) 'Children, Crime, Policy and Practice: Neither Welfare nor Justice', *Children and Society*, 11(2): 77–88.

Goldson, B. (2002a) 'New Punitiveness: The Politics of Child Incarceration', in J. Muncie, G. Hughes and E. McLaughlin (eds) *Youth Justice: Critical Readings*. London: Sage.

Goldson, B. (2002b) *Vulnerable Inside: Children in Secure and Penal Settings*. London: The Children's Society.

Goldson, B. and Coles, D. (2005) *In the Care of the State? Child Deaths in Penal Custody in England and Wales*. London: INQUEST.

Goldson, B. and Peters, E. (2002) *The Children's Society National Remand Review Initiative:* Final Evaluation Report (1 December 1999 – 30 November 2001), Prepared for the Youth Justice Board for England and Wales. Unpublished.

Graham, J. and Moore, C. (2004) *Trend Report on Juvenile Justice in England and Wales*, European Society of Criminology Thematic Group on Juvenile Justice, http://www.esc-eurocrim.org/workgroups.shtml#juvenile_justice – accessed 24 August 2004.

Hagell, A. (2005) 'The Use of Custody for Children and Young People', in T. Bateman and J. Pitts (eds) *The RHP Companion to Youth Justice*. Lyme Regis: Russell House Publishing.

Hagell, A. and Hazel, N. (2001) 'Macro and Micro Patterns in the Development of Secure Custodial Institutions for Serious and Persistent Young Offenders in England and Wales', *Youth Justice*, 1(1): 3–16.

Hagell, A., Hazel, N. and Shaw, C. (2000) *Evaluation of Medway Secure Training Centre*. London: Home Office.

Haines, K. and Drakeford, M. (1998) *Young People and Youth Justice*. Basingstoke: Macmillan.

Hazel, N., Hagell, A., Liddle, M., Archer, D., Grimshaw, R. and King, J. (2002) *Detention and Training: Assessment of the Detention and Training Order and its Impact on the Secure Estate across England and Wales*. London: Youth Justice Board.

Hennessey, P. (2005) 'Blair Humiliates Clarke for Going Soft in the Fight against Crime', *The Sunday Telegraph,* 3 July.

Her Majesty's Chief Inspector of Prisons (1999a) *Suicide is Everyone's Concern: A Thematic Review by HM Chief Inspector of Prisons for England and Wales*. London: Home Office.

Her Majesty's Chief Inspector of Prisons (1999b) *Report on an Announced Inspection of HMP YOI Portland 24 October–3 November 1999 by HM Chief Inspector of Prisons*. London: Home Office.

Her Majesty's Chief Inspector of Prisons (2000) *Unjust Deserts: A Thematic Review by HM Chief Inspector of Prisons of the Treatment and Conditions for Unsentenced Prisoners in England and Wales*. London: Her Majesty's Inspectorate of Prisons for England and Wales.

Her Majesty's Chief Inspector of Prisons (2002) *Annual Report of HM Chief Inspector of Prisons for England and Wales, 2001–2002*, London, The Stationery Office.

Her Majesty's Chief Inspector of Prisons (2004) *Report on an Announced Inspection of HMP Eastwood Park 22–26 September 2003 by HM Chief Inspector of Prisons*. London: Home Office.

Her Majesty's Chief Inspector of Prisons (2005) *Annual Report of HM Chief Inspector of Prisons for England and Wales, 2003–2004*, London, The Stationery Office.

Her Majesty's Chief Inspector of Prisons and The Office for Standards in Education (2001) *A Second Chance: A Review of Education and Supporting Arrangements within Units for Juveniles Managed by HM Prison Service*. London: Home Office.

Holmes, C. and Gibbs, K. (2004) *Perceptions of Safety: Views of Young People and Staff Living and working in the Juvenile Estate*. London: Her Majesty's Prison Service.

Home Office (1997a) *Tackling Youth Crime: A Consultation Paper*. London: Home Office.

Home Office (1997b) *Tackling Delays in the Youth Justice System: A Consultation Paper*. London: Home Office.

Home Office (1997c) *New National and Local Focus on Youth Crime: A Consultation* Paper. London: Home Office.

Home Office (1997d) *No More Excuses – A New Approach to Tackling Youth Crime in England and Wales*. London: The Stationery Office.

Home Office (2003a) *Prison Statistics England and Wales*. London: The Stationery Office.

Home Office (2003b) *World Prison Population List*, Findings 234. London: Home Office.

Hough, M., Jacobson, J. and Millie, A. (2003) *The Decision to Imprison: Key Findings*. London: Prison Reform Trust.

House of Commons Committee of Public Accounts (2004) *Youth Offending: The Delivery of Community and Custodial Sentences*, Fortieth Report of Session 2003–04. London: The Stationery Office.

Howard League for Penal Reform (1995) *Secure Training Centres: Repeating Past Failures*, Briefing Paper. London: The Howard League for Penal Reform.

Howard League for Penal Reform (2004a) *Prison Overcrowding: 75,000 Behind Bars*, Briefing Paper. London: The Howard League for Penal Reform.

Howard League for Penal Reform (2004b) 'Girls Held in Adult Prisons Against their "Best Interests"', Press Release 20 January. London: The Howard League for Penal Reform.

Howard League for Penal Reform (2005) *Children in Custody: Promoting the Legal and Human Rights of Children*. London: The Howard League for Penal Reform.

Jones, D. (2002) 'Questioning New Labour's Youth Justice Strategy: A Review Article', *Youth Justice*, 1(3): 14–26.

Jones, T. and Newburn, T. (2004) 'The Convergence of US and UK Crime Control Policy: Exploring Substance and Process', in T. Newburn and R. Sparks (eds) *Criminal Justice and Political Cultures: National and International Dimensions of Crime Control*. Cullompton: Willan.

Labour Party (2005) *Britain Forward not back: The Labour Party Manifesto*, London: The Labour Party.

Leech, M. and Cheney, D. (2001) *The Prisons Handbook*. Winchester: Waterside Press.

Liberal Democratic Party (2004) 'Tough Liberalism', speech presented by Rt. Hon. Charles Kennedy, 30 March, http://www.libdems.org.uk/parliament/feature.html?id=6453 – accessed 29 April 2005.

Magarey, S. (1978) 'The Invention of Juvenile Delinquency in Early Nineteenth-Century England', *Labour History*, 34: 11–25.

Mental Health Foundation (1999) *Bright Futures: Promoting Young People's Mental Health*. London: Salzburg-Wittenburg.

Miller, J. (1991) *Last One Over the Wall: The Massachusetts Experiment in Closing Reform Schools*. Ohio: Ohio State University Press.

Monaghan, G., Hibbert, P. and Moore, S. (2003) *Children in Trouble: Time for Change*. London: Barnardo's.

Morgan, R. (2004) 'Where Does Child Welfare Fit into Youth Justice?', paper presented at *Children First, Offending Second?*, Nacro Youth Crime Conference, April, Loughborough University, unpublished.

Munby, The Honourable Mr Justice (2002) *Judgment Approved by the Court for Handing Down in R (on the application of the Howard League for Penal Reform) v. The Secretary of State for the Home Department*, 29 November. London: Royal Courts of Justice.

Muncie, J. (1990) 'Failure Never Matters: Detention Centres and the Politics of Deterrence', *Critical Social Policy,* 28: 53–66.

Muncie, J. (1999) 'Institutionalised Intolerance: Youth Justice and the 1998 Crime and Disorder Act', *Critical Social Policy,* 19(2): 147–75.

Muncie, J. (2002) 'Policy Transfers and What Works: Some Reflections on Comparative Youth Justice', *Youth Justice*, 1(3): 27–35.

Muncie, J. (2003) 'Juvenile justice in Europe: Some Conceptual, Analytical and Statistical Comparisons', *Childright*, 202: 14–17.

Muncie, J. (2005) 'The Globalization of Crime Control – the Case of Youth and Juvenile Justice: Neo-liberalism, Policy Convergence and International Conventions', *Theoretical Criminology*, 9(1): 35–64.

Muncie, J. and Goldson, B. (eds) (2006) *Comparative Youth Justice: Critical Issues*. London: Sage.

Nacro (1989a) *Phasing Out Prison Department Custody for Juvenile Offenders*. London: Nacro.

Nacro (1989b) *Replacing Custody: Findings from Two Census Surveys of Schemes for Juvenile Offenders Funded Under the DHSS Intermediate Treatment Initiative Covering the Period January to December 1987*. London: Nacro.

Nacro (2003) *A Failure of Justice: Reducing Child Imprisonment*. London: Nacro.

Nacro (2005) *A Better Alternative: Reducing Child Imprisonment*. London: Nacro.

Newburn, T. (1997) 'Youth, Crime and Justice', in M. Maguire, R. Morgan and R. Reiner (eds) *The Oxford Handbook of Criminology*. (2nd edn) Oxford: Clarendon Press.

Office for the Commissioner for Human Rights (2005) *Report by Mr Alvaro Gil-Robles, Commissioner for Human Rights, on His Visit to the United Kingdom 4–12 November 2004*. Strasbourg: Council of Europe.

Pitts, J. (2000) 'The New Youth Justice and the Politics of Electoral Anxiety', in B. Goldson (ed.) *The New Youth Justice*. Lyme Regis: Russell House Publishing.

Pitts, J. (2001) *The New Politics of Youth Crime: Discipline or Solidarity*. Basingstoke: Palgrave.

Pratt, J. (1987) 'A Revisionist History of Intermediate Treatment', *British Journal of Social Work*, 17(4): 417–35.

Pratt, J. (2000) 'Emotive and Ostentatious Punishment: its Decline and Resurgence in Modern Society', *Punishment and Society*, 2(4): 417–39.

Prison Reform Trust (2004) *Prison Reform Trust Factfile: July 2004*. London: Prison Reform Trust.

Rutherford, A. (1984) *Prisons and the Process of Justice*. London: Heinemann.

Rutherford, A. (1995) 'Signposting the Future of Juvenile Justice Policy in England and Wales', in Howard League for Penal Reform, *Child Offenders: UK and International Practice*. London: Howard League for Penal Reform.

Rutherford, A. (2002) 'Youth Justice and Social Exclusion', *Youth Justice*, 2(2): 100–07.

Scraton, P. (ed.) (1997) *'Childhood' in 'Crisis'?* London: UCL Press.

Social Exclusion Unit (2002) *Reducing Re-offending by Ex-prisoners*. London: Social Exclusion Unit.

Social Services Inspectorate, Commission for Health Improvement, Her Majesty's Chief Inspector of Constabulary, Her Majesty's Chief Inspector of the Crown Prosecution Service, Her Majesty's Chief Inspector of the Magistrates' Courts Service, Her Majesty's Chief Inspector of Schools, Her Majesty's Chief Inspector of Prisons and Her Majesty's Chief Inspector of Probation (2002) *Safeguarding Children: A joint Chief Inspectors' Report on Arrangements to Safeguard Children*. London: Department of Health Publications.

Stern, V. (2005) 'The Injustice of Simple Justice', in D. Conway (ed.) *Simple Justice*. London: CIVITAS.

Tonry, M. (2004) *Punishment and Politics: Evidence and Emulation in the Making of English Crime Control Policy*. Cullompton, Willan.

United Nations Committee on the Rights of the Child (2002) *Concluding Observations of the Committee on the Rights of the Child: United Kingdom of Great Britain and Northern Ireland*. Geneva: United Nations.

Young, J. (1999) *The Exclusive Society*. London: Sage.

Youth Justice Board for England and Wales (2004) *Strategy for the Secure Estate for Juveniles: Building on the Foundations*. London: Youth Justice Board for England and Wales.

Youth Justice Board for England and Wales (2005a) *Youth Justice Annual Statistics 2003/04*. London: Youth Justice Board for England and Wales.

Youth Justice Board for England and Wales (2005b) *Secure Estate Bulletin: September 2005*. London: Youth Justice Board for England and Wales.

Youth Justice Board for England and Wales (2005c) *Secure Estate Bulletin: October 2005*. London: Youth Justice Board for England and Wales.

Community Safety, Youth and the 'Anti-Social'

Gordon Hughes and Matthew Follett

Introduction

In this chapter an overview of current developments in the field of community safety with regard to the 'youth question' in the UK is provided. Much of the discussion necessarily focuses on the exclusionary consequences of the national governmental drive to address the problem of 'anti-social behaviour' in localities and communities across the country. Indeed the seemingly newly 'discovered' problem of anti-social behaviour appears to be increasingly recoded as a problem of young people in deprived and marginalised communities and neighbourhoods. The consequences of these processes for young people so designated as anti-social will be explored through a critical interrogation of the (by no means unproblematic) evidence generated to date from often competing constituencies, researching variously at the national and local levels.

The evaluation of local governmental trends in community safety remains complex and uncertain. This accords with Newburn's (2002: 453) conviction that: 'the nature of youth justice and crime prevention under New Labour is somewhat tricky to characterise'. Indeed it is important to capture the messy instabilities of 'community governance' (Edwards and Hughes, 2002). Both supporters and critics alike – of the New Labour project on the problem of 'anti-social' youth – have tended to downplay such complexity in their efforts to characterise the local implementation of crime and disorder strategies, either as a managerial, evidence-based and communitarian success, or as a clear manifestation of a new institutionalised intolerance and populist authoritarianism. Nor should we assume that the New Labour message on crime and communities is mono-vocal. Rather we might expect to see ambivalences and contradictions expressive of competing networks and cabals, even in this seemingly 'presidentially' ruled administration. In particular, whilst this chapter argues that there is a dominant trend towards the social exclusion of specific categories of youth (often the most marginalised, vulnerable, already 'outcast' and angry young people), at the same time, when we examine practices in depth and *in situ* in specific contexts, the picture is far from monochromal or finished. Compromise, contestation, even resistance, are all present in the day-to-day realities of the local implementation and delivery of community safety strategies that focus upon the perennial youth issue. As a site of governance, community safety partnership work with regard to youth remains unstable and the actions of key players are, to varying degrees, 'unpredictable' (Clarke, 2004). Furthermore, despite the central government project of rolling out a common approach to youth crime and disorder reduction across the country, the uneven development of policy and practice in distinct localities, with their own 'geohistories' of crime control and safety (Edwards and Hughes, 2005), should not be under-estimated by social scientists and commentators. As Muncie and Hughes conclude in their overview of the changing and competing modes of youth governance under neo-liberalism:

> No reading of the future can ever be clear. The logics of welfare paternalism, justice and rights, responsibilization, remoralization, authoritarianism and managerialism will continue their 'dance' and new spaces for resistance, relational politics and governmental innovation will be opened up. (Muncie and Hughes, 2002: 16)

The structure of the chapter is as follows. First, a brief overview of the policy field of local community safety and of the place of the 'youth problem' within this field is presented. Second, the changing discourses on, and governing practices of, the 'anti-social' both nationally and locally are discussed. Third, the possibly countervailing dynamics around local, conditionally inclusionary strategies towards the problem both *with* and *of* 'anti-social' youth are analysed. Fourth, the chapter concludes by noting the normative and political challenges that are opened up by the debate on the place of young people in discourses of community safety and the 'anti-social'.

Community safety and the perennial 'problem' of youth

In this section the main features of the New Labour government's crime and disorder reduction policy with regard to the problem of the 'anti-social' in the first decade of the twenty-first century are considered. This ambitious political project and programme of policy implementation can be particularly associated with two inter-connected governmental imperatives. Namely, the development and implementation of a national and centralised 'what works', 'evidence-based' paradigm for crime and disorder reduction policy and practice; and the institutionalisation of local Crime and Disorder Reduction Partnerships through which responsibility for the production and implementation of community safety strategies, targeted at crime, disorder and increasingly the 'anti-social', is seemingly handed over to a plurality of 'responsibilised' local actors in the 'community'.

There now exists a statutory duty on local authorities and police forces, in co-operation with probation services, primary health care and a growing number of other agencies, to formulate and implement strategies for the reduction of crime and disorder in their area. The most striking contrast with the previous models of partnership working which influenced New Labour reforms, is that post-Crime and Disorder Act 1998 reduction partnerships have a *statutory* footing in England and Wales. Furthermore, since 1998 all 376 statutory Crime and Disorder Reduction Partnerships in England and Wales have had to:

- carry out audits of local crime and disorder problems;
- consult with all sections of the local community;
- publish three-year crime and disorder reduction strategies based on the findings of the audits;
- identify targets and performance indicators for each part of the strategy, with specified time scales;
- publish the audit, strategy and targets; and
- report annually on progress against the stated targets.

The routine operation of local Crime and Disorder Reduction Partnerships, therefore, is massively affected by this paradigm of measurable 'success' in policy and practice. However, it is only post-2003 that the requirement to both audit the extent of disorder-qua-'anti-social behaviour' and set targets on disorder, has been given serious attention across most Crime and Disorder Reduction Partnerships – largely as a result of central government pressure. We are, in effect, entering a phase of crime *and disorder* reduction after an earlier phase which was in name and practice a 'crime reduction' programme, centrally devised and locally implemented.

'Community safety' remains a profoundly vague, slippery and contested signifier; at the same time its rise has been exponential and its political appeal increasingly prominent over the last two decades. At its most prosaic, it is a short-hand term to capture the move from single agency-focused crime prevention, to a shared agency responsibility for prevention in which it is also assumed, often mostly at the rhetorical level, that non-statutory actors-qua-*communities* will also play a key role in the promotion and delivery of 'community-based crime prevention'. At its most ambitious, community safety has broadened the concern with crime prevention *per se* to cover a range of other harms and fears, including various forms of 'anti-social' behaviour from rowdiness, nuisance neighbours to speeding cars and environmental 'pollution'. Given this mandate to broaden the agenda on what is harmful and destructive of 'safety' in local communities, it is not surprising that the problem of the 'anti-social' has consistently figured in local community safety practice, albeit without the more recent emphasis on auditing the extent of 'anti-social' behaviour and defining reduction targets. Furthermore, in the post-1997 New Labour context the methods and modes of local practice have been reformulated. A combination of situational and social crime *prevention* techniques for governing the 'anti-social' has been overshadowed by an agenda in which central government wishes to prioritise *enforcement* and *repression* alongside a preventive rationality. It is also crucial to note that the meaning (and practice of) 'community safety' have been increasingly recoded in official government discourse by the rather different term 'crime and disorder reduction', which is narrower in scope and more amenable to performance management targets than the more generic community safety (Hughes and Gilling, 2004).

Despite these important semantic slippages and shifts in policy and practice priorities, what becomes clear from scanning the field of local community safety over two decades is that the 'problem of youth' has always held a pivotal place in the local work of the multi-agency partnerships. This has remained evident from the Morgan Report (Home Office, 1991) to the latest round of local community safety strategies issued in 2005. In all three rounds of the triennial local crime and disorder reduction strategies launched since 1999 in every local authority across England and Wales, the problem of youth as offenders and victims is a universal theme, which in turn is linked to specific crime and disorder reduction targets. Despite the co-existence of separate 'youth offending teams' (YOTs) and a separate line of management to the National Youth Justice Board, it is impossible to imagine local Crime and Disorder Reduction Partnerships functioning without the presence of youth issues on their agendas.

Accordingly, there is much continuity in community safety practice over the last two decades, given the central focus on the problems of crime, disorder and safety linked to young people as both offenders and victims. However, it is widely acknowledged that there is also an increasingly marked 'punitive' turn in the field of community safety in recent years. This is most clearly exemplified in the growing centrality of the problem of 'anti-social behaviour' particularly following the Police Reform Act 2002 and the Anti-Social Behaviour Act 2003. Each of these acts have sought to both give local authorities (and an expanded array of other agencies) greater and more permissive powers to enforce measures targeted at 'anti-social behaviour' and, more implicitly, to bring recalcitrant local partnerships into line with central government's desire to be seen as 'tough', not just on crime but on disorder and 'anti-social behaviour'.

Youth, exclusion and the crusade against the 'anti-social'

It is important to ask why is there such a heightened concern and public debate over 'anti-social behaviour' now, when the official rate of crime, including offences associated with street disorder, is apparently in decline? To answer this we need to take note of both the broader socio-historical conditions of our times and the cultural sensibilities associated with late modernity, as well as the specific political developments in recent decades.

Tracing the roots of the problem of the 'anti-social'

As a newly recognised social problem, 'anti-social behaviour' does speak to real individual and collective concerns and harms, especially those affecting Britain's poorest communities which have been left behind following the great marketising and consumerist onslaught of the 1980s and 1990s (Lea, 2001). Indeed, as Burney (2004a: 470) notes, it was in part local authority pressure which lay behind the introduction of the exclusionary anti-social behaviour order (ASBO) in the 1998 Crime and Disorder Act, expressing the concerns of councillors and housing managers who had to deal with a rising volume of complaints of un-neighbourly and predatory behaviour, mainly from Labour-controlled poor council estates in areas of high unemployment.

In contrast, the problem of 'anti-social behaviour' may also be interpreted as a classic 'moral panic', stoked up by politicians seeking votes and mass media campaigners chasing improved readership figures by trading on the politics of fear, whether it be the *stranger* both without and within the nation (epitomised by the asylum seeker, Hughes, 2005) or, in this case, the 'anti-social' *outcast* from the domestically reared 'underclass'. Within this 'underclass', youths 'hanging about' and 'out of control' have become the almost universal symbol of disorder and menace (Burney, 2004a: 473).

For others, most famously left realist criminologists (Lea and Young, 1983), the problem of 'anti-social behaviour' is indicative of a political crisis associated with blighted communities and the ever-widening divisions between the socially and politically included and the excluded and marginalised. The concerns expressed by the left realist criminologists in the 1980s in part reflected fears in working-class areas identified in local victim surveys. In turn, the 'solutions' they offered – in terms of multi-agency responses based on 'the planned, co-ordinated response of the major social agencies to problems of crime and incivilities' (Young, 1991: 155) – reflected initial local authority community safety work in certain localities and came to influence local and central policy debates in the UK. Much of their thinking resonates within the Home Office-sponsored Morgan Report of 1991 (in which the discourse of community safety first gained a national profile) and the subsequent pronouncements of New Labour politicians.

It would, however, be misleading to assume that the roots of the new political and moral salience of the crusade against the 'anti-social' in the public imagination are reducible to purely indigenous UK trends. A lively export trade in ideas and practices of crime control from across the Atlantic, has been starkly evident for several decades. Indeed, much of the current hegemony of 'anti-social' measures in policy discourses across the world is associated with possibly the most influential criminological essay produced in recent decades: Wilson and Kelling's (1982) 'Broken Windows'. This essay has been 'translated' and deployed within local policing and safety strategies across many Western societies (Edwards and Hughes, 2005), and the UK is no exception. The logic that seemingly minor sub-criminal misdemeanours, incivilities and acts of 'anti-social behaviour' need 'nipping in the bud' by means of 'zero-tolerance' community policing and the rigorous cleansing of the streets and public places has proven to be profoundly seductive. Put simply, the argument goes that if cultures and climates of disorder are allowed to develop and take root, then more serious crime will grow as surely as night follows day. Indeed, the simplicity of the thesis makes it practically and commonsensically attractive, whatever its conceptual flaws. Burney is not alone in observing that:

> the well-documented features of neighbourhood decline are mainly correlations, not causes, with a common root in poverty, structural weakness, and lack of social cohesion. It becomes increasingly hard for government rhetoric to blame individual nastiness for the destruction of communities. (2004a: 473)

Proponents of the 'broken windows' thesis, both within and without government circles, continue to do just that!

New Labour and 'anti-social behaviour'

'Anti-social behaviour' is notoriously difficult to define. Section 1 of the Crime and Disorder Act provides that it is acting 'in a manner that caused or was likely to cause harassment, alarm or distress to one or more persons not of the same household'. Nor is the problem 'new' to any complex social order: there have always been concerns over the 'anti-social' in local areas at certain times and it is important to be wary of assuming the 'newness' of both contemporary social problems and the responses to them (Pearson, 1983). Instead, perhaps what is most striking about the current crusade against the 'anti-social', and the preferred means of managing it, is that it departs radically from the era of state welfare and conditionally inclusive collective risk management strategies for dealing with social problems, perhaps ushering in a new period characterised by 'the criminalization of social policy' (Hughes, 1998; forthcoming). Since the 1997 election, a raft of legal remedies aimed at holding accountable and punishing the perpetrators of 'anti-social' acts have been introduced. In turn, Parr has observed:

> the choice of legal remedies designed to deal with 'anti-social behaviour' has widened, so has the range of behaviours and potential offenders liable for prosecution ... Now a touchstone of the New Labour Government's policy-making agenda, it is increasingly difficult to remember when 'anti-social behaviour' was not a familiar policy concern. (2005: 1)

It is now more-or-less taken for granted – by ministers, the Home Office and its specialist Anti-Social Behaviour Unit – that 'anti-social behaviour' is a widespread and increasingly urgent problem. It follows that tackling this problem is, along with the 'war on terrorism', viewed by government as one of the greatest challenges facing 'our' communities.

One of the most radical features of the Crime and Disorder Act lay in imposing a statutory duty on local partnerships to reduce crime *and* disorder. In the context of 'anti-social behaviour', the key significance of the Act was that it provided new *civil* orders and powers. This civilianisation of law is clearly moralising in tone and it served to 'define deviance up'. An ASBO is a civil order that can be made by the police, local authority (and several other agencies since 2002) on anyone over the age of ten whose behaviour is thought likely to cause alarm, distress or harassment. Perhaps most significantly, 'breach' of such a *civil* order is punishable by up to five years' imprisonment.

Burney (2004a: 473) observes that in the build-up to the implementation of the Crime and Disorder Act, youths were not a prominent part of the 'anti-social' paradigm and in the draft guidance issued by the Home Office immediately after the Act, imposing orders on under-18-year-olds was specifically discouraged. However, Burney argues that this was not 'what local authorities wanted' (at least not what a powerful lobby among local authorities wanted). In the final version of the guidance on ASBOs published in March 1999, therefore, young people aged between 12–17 were identified as appropriate groups for the routine application for ASBOs (Burney, 2004a: 474). In the first two and a half years following the implementation of ASBOs, 58 per cent of all the orders imposed were made on under-18s and a further 16 per cent on people aged 18–21 years (Campbell, 2002). The *total* number of ASBOs remained relatively low, however, and in many Crime and Disorder Reduction Partnerships they were hardly employed at all. Accordingly, the picture across the country – up to 2003 – was not one in which there was a local authority consensus with regard to ASBOs. Across the 376 Crime and Disorder Reduction Partnership areas between April 1999 to March 2001, only 317 ASBOs were issued, a third being served on young people (House of Commons Select Committee Inquiry into Anti-Social Behaviour, 2004). The uneven appeal of ASBOs across the often very different contexts of local community safety practice is important, therefore. It is sanguine, for example, to note that to date approximately a sixth of all ASBOs imposed have been in the Greater Manchester area alone.

Since the implementation of the Anti-Social Behaviour Act 2003, the legal powers of local authorities and Crime and Disorder Reduction Partnerships for dealing with 'anti-social behaviour' have been extended and the process for imposing an ASBO has been made simpler and speedier. It would seem that the 2003 Act was introduced to make the generally resistant local Crime and Disorder Reduction Partnerships and local authorities – outside a number of prominent metropolitan authorities – comply with the new exclusionary statutory powers which central government had provided. Furthermore, the legitimising discourses and primary targets for local 'anti-social behaviour' measures have shifted in large part from (adult) 'neighbours from hell' to young people. Such shifts have been accompanied by the growing profile of 'anti-social behaviour' work within community safety units where there are increasing numbers of staff employed in specialist 'anti-social behaviour' teams.

1. Prohibits from:

- entering the whole of a named council estate;
- engaging in conduct which causes or is likely to cause alarm, distress or harassment to others, or inciting others to do so;
- causing or attempting to cause criminal damage; and
- engaging in behaviour which is or is likely to be threatening, abusive or insulting to others, or encouraging or inciting others to do so.

(January 2000, Huddersfield Magistrates' Court)

2. Prohibits for a period of two years:

- Shouting, spitting, using verbal/physical and/or racial abuse, swearing, drinking alcohol;
- Smashing bottles, throwing eggs, stones or other items at vehicles or property in any street in the London Borough of Haringey including inciting or encouraging others in the commission of any of the above;
- Entering the Park Ward of Tottenham (other than to remain at his house address) for one hour before and after the scheduled kick-off time of any football match held at White Hart Lane football stadium; and
- Leaving his home address between the hours of 8.00 pm and 7.00 am unless under the direct supervision of a youth worker from the London Borough of Haringey on an organised event.

(May 2000, Haringey Magistrates' Court)
Adapted from Burney, 2004a: 476–7.

Figure 11.1 Examples of Anti-Social Behaviour Orders

Not surprisingly typical conditions of ASBOs (see Figure 11.1) have attracted intense criticism for their 'all-embracing and subjective basis; [the] potential criminalization of non-criminal conduct; [the] deliberate confusion of civil and criminal law; for allowing evidence from "professional witnesses"; [the] potential disproportionality; and ... its stigmatising and exclusionary effects' (Burney, 2004a: 471; See also Ashworth et al., 1999).

Straddling adaptation and denial? Local community safety work and the 'anti-social'

As noted, the majority of Crime and Disorder Reduction Partnerships largely avoided using their 'anti-social behaviour' powers – from local child curfews to ASBOs – between 1999–2003. The talk was often 'tough' but local practices and actions were more measured in the years immediately prior to the Anti-Social Behaviour Act 2003. Newburn (2002), for example, observed that in practice 'there has been a remarkable reluctance on the ground to use such powers'. More conditionally inclusive measures such as Acceptable Behaviour Contracts (ABCs) proved to be more popular. In retrospect the period between 1999 and 2003 appears to have been characterised by what Garland (2001) has termed 'adaptive' pragmatic preventive responses led by officers/practitioners which, in turn, reflected the 'habitus' of this professional group and resulted in localised modes of reworking and contestation (Hughes, 2004, Hughes and Gilling, 2004).

Since that time, however, local Crime and Disorder Reduction Partnerships have been under increasing pressure from central government to deliver on the 'tough' aspects of the Crime and Disorder Act and the Anti-Social Behaviour Act. Added to this, there is a more visible presence of locally elected politicians with specific 'portfolios' on crime and disorder reduction and community safety as a result of the 'modernising' agenda in local government, and the new legal powers institutionalised in the Local Government Acts of 1999 and 2000. There are now new powers and liabilities for elected councillors who are often under sustained pressure to respond to local concerns and whose political careers and aspirations are at stake. The local espousal of a 'tough on crime and disorder' agenda may be a 'win/win' situation, not just for a growing number of councillors, but also for beleaguered community safety teams (including the police). Furthermore, the high profile of 'anti-social behaviour' practice and a prevailing context in which 'tough' responses are viewed as being indicative of local authorities 'at long last' doing something tangible, consolidate such tendencies. This appears to be indicative of a new phase of an 'expressive' and 'symbolic' politics of local crime control emphasising the exclusion and expulsion of a range of 'undesirables'. Indeed, at the national level whereas only 466 ASBOs were imposed in the two and a half years after 1999, 2,633 were issued in the 12 months between October 2003 and September 2004 alongside 5,383 ABCs during the same period (Home Office, 2005).

Despite these broad shifts towards a more overtly repressive crime and disorder prevention politics, the nature of the new practices across the range of localities and contexts in England and Wales, and their actual outcomes for those identified as 'anti-social', remain complex and under-researched. Overall, it is important to note the paucity of detailed empirical research on the new 'anti-social behaviour' measures and their human consequences. On the basis of the limited research undertaken, particularly outside government-sponsored surveys and evaluations, the story across different locations and occupational contexts appears to be characterised by an uneven mix of enthusiasm, co-operation alongside wary compliance and gentle contestation with the government's moral communitarian and popular punitive agenda. However, what is abundantly evident is that the problem of youth 'hanging around' is a constant area of concern in most community safety strategies. Hill and Wright (2003), for example, on the basis of their ethnographic research on two estates in the

Midlands, suggest that community safety is predominantly about the local management of crime and incivilities, and not about issues of empowerment and inclusion:

> 'Community' becomes a setting in which only the interests of adults are identified, interests which underpin a moral authoritarianism which operate to exclude marginal groups such as 'dangerous' youth. 'Safety' becomes a notion to be secured by blaming, isolating and silencing youth. (Hill and Wright, 2003: 291)

Whether this conclusion can be generalised across the practices of most Crime and Disorder Reduction Partnerships is difficult to say. There are important qualifications to such a blanket foreclosure on the possibilities of inclusive community safety work on youth and the 'anti-social' from other research studies, however. Evidence from Hughes and Gilling's (2004) national survey of community safety managers, for example, points to a continuing professional commitment to inclusive, social democratically-influenced preventive approaches to the 'problem of youth'. Even Hill and Wright note that on one of the estates they studied, parents do recognise the need for the authorities to take account of 'their' children's views. This accords with Girling et al.'s (2000) finding in Macclesfield, which confirms that adults are willing to take account of the needs of 'their' youth whilst simultaneously perceiving youth from different areas as 'other' (Hill and Wright, 2003: 295).

In Thomas et al.'s (2004/5) study of 85 youth offending teams (YOTs) and the use and impact of ASBOs, they found that there was uneven use of such excluding orders across the YOTs. YOTs in Greater Manchester had a very high number of young people on orders (with the highest being 102) but most YOTs in the survey had fewer than 10 young people subject to ASBOs. Officially ASBOs are not considered to be a measure of last resort but many practitioners do view them as such and in turn prefer to employ other approaches first. The most common alternatives offered were ABCs, warning letters, interviews and referrals to youth inclusion and support panels (Thomas et al., 2004/5: 25). More worryingly they found that breaches of ASBOs, itself a criminal offence, were common, with more than half of ASBOs being breached. Half of breaches were for criminal or 'anti-social behaviour' but a quarter were breached for lesser matters such as associating with named individuals. Furthermore, adverse publicity about the young people on ASBOs appeared to be the norm including coverage in newspapers, leaflets to residents and the distribution of posters. Finally, Thomas et al. found that the main priority of local authorities and the police in applying ASBOs and addressing 'anti-social behaviour' more generally, is to respond to the concerns of local communities and provide reassurance that their problems will be reduced rather than changing the behaviour of young people (Thomas et al., 2004/5: 26). Although rigorous data are in short supply, there is emerging research evidence that ASBOs are disproportionately used against the most vulnerable and 'troubled' as well as 'troublesome' children and young people (and adults). As Krudy and Stewart (2004: 11) note, the 'anti-social behaviour' associated with ASBOs is very often behaviour influenced by a matrix of underlying problems that include lack of suitable educational provision, strained parenting, social exclusion and drug dependency.

The uneasiness over the use of ASBOs among local practitioners and community safety managers is evident in Follett's ongoing and, as yet, unpublished research on Crime and Disorder Reduction Partnerships. For example, the YOT manager of the Crime and Disorder Reduction Partnership under scrutiny self-consciously sought to broaden out the partnership's debate on ASBOs and children and young people explaining that:

> The problem with ASBOs in X, and elsewhere is that the context around anti-social behaviour has been driven around the crime and disorder silo, and there hasn't been a child-centred perspective. And yet all the services in place that deal with kids who are involved in anti-social behaviour are children's services – health, education, social care etc. So I try and make sure that the crime and disorder and the children's side are talking to each other ... Principally the whole ASBOs thing is about protection of victims and public confidence. We are about that too, but you have to do something with the kids involved, you can't just shut them away somewhere. (Follett, unpublished)

While such 'talk' cannot be read as being unproblematically translated into local strategy and practice, the Crime and Disorder Reduction Partnership in question foregrounded preventive approaches on 'anti-social behaviour', including a long-established mediation scheme as part of what it terms a 'pyramid approach' to 'anti-social behaviour' whereby ASBOs comprise the last resort following a series of preventive stages.

It is possible that such an approach might lead to 'widening the net' of social control Cohen (1984) or even the 'soft end' of 'a strategy of "lockdown" leading inexorably and inevitably to differential policing, discriminatory targeting, universal surveillance, criminalisation and an escalation in the prison population' (Scraton, 2002: 31). However, to date this totalising and dystopian prediction remains one that apparently overlooks the uneven and uncertain implementation of such a 'strategy' across different sites, despite the undoubted general shift towards greater punitiveness in local crime control measures across England and Wales. To date, in the area covered by Crime and Disorder Reduction Partnership X (see above), 13 ASBOs had been taken out over the past six years. How long this minimalist 'adaptive' position might last is uncertain of course, given that 'in the eyes of politicians, and increasingly, the public at large, "success" in dealing with perpetrators of "anti-social" acts tends to be seen entirely in terms of ASBO statistics' (Burney, 2004b: 4). At the same time, Burney notes that the recent growth in the use of ASBOs is largely attributable to changes introduced in the Police Reform Act 2002. 'Most importantly [ASBOs] can be obtained on top of a criminal sentence if proof of anti-social behaviour ... can be shown. The police have seized on this opportunity to extend control over persistent offenders and thus have sharply driven up the total of orders granted' (ibid.). It is estimated that of the 16,670 ASBOs imposed between December 2002 and March 2004, 43 per cent were obtained on the back of conviction and increasingly ASBOs have become 'just another policing tool' (Burney, 2004b: 5).

At the national level of politics, the exponential rise of the government's 'anti-social behaviour' agenda would not seem to be about finding evidence-based measures which can be shown to 'work'. Instead it serves more complex and less easily measurable political ends. With regard to the White Paper on 'Anti-Social Behaviour', Matthews (2003: 8) argues that the general level of vagueness and lack of specificity was essential since it rationalised a wide range of sanctions which otherwise would be difficult to justify, and he notes that there is an assumption that: 'if a large enough armada can be mobilised then the offensive will be successful, even if it is not sure where it is going or what it should be aiming at'. However, what seems clearer is that the nationally orchestrated crusade against the anti-social is 'not going to be directed at those who pollute our environment for profit, those who recycle foodstuffs and inject meat with additives or those involved in multi-million pound pension swindles. This is an offensive aimed at the feckless, the marginalised and the poor' (Matthews, 2003: 6).

Making local youth safer? Conditional inclusions of troublesome and troubled young people

It is widely acknowledged that the emphasis on partnership working in community safety strategies holds the potential for greater co-ordination and less isolated practices by specific agencies. The survey work of Hunter et al. (2001) and Campbell (2002) on 'anti-social behaviour' measures indicated that agencies placed great value on the time-consuming 'case conferences' and that these often had unintended consequences. In particular, some social landlords found the process of initiating ASBOs particularly useful due to the 'problem-solving' component involved, and Burney (2004a: 481) observes that once a case was looked at from a multi-agency perspective, solutions at times emerged that rendered it unnecessary to pursue an ASBO. In many cases the problematic behaviour was seen to arise from social and health-related problems that needed addressing. Harm reduction initiatives may be developed, particularly given the key role played by alcohol and drug abuse in many 'anti-social behaviour' cases. Overall, Burney's research has suggested that most local Crime and Disorder Reduction Partnerships and corresponding professional/practitioner bodies have remained unimpressed by the central government criticisms of their perceived failure to impose ASBOs. Her conclusion is relatively optimistic, arguing that the local partnerships are now developing their own ways of dealing with their own problems 'exactly what the partnership structures were to be intended for' (Burney, 2004a: 482). In turn, Burney suggests that 'responsibilisation' or 'government by proxy' might mean that the methods adopted by the local proxy agents such as Crime and Disorder Reduction Partnerships, given the encouragement and means to develop their own 'local solutions to local problems', diverge from the central government 'vision'. Although there is clear evidence that all local community safety strategies prioritise the reduction of incidents of, and fears about, disorder and 'anti-social behaviour' (not least given the national targets set by government), the specific form that such work may take results at times in the promotion of preventive approaches to 'anti-social behaviour'.

Tackling and reducing 'anti-social behaviour' are now ingrained within the policies and practices of all Crime and Disorder Reduction Partnerships. Despite this seemingly smooth unfolding of the central state's policy agenda on 'anti-social behaviour', however, local implementation is by no means a uniform or uncontested tale of growing authoritarianism and institutionalised intolerance. In summary, we submit that any accurate interpretation of the broad trends at work in the social control of 'anti-social' young people associated with partnership-based community safety policies and practices, must centre three key inter-related issues. First, the distinction between central government rhetoric and actual practice at the local level. Second, the power-dependence of would-be sovereign actors on local actors and institutions. Third, the means by which the specificities and geohistories of particular localities can serve to neutralise dominant national trends and discourses.

Conclusion

Within the contemporary policy agenda on community safety, anti-social behaviour and youth justice, there is a seemingly contradictory espousal of both an evidence-based policy and adaptive pragmatic strategies of local prevention partnerships, alongside a continuing recourse to a symbolic, visceral and expressive politics of exclusion, banishment and penal segregation. The crusade against 'anti-social behaviour' may be a bridging device across these supposedly distinct political strategies due to its commonsensical populism and moral communitarian appeal (Hughes, 2004). It is difficult to deny that we are witnessing a concerted political drive to 'define deviance up' which has also had the paradoxical result that public tolerance to incivility is progressively lowered and public fear of young people, as well as other adult 'outcasts', is significantly increased. Positive communication between the generations is put in jeopardy (Muncie, 2004: 238–9). The dominant discourse on youth and community sees the latter as needing protection from the former rather than being associated with a politics of recognition whereby young people are also seen as victims (as well as perpetrators) of crime and disorder and as citizens in waiting. At the same time, we have emphasised the importance of specific geohistories in different localities and contexts across

Britain and both the unpredictability and uneven development of local governmental strategies of safety and crime control. The current situation remains uncertain and precariously balanced. It is as yet unclear whether the increasingly embattled countervailing forces of conditional inclusion may be powerful and resilient enough to resist the dominant tendency towards the exclusion of the 'anti-social' through censure and banishment.

References

Ashworth, A., Garner, J., von Hirsch, A., Morgan, R., Wasik, M. (1998) 'Neighbouring on the Oppressive: the Government's Community Safety Orders', *Criminal Justice*, 16(1): 7–14.

Burney, E. (2004a) 'Talking Tough, Acting Coy: What Happened to the Anti-Social Behaviour Order?', *Howard Journal,* 41(5): 469–84.

Burney, E. (2004b) 'Nuisance or Crime? The Changing Uses of Anti-Social Behaviour Control', *Criminal Justice Matters,* 57: 4–5.

Campbell, S. (2002) *A Review of Anti-social Behaviour Orders.* London: Home Office Research Series.

Clarke, J. (2004) *Changing Welfare, Changing States.* London: Sage.

Cohen, S. (1985) *Visions of Social Control.* Cambridge: Polity Press.

Edwards, A. and Hughes, G. (2002) 'Introduction: the Community Governance of Crime Control', in G. Hughes and A. Edwards (eds) *Crime Control and Community.* Cullompton: Willan Publishing.

Edwards, A. and Hughes, G. (2005) 'Comparing the Governance of Safety in Europe: a Geohistorical Approach', *Theoretical Criminology,* 9: 3.

Follett, M. (unpublished PhD in progress) 'Local Governance of Crime and Disorder: an Ethnographic Case-Study'. Miltan Keynes: The Open University.

Garland, D. (2001) *The Culture of Control.* Oxford: OUP.

Girling, E., Loader, I. and Sparks, R. (2000) *Crime and Social Change in Middle England.* London: Routledge.

Hill, J. and Wright, G. (2003) 'Youth, Community Safety and the Paradox of Inclusion', *The Howard Journal*, 42(3): 282–97.

Home Office (1991) *Safer Communities.* London: HMSO.

Hughes, G. (1998) *Understanding Crime Prevention: Social Control, Risk and Late Modernity.* Buckingham: Open University Press.

Hughes, G. (2004) 'Straddling Adaptation and Denial: Crime and Disorder Reduction Partnership in England and Wales', *Cambrian Law Review,* 38: 1–22.

Hughes, G. (2006 forthcoming) 'The Politics of Safety and the Problem of "the Stranger"', in G. Brannigan and G. Pavlich (eds) *Adventures in the Sociologies of Law.*

Hughes, G. (forthcoming) *The Politics of Crime and Community.* London: Palgrave.

Hughes, G. and Gilling, D. (2004) 'Mission Impossible? The Habitus of the Community Safety Manager and the New Expertise in the Local Partnership Governance of Crime and Safety', *Criminal Justice,* 4(2): 129–49.

Hunter, C. et al. (2001) 'Social landlords' Use of Anti-Social Behaviour Orders', Sheffield: Sheffield Hallam University (unpublished).

Krudy, M. and Stewart, G. (2004) 'Real-Life ASBOs: Trouble-Makers or Merely Troubled?' *Criminal Justice Matters,* 57: 1011.

Lea, J. (2001) *Crime and Modernity.* London: Sage.

Lea, J. and Young, J. (1983) *What Is to Be Done about Law and Order?* London: Pluto.

Matthews, R. (1992) 'Replacing Broken Windows: Crime, Incivilities and Urban Change', in R. Matthews and J. Young (eds) *Issues in Realist Criminology.* London: Sage.

Muncie, J. (2004) *Youth and Crime.* (2nd edn) London: Sage.

Muncie, J. and Hughes, G. (2002) 'Modes of Youth Governance: Political Rationalies, Criminalization and Resistance', in J. Muncie, G. Hughes and E. McLaughlin (eds) *Youth Justice: Critical Readings.* London: Sage.

Newburn, T. (2002) 'The Contemporary Politics of Youth Crime Prevention', in J. Muncie, G. Hughes and E. McLaughlin (eds) *Youth Justice: Critical Readings.* London: Sage.

Parr, S. (2005) 'Anti-Social Behaviour and New Labour', Unpublished Paper.

Pearson, G. (1983) *Hooligan: A History of Respectable Fears.* London: Macmillan.

Scraton, P. (2002) 'Defining "Power" and Challenging "Knowledge": Critical Analysis as Resistance in the UK', in K. Carrington and R. Hogg (eds) *Critical Criminology.* Cullompton: Willan Publishing.

Thomas, et al. (2004/5) *Criminal Justice Matters*

Wilson, J. Q. and Kelling, G. (1982) 'Broken Windows', *Atlantic Monthly,* March, pp. 29–38.

Young, J. (1991) 'Left Realism and the Priorities of Crime Control', in D. Cowell and K. Stenson (eds) *The Politics of Crime Control.* London: Sage.

Urban Regeneration, Young People, Crime and Criminalisation

12

Lynn Hancock

It is claimed that many British cities are now experiencing an urban renaissance because of regenerative strategies and the strength of national and regional economies more generally. Local partnerships, in attempts to secure inward investment, are vigorously marketing their localities. The provision of 'safe', 'clean' and 'orderly' spaces are regarded as crucial to their success (Coleman, 2004). At the neighbourhood level, a range of initiatives have been introduced by New Labour governments since 1997 to regenerate localities experiencing deprivation measured against a range of indicators (Hancock, 2003). Reducing 'anti-social behaviour' and 'crime', and securing the involvement of 'communities', are now seen as being pivotal to the regenerative task. The importance of young people's participation in urban regeneration has been stressed in similar fashion (Fitzpatrick et al., 1998). Too frequently, however, commentators regard the relationships, connections and tensions between regeneration, crime reduction, social inclusion and social control in an unproblematic and uncritical fashion.

The aim of this chapter is to unpack the taken-for-granted assumptions in the urban regeneration–youth crime and disorder reduction relation and to open them up to critical scrutiny. This is particularly important given that few academic studies centre the role of young people in this relation. It is argued that regeneration strategies, as currently conceived, are re-configuring patterns and experiences of social exclusion (Coleman, 2004; Johnstone, 2004; Jones and Wilks-Heeg, 2004), and the consequences for youth crime and criminalisation are considered within this context. The chapter advances the contention that current policies are ideologically driven rather than the product of 'evidence-based' policy-making. The government's adherence to a neo-liberal *economic* agenda coupled with a moral communitarian *social* agenda, both frames current developments and exposes their contradictions and limitations.

One of the first issues to emerge when we consider the urban regeneration and crime/disorder reduction relation is the extent to which recent developments reflect the further 'criminalisation of social policy' (Crawford, 1997; Gilling and Barton, 1997). It also reveals the tension between these tendencies and the political appeal, or potential gains to be made, from seeing initiatives like the *New Deal for Communities* going some way at least towards recognising that crime is best addressed 'holistically' and urban social policy interventions are a step toward 'social justice' (Donnison, 1995; Hope, 2001). Whatever position is taken, it is important to consider the contradictions between different policies and governmental agendas, and the thinking underpinning them, which become manifest when considering urban regeneration, youth inclusion, crime and social control. We must also assess the extent to which economic inclusion is achieved, and situate urban social policies against the backdrop of market responses and 'cultural injustice', if the tensions and contradictions are to be fully appreciated.

Urban regeneration and 'inclusion' strategies

Urban regeneration in the current period can be characterised as a market-driven enterprise, 'facilitated' by local authorities and their 'strategic' partners who compete with each other to attract potential investors. In this context, places are 're-branded' and space 'reconstructed' in efforts to attract wealthy visitors, tourists and shoppers (Raco, 2003), and consumption-based and 'culture-led' projects lie at the heart of the regeneration process (Jones and Wilks-Heeg, 2004; Mooney, 2004). In this context, 'safety', 'cleanliness' and 'order' in city-centre spaces are prioritised (Coleman, 2004).

The idea that regenerative efforts should benefit disadvantaged communities is a priority in government policy (Munck, 2003). The stated aim of the *New Commitment to Neighbourhood Renewal: A National Strategy Action Plan*, for example, was to close the gap between the poorest neighbourhoods and the rest of the country over 10–20 years (Social Exclusion Unit, 2001). There are several ways in which this is envisaged, but the idea that social inclusion is to be achieved through participation in the labour market is the hallmark of other government policies, and is reflected as such in the national strategy for neighbourhood renewal (Young, 2001). Key approaches include old 'Thatcherite' notions that economically disadvantaged groups will benefit from the 'trickle down effect', alongside the idea that developing 'social capital', 'community involvement' and 'participation' will help to secure benefits (including employment) for disadvantaged groups. The combined influences of Etzioni's communitarianism (1993; 1997; Hancock and Matthews, 2001), and New Labour's 'third way' political agenda (see Crawford, 2001), have inspired a programme of initiatives to re-invigorate civic engagement, public participation and partnership working since 1997. More recently, the government's ideological commitment to communitarianism was reflected in its *Civil Renewal Agenda* (Blunkett, 2003) and other efforts to promote 'active citizenship'. An *Active Citizenship Centre* was established in 2003 and New Labour's commitment to 'citizenship education' was extended from a primary concern with young people (through the National Curriculum) (Goldson, 2003: 148) to the adult population in *Active Learning for Active Citizenship*.[1] It is further envisaged that reducing the gap between the most affluent and the most disadvantaged will be achieved by reform of welfare benefits and tax policies (*New Tax Credits*, for example) and extended access to childcare (*Sure Start* and the *New Deal for Lone Parents*, for example), each of which also aim to 'facilitate' access to paid work.

Considerable emphasis has been placed on the inclusion of young people in regeneration projects since the early 1990s (Fitzpatrick et al., 1998) and the more general focus on 'active citizenship' has added weight to youth involvement. The rationale is to improve the sustainability of regeneration, to make 'better' (less wasteful) decisions and to give young people a 'voice' (Fitzpatrick et al., 1998). Their role as future workers is prioritised; employment, training and educational needs were the priorities found most frequently in the regeneration projects included in Fitzpatrick et al.'s study. Leisure and cultural activities are viewed as an aid to securing young people's involvement and as a diversion from anti-social behaviour (Fitzpatrick et al., 1998). Fitzpatrick et al. note, however, that there were clear differences to be observed between the priorities of young people and those of adult decision-makers: Young people shared adults' views that employment and leisure facilities were important, but they also prioritised police harassment and negative adult perceptions of young people as their main problems. These concerns, however, remained the 'most significant gap in these youth-oriented regeneration initiatives' (ibid.: 2; see also Goldson, 2003).

Regeneration and 'anti-social behaviour'

There is a clear tension between activities designed to 'include' young people in the regeneration of urban neighbourhoods, and the widespread perception that 'anti-social behaviour' (often centred on young people) is a 'threat' to regenerating communities. The 'Number 10' website, for example, states:

> Anti-social behaviour] can hold back the regeneration of our most disadvantaged areas, creating the environment in which crime can take hold. It damages the quality of life for too many people – one in three people say it is a problem in their area.[2]

1. http://www.active-citizen.org.uk/
2. http://www.number-10.gov.uk/output/Page6210.asp

Inspired by Wilson and Kelling's (1982) 'Broken windows' thesis, government and local authorities stress the importance of addressing anti-social behaviour and crime as a pre-requisite for regeneration. Manchester's 'Community Strategy', for example, claims that:

> Action to control crime and anti-social behaviour is often required as a fore-runner to the regeneration of local areas and the full engagement of communities. Improving the quality of housing and the physical environment will be to no avail, without action to tackle crime and anti-social behaviour and to support good neighbours.[3]

Moreover, in his foreword to the White Paper *Respect and Responsibility,* David Blunkett (the Home Secretary at the time) argued that:

> It's time to stop thinking of anti-social behaviour as something that we can just ignore. Anti-social behaviour blights people's lives, destroys families and ruins communities. It holds back the regeneration of our disadvantaged areas and creates the environment in which crime can take hold. (Home Office, 2003a)

Further:

> At the heart of this Government's determination to tackle social exclusion is the National Strategy for Neighbourhood Renewal. That strategy must tackle and reduce the incidence and perception of anti-social behaviour if the Government is to achieve its aims of revitalising the most deprived communities. Communities drive this agenda. It is Government's role to empower them to succeed. (Home Office, 2003a: para 4.53)

The ambiguity and confusion surrounding the role and nature of working-class communities are neatly reflected in these quotations. Variously, 'communities' 'drive' these efforts, despite being 'blighted', and at the same time they need 'empowering'. Notions that communities are both the 'object of policy' and a 'policy instrument' (Imrie and Raco, 2003: 6) permeate recent official discourses around urban policy and community crime reduction. This elision arises because the government 'operate[s] with a simplistic communitarian vision' (Matthews, 2003:7). There are further confusions of course, not least those derived from the 'anti-social behaviour'–'crime' relation. On the one hand it is claimed that anti-social behaviour *leads* to crime, yet on the other, some behaviours centred in the White Paper clearly *are* crimes proscribed in the criminal law (such as drugs dealing in 'crack houses'). Furthermore, there is no distinction between the differential impacts that various kinds of behaviour may have, despite empirical evidence confirming that it is difficult to generalise (see Hancock, 2001; Matthews, 1992).

---

3. http://www.manchester.gov.uk/regen/strategy/section5.htm

The *National Strategy for Neighbourhood Renewal*, together with supporting documentation from various Social Exclusion Unit *Policy Action Team* reports, recognises that factors other than crime and disorder – external to neighbourhoods and related to the restructuring of local and national economies (as well as local and national government policies) – have led or furthered a spiral of neighbourhood decline (Hastings, 2003). Nevertheless, regenerative efforts remain focused on the deficiencies of working-class families and 'communities'. As far as the link with crime and/or anti-social behaviour is concerned (implied in the quotations above), local and national government strategies rely wholly on an uncritical acceptance of 'broken windows' (Wilson and Kelling, 1982), and the rather flawed direction of causality (disorder leads to neighbourhood decline) to which such logic gives rise (Hancock, 2001; Matthews, 1992; 2003). The complex *range* of conditions which may cause distress in neighbourhoods, or promote outward migration, are ignored or downplayed.

The 'problem' of young people 'hanging around' receives high-profile attention in the official documents of national and local government, though variously there is slippage between using the term 'hanging around' to 'youth nuisance', and in some cases 'youth gangs', with little differentiation of the precise behaviours involved. In this respect, the British Crime Survey is more helpful in terms of illuminating a sense of context (Wood, 2004). 'Teenagers hanging around' is ranked *lower* than 'vandalism and graffiti', 'misuse of fireworks', problems associated with 'rubbish and litter', and 'illegal' or 'inconveniently parked vehicles' as 'very' or 'fairly' big problems for survey respondents. Indeed, the most important cause for concern, and heading the list of most frequently mentioned problems, is 'speeding traffic', which was also considered the 'biggest problem'. Importantly, a significant proportion of 'incidents' in the 'teenagers hanging around' category involved young people 'just being a general nuisance' (43 per cent) or 'not doing anything in particular' (6 per cent), especially in more affluent areas. Moreover, '[i]n over a third of incidents (36 per cent), those perceiving problems acknowledged that the young people were not being deliberately anti-social' (Wood, 2004: 25). Significantly, the survey showed also that in these instances, for the most part, those involved were strangers.

The relationship between those who observe or report anti-social behaviour, and those who are regarded as perpetrators, is important. Where young people causing 'annoyance' are regarded as 'part of the community', not an 'out group', there is evidence to suggest that residents are more likely to be more sympathetic to the plight of young people (Goldson, 2003; Hancock, 2001). This is not to say they 'tolerate'[4] 'anti-social behaviour'. However, the reporting of particular behaviours in surveys, or to the police, does not automatically mean that a punitive response is desired (many people will simply want it to stop if it is causing annoyance). People may exercise toleration precisely because the

---

4. 'The deliberate choice not to interfere with conduct or beliefs, with which one disapproves' (Hancock and Matthews, 2001: 99).

impact of a criminal justice response is seen as being more damaging for the alleged 'perpetrator' than the 'annoying' behaviour they witness or experience. This may be especially the case where the relationship between the 'community' and key agencies such as the police and local authority has, historically, been one of antagonism (see Hancock, 2001). That said, in localities where regenerative effects can be observed, the presence of 'strangers' is more likely and a more 'punitive' response may emerge.

Communitarianism and regeneration: Uncomfortable bedfellows?

Lees (2003) has argued that much of what is advocated as 'urban renaissance' is in fact a thinly veiled attempt to gentrify urban areas. If this position is accepted, the ideals of 'community cohesion', and the government's communitarian vision, come under question. As Skogan (1988) has argued:

> in gentrifying areas there may be divisions that preclude community-wide support as new residents and property developers' interests (exchange values) may not coincide with those of long-term residents. Their influence may result in actions against undesirable people and land uses. (cited in Hancock, 2001: 153)

There are a variety of influences, of course, which impact on the nature of community responses to crime and other neighbourhood problems – not least the socio-cultural and historical context of neighbourhoods and the relationships between community members and 'dominant authorities'. Class and other status divisions may not *always* inhibit action (Hancock, 2001), but we need to examine these in the context of the wider changes in cities, which may indeed exacerbate conflict.

The government's communitarian agenda has placed increasing significance on enforcing 'community values' and responding to 'public opinion'. However, the ways in which public perceptions are gathered and used as an aid to crime and criminal justice policy-making are rarely subjected to scrutiny (Hancock, 2004), and young people's perceptions and experiences are largely absent from mainstream policy documents. It should also be borne in mind that where resources are scarce and, to the extent that the focus on anti-social behaviour secures investment in facilities that would not otherwise be available in marginalised localities, there are likely to be few benefits associated with promoting a view that anti-social behaviour is diminishing (Hancock, 2001). For example, 600 young people in Knowsley, Merseyside, were offered football coaching sessions in 2005 with the explicit aim of diverting them from anti-social activities.[5] Whether these resources would be available, were there not such a focus on anti-social behaviour in the current period, is a moot point.

---

5. http://www.merseyside.police.uk/html/news/news/july/kh28-07d-knowsleyasb.htm

The Home Office's guidance to agencies in *Working Together: Tackling Not Tolerating Anti-Social Behaviour* reminds them that youth facilities should be available, but that action 'must' be taken if they are not utilised to 'protect the community' (Home Office, 2003b: 10–11). Not only is the *adequacy* of youth provision in young people's opinions not placed under examination, but the emphasis on enforcement is likely to be counter-productive for a number of reasons. For example, the government has stressed the importance of communicating the fact that action has been taken (via the media, leaflets, public meetings and so on) to improve 'community confidence' and to facilitate the reporting of sanction breaches. But the aim is not just to tackle 'incidents' of anti-social behaviour; rather, *perceptions* must also be addressed; they influence inward investment. Indeed, the British Crime Survey 2003/04 shows that: 'for those measures where trends are available, there have been significant recent falls in the level of [specific] problems perceived' (Wood, 2004: 6), although at a *general* level respondents regarded anti-social behaviour as a growing problem. Thus, unlike government pronouncements about the falling *crime* rate, where similar trends can be observed (Wood, 2004), there is no such effort where anti-social behaviour is concerned. Moreover, if addressing 'perceptions' is the key concern, and the value of 'regeneration' or the 'community' is stressed above individual interests (including human rights and civil liberties) – as it is in the most conservative communitarian thought (see Hancock and Matthews, 2001) – it is important to recognise the limitations of this stance. As Allen Buchanan has shown, in more moderate versions of communitarian thought, the rights of individuals are recognised for the part they play in *protecting communities* (cited in Hancock and Matthews, 2001).

In view of the large number of incidents of anti-social behaviour reported in the British Crime Survey which concerned young people 'just being a general nuisance', or 'not doing anything in particular', 'evidence-led policy' would suggest the need for a more critical focus on the frequently negative perceptions adults hold of young people (Goldson, 2003; Fitzpatrick et al., 1998). In one project for example – involving Save the Children and Groundwork in partnership with CDS Housing in the West Everton district of Liverpool – residents had complained about young people 'loitering' on street corners. The 'Young Voices' initiative ('We All Live Here') worked with young people *and* local residents to arrive at a solution. Young people wanted their own (safe) place to meet. Residents were also keen that it should be safe and clearly visible. Following the identification of suitable premises, young people themselves led the process of setting up a 'youth shelter' where they could 'hang out', including getting the necessary planning permissions and overseeing construction. The evaluation of the project established that young people had well-structured ideas about solutions, which were not costly. They valued having a 'real' rather than 'tokenistic' voice. Moreover, this and other Young Voices' projects also demonstrated that: 'one of the biggest barriers to involving young people more meaningfully in their communities was local adults' negative attitudes towards them' (Renewal. net, no date). Examples such as this receive limited profile. As Worpole (2003: 9) noted with regard to discourses around urban regeneration: 'the concept of "public space" has never been so popular, but never so poorly conceptualised or understood, especially in its use by children and young people'. Indeed:

> ... the government's Neighbourhood Renewal Unit has now instigated three different programmes for street cleanliness and safety involving paid staff: Neighbourhood Wardens, Street Wardens and Street Crime Wardens ... Nowhere is it suggested that encouraging more people to be out and about on the streets, especially children, is something to be desired, and which may, in the long run, be more conducive to neighbourhood renewal through a vision of the 'walkable community' advocated, for example, by the Urban Green Spaces Taskforce in its report ...
>
> One might be tempted to think that such initiatives not only want to clean the streets of litter, but of young people as well. It is telling that the Minister for Children and Young People also doubles up as Community and Custodial Provision Minister, based at the Home Office, rather than being a minister located within the more permissive and developmental settings of Health, Education or even Culture, Media and Sport ministries. (Worpole, 2003: 9)

There are, of course, problems associated with 'anti-social behaviour'; young people are more likely to be the victims of actions or conditions that cause 'alarm, distress and intimidation'. What is clear is that, in contrast with the Young Voices initiatives in Liverpool, the more frequently cited and draconian types of responses, such as designated zones under section 30 of the Anti-Social Behaviour Act 2003 (HMSO, 2003), increase fear among young people and promote hostile feelings towards the police. By way of illustration, designated areas under section 30 were introduced in parts of south Liverpool in summer 2005 on the grounds that 'anti-social behaviour' was 'a significant and ongoing problem'[6] in specified areas. Attempts to disperse young people in one designated zone in the Garston district of South Liverpool prompted young people to voice concerns about being bullied by the police. It heightened their anxieties about safety as avoidance strategies took them to unfamiliar places in response to a policy which failed to recognise that young people congregate in groups because of concerns about safety (Rice et al., 2005). Also, the increasingly popular 'Acceptable Behaviour Contracts' (ABCs), have produced feelings of 'injustice', their 'success' has relied on fear (of eviction) and they have adversely affected the siblings of the young people subject to such sanctions. While some families have reported that they have welcomed greater levels of support in the face of hardships, such interventions have also increased tensions within households, and the likelihood of restoring good neighbour relations at the end of the

---

6. www.merseyside.police.uk/livsouth/asb/designated-areas/

'Acceptable Behaviour Contract' period remained highly questionable (Stephen and Squires, 2003).

Urban regeneration, social inclusion and cultural injustice

A more liberal-communitarian 'peace-making' approach might serve to restore good neighbour relations, without the prospect of intensifying tensions in the way in which 'Acceptable Behaviour Contracts' have been shown to do. This prospect is thrown into question, however, by market-led approaches to regeneration. 'As inequality increases, the basis of the communitarian vision begins to collapse since it undermines the realisation of both social and distributive justice, while creating new conflicts and antagonisms' (Walzer, cited in Hancock and Matthews, 2001: 113). Not only does material inequality become more manifest and proximate in this context, the discourses around 'social exclusion' 'reproduce, rather than successfully address, cultural aspects of injustice' (Morrison, 2003: 139. See also Haylett, 2001; 2003; Young, 1999). Drawing on the work of Nancy Fraser, where 'respect' and 'recognition' are centred in her discussion of cultural subordination and domination, Morrison (2003) demonstrates how the 'socially excluded' are constructed as 'the problem to be fixed' or corrected. The nature of excluded communities, together with their families, skills-base, and bodies and so on are devalued; they are contrasted with the 'included' – the 'we' in the policy documents. 'They' are 'misrecognised'.[7] Using the case study of Blackbird Leys in Oxford, Morrison shows how a locality that had been stigmatised in local and national discourses, especially following urban disorders in 1990, saw the same stereotypes reproduced locally with the establishment of the Single Regeneration Budget initiative in the area. As elsewhere, the bidding process relied upon authorities demonstrating that the community was amongst the 'worst off' on a range of indicators. 'Communities' in this context are portrayed as being victimised and problematic. People are described by their deficiencies and young people are portrayed as 'threatening and potentially dangerous' (Morrison, 2003: 152). As Young (1999) has argued, these kinds of essentialising processes effectively locate deviance within the individual or group and *not* in the included majority; simultaneously they 'reaffirm the normality' of the included and in this way 'allow, in a Durkheimian fashion the boundaries of normality to be drawn more definitely and distinctly' (Young, 1999: 113).

As Young reminds us, it is not with the wealthiest that people compare themselves and nowhere is this more apparent than in the recent popular discourses

---

7. 'To be misrecognised ... is to be denied the status of a full partner in social interaction, as a consequence of institutionalised patterns of cultural value that constitute one as comparatively unworthy of respect and esteem' (Fraser, cited in Morrison, 2003: 140).

around 'Chavs', 'Scallies', and 'Neds'. These groups are, we are told, defined by a disposition to criminality, anti-social behaviour, welfare dependency, and particular behaviour as consumers of cheap or illicit goods and in the display of hyperfeminine and masculine identities. The object of the humour attendant in the discourses around 'Chavs' is to point out the difference between 'them' and 'us' (see for example, www.chavscum.co.uk); it serves to denigrate lifestyles, practices and cultures shaped by structural location (class) and, in turn, disguises it. Young people labelled in this way, like other members of the white working class, are accorded no positive meaning to their existence (Haylett, 2001). What is more, these popular views of the young urban poor find expression in 'respectable' and institutionalised – but arguably more damaging – forms in urban renewal policies (see Haylett, 2003).

Regeneration and the reconfiguring of inequality

Haylett (2003) and Young (1999; 2001) in their different ways are both concerned to highlight the importance of 'a politics of distribution' and a 'politics of recognition'. For Haylett:

> a politics of social justice needs to address more than structural or even distributional issues of inequality. In particular, it needs to accord positive meaning and value to working-classness on the basis of something more than labour market utility, in order that welfare might be remade as a site of cultural dignity and economic justice. (2003: 69)

However, instead, it is often assumed that social exclusion can be addressed by economic investment aimed at reducing 'worklessness' and the development of 'social capital', through participation and community involvement, and that, as a consequence, crime and anti-social behaviour will diminish. Indeed, social capital is thought to 'cure' a number of social problems (Fine, 2001). There is a growing literature critiquing the idea of social capital, which need not be reviewed here. Suffice to note that the construct says more about the way New Labour perceives economically marginal working-class communities than evidence-led policy (Johnstone and Mooney, 2005). One immediate challenge to the approach which emphasises perceived deficiencies, is derived from evidence concerning the networks, self-help and organisation of many working-class communities (see Hancock, 2001). This points up the flaws in the idea that the 'included' possess qualities that the 'excluded' do not (Young, 1999). Similarly, there is a wealth of criminological literature that shows how communities can be both organised and disorganised and, in different ways, both can contribute to crime, and its control (Bottoms and Wiles, 2002; Hancock, 2001). But, the concern in this section is more modest: the aim is to show how inequality is reconfiguring and becoming more visible in the contemporary period before considering some of its consequences for research on young people, crime and criminalisation.

At the national level, analysis of the 2001 Census showed that 'wealthy achievers' increased from 19 per cent to 25 per cent of the population, while those of 'moderate means' and the 'hard pressed' grew to 37 per cent; 15 per cent and 22 per cent respectively in the period from 1991 (Doward et al., 2003: 7). While there is no simple geographic distribution pattern as far as income inequality is concerned, the large concentrations of poverty in the post-industrial towns and cities like Glasgow, Liverpool and Middlesbrough are thoroughly documented. Regeneration has brought about improvement on some indicators. Since the 1990s in Liverpool, for example, private investment in retail, hotels, offices, call centres and tourism has increased the number of employment opportunities in these sectors, but by the same token, (better) jobs have been lost, especially in manufacturing. While there has been a marked increase in affluence in some post-code areas, entrenched poverty remains (Jones and Wilks-Heeg, 2004). Analysis of *Index of Deprivation* data (despite some methodological problems associated with comparison over time) shows that: 'by and large Merseyside's position was unchanged' between 2000 and 2004, although some areas experienced improvement and others deterioration (Mersey Partnership, 2005: 13). Despite some progress, child poverty remains entrenched (Hirsch, 2004). In contrast, house prices in Liverpool have increased dramatically (22 per cent in 2004), taking average prices (£136,262)[8] well beyond the means of many local families.

The gentrification of urban neighbourhoods has meant that inequalities in income and wealth are increasingly proximate and visible (Hancock, 2001). It is clear that there are a range of exclusionary forces at work in city centre spaces (Coleman, 2004; Raco, 2003). However there are also contradictory processes at play which show evidence of 'inclusionary' dimensions, which sustain and reflect the dominant cultural value placed on consumption (often conspicuous). At the city level, they arise because city centre retail, residential or commercial investment is frequently less forthcoming than city planners would wish (Hobbs et al., 2000) and in this context, 'the type of "culture" promoted is often *popular*, rather than so-called "high" culture' (O'Connor, 1998; in Hobbs et al., 2000: 703). In particular, the further expansion of licensed premises is encouraged by city authorities, although not without some disquiet, despite the high prevalence of bars in many city centre spaces. The response to such congestion is to offer cheap drink and other promotions that effectively encourage excessive alcohol consumption (particularly mid-week). The tension that becomes manifest in this context is reflected in the liberalisation of the licensing regime on one hand, and the concern to more closely regulate anti-social behaviour, disorder and crime on the other. Thus, Liverpool City Council's response to the Licensing Act (2003) states:

> Potential benefits to Liverpool's economy (in terms of business viability and success, increased customer choice and access, increased job opportunities

---

8. http://www.liverpool.gov.uk/The_City/City_suburbs/index.asp

and greater visitor/tourist potential) must however be balanced against any potential disadvantages, such as an increase in anti-social behaviour, noise nuisance and crime. (Liverpool City Council, 2005: para 1.3.1)

Hall and Winlow (2005) emphasise the centrality of the 'nocturnal economy' to young people's social relations in the post-industrial North East. They locate the changing relations between young people against the backdrop of dominant economic and cultural forces under neo-liberalism. The shift from the industrial city to the neo-liberal consumption-led city has fractured working-class social relations that were characterised by mutualism, inter-dependence and a depth of knowledge about the life events of others. In the contemporary context, there is some evidence that young people's inter-personal relationships and friend-ships centre upon individual self-interest and instrumentalism, often concerned with 'going out'. These shifts, it is argued, have profound consequences for social cohesion and criminality (Hall and Winlow 2004; 2005). The picture pre-sented is bleak and research questions remain about whether social relations among young people are capable of resisting the kinds of 'atomising' forces exposed by Hall and Winlow's (2004; 2005) accounts.

Urban regeneration, youth crime and criminalisation: Concluding thoughts

Young (1999) emphasises the significance of 'inclusion' in the dominant culture – which centres individualism, consumerism, competition and success – for understanding crime in the modern period. In this view, 'cultural inclusion' coupled with 'structural exclusion' is crucial for an understanding of discontent and crime in late modernity. Furthermore, as this chapter has shown, 'relative deprivation' is not only persisting but inequalities are becoming more visible and proximate in urban space, as well as in mediated forms. For Young, relative deprivation creates sources of discontent which are liable to generate high crime rates, but relative deprivation needs also to be understood alongside 'mis-recognition', which causes disaffection. Both concepts are crucial for under-standing crime (Young, 2001). The preceding analysis suggests support for Young's criminology (1999: 2001). His analysis, which centres the increasingly precarious nature of life in late modernity, where insecurity abounds, explains the attraction of essentialisms. Space precludes a more detailed discussion, but taken in total, his analysis provides a useful way of making sense of youth crime, intolerance and punishment in the neo-liberal, consumption-led city.

The growing expressions of intolerance towards young people and other mar-ginalised groups are deeply rooted in the social divisions and inequalities which flow from economic restructuring. These conditions replicate, re-work but always sustain the 'cultural injustices' that have been perpetrated against the urban poor since the emergence of the modern city in the nineteenth century. The precarious nature of renewal in cities (despite talking local economies up) suggests a sustained focus on the 'threat' of marginalised groups, especially young people. In this way, we must also place emphasis on the moral communitarianism underpinning urban renewal and crime and disorder reduction policies, underpinned by changing conceptions of the role of the state, as well as failure of classical liberal defences of individual freedoms against these backdrops,[9] rather than simply regard the current clampdown on anti-social behaviour as the product of short-sighted and rather ill-informed political decisions. Although in many respects the evidence in this chapter has suggested that they are that too.

References

Blunkett, D. (2003) *Civil Renewal: A New Agenda: The CSV Edith Kahn Memorial Lecture*, 11 June. http://www.homeoffice.gov.uk/docs2/civilrennewagenda.pdf

Bottoms, A. and Wiles, P. (2002) 'Environmental Criminology', in M. Maguire, R. Morgan, R. Reiner (eds) *The Oxford Handbook of Criminology*. (3rd edn) Oxford: Clarendon Press.

Coleman, R. (2004) *Reclaiming the Streets: Surveillance, Power and Social Order*. Cullompton: Willan Publishing.

Crawford, A. (1997) *The Local Governance of Crime: Appeals to Community and Partnerships*. Oxford: Clarendon.

Crawford, A. (2001) 'Joined-up but Fragmented: Contradiction, Ambiguity and Ambivalence at the Heart of New Labour's "Third Way"', in R. Matthews and J. Pitts (eds) *Crime, Disorder and Community Safety*. London: Routledge.

Donnison, D. (1995) 'Crime and Urban Policy: A Strategic Approach to Crime and Insecurity', in C. Fijnaut, J. Goethals, and L. Walgrave (eds) *Changes in Society: Crime and Criminal Justice in Europe*. The Hague: Kluwer.

Doward, J., Reilly, T. and Graham, M. (2003) 'Census Exposes Unequal Britain', *The Observer*, 23 November (page 7).

Etzioni, A. (1993) *The Spirit of Community*. New York: Crown Publishing.

Etzioni, A. (1997) *The New Golden Rule*. London: Profile Books.

Fine, B. (2001) *Social Capital Versus Social Theory*. London: Routledge.

Fitzpatrick, S., Hastings, A. and Kintrea, K. (1998) *Including Young People in Urban Regeneration* Findings 918. York: Joseph Rowntree Foundation.

Gilling, D. and Barton, A. (1997) 'Crime Prevention and Community Safety: a New Home for Social Policy?', *Critical Social Policy*, 17: 63–83.

Goldson, B. (2003) 'Youth Perspectives', in R. Munck (ed.) *Reinventing the City? Liverpool in Comparative Perspective*. Liverpool: Liverpool University Press.

Hall, S. and Winlow, S. (2004) 'Barbarians and the Gate: Crime and Violence in the Breakdown of the Pseudo-Pacification Process', in J. Ferrell, K. Hayward, W. Morrison and M. Presdee (eds) *Cultural Criminology Unleashed*. London: Glasshouse Press.

Hall, S. and Winlow, S. (2005) 'Anti-Nirvana: Crime, Culture and Instrumentalism in the Age of Insecurity', *Crime, Media, Culture*, 1(1): 31–48.

---

9. See Hancock and Matthews (2001) for a further discussion of the concept of 'toleration' and community safety.

Hancock, L. (2001) *Community, Crime and Disorder: Safety and Regeneration in Urban Neighbourhoods*. Basingstoke: Palgrave.

Hancock, L. (2003) 'Urban Regeneration and Crime Reduction: Contradictions and Dilemmas', in R. Matthews and J. Young (eds) *The New Politics of Crime and Punishment*. Cullompton: Willan Press.

Hancock, L. (2004) 'Criminal Justice, Public Opinion, Fear and Popular Politics', in J. Muncie and D. Wilson (eds) *The Cavendish Student Handbook of Criminal Justice and Criminology*. London: Cavendish.

Hancock, L. and Matthews, R. (2001) 'Crime, Community Safety and Toleration', in R. Matthews and J. Pitts (eds) *Crime, Disorder and Community Safety*. London: Routledge.

Hastings, A. (2003) 'Strategic, Multi-Level Neighbourhood Regeneration: an Outward Looking Approach At Last?', in R. Imrie and M. Raco (eds) *Urban Renaissance? New Labour, Community and Urban Policy*. Bristol: Policy Press.

Haylett, C. (2001) 'Illegitimate Subjects? Abject Whites, Neoliberal Modernisation and Middle-Class Multi-culturalism', *Environment and Planning D: Society and Space*, 19: 351–70.

Haylett, C. (2003) 'Culture, Class and Urban Policy: Re-considering Equality', *Antipode*, 35(1): 55–73.

Her Majesty's Stationery Office (2003) *Anti-Social Behaviour Act*. London: HMSO.

Hirsch, D. (2004) *Strategies Against Poverty: A Shared Roadmap*. York: Joseph Rowntree Foundation.

Hobbs, D., Lister, S., Hadfield, P., Winlow, S., and Hall, S. (2000) 'Receiving Shadows: Governance and Liminality in the Night-Time Economy', *British Journal of Sociology*, 51(4) (December): 701–17.

Home Office (2003a) *White Paper: Respect and Responsibility – Taking A Stand Against Anti-Social Behaviour*, CM 5778. London: The Stationery Office.

Home Office (2003b) *Working Together: Tackling Not Tolerating Anti-Social Behaviour*. London: Home Office.

Hope, T. (2001) 'Community, Crime Prevention in Britain: A Strategic Overview', *Criminal Justice*, (4): 421–39.

Imrie, R. and Raco, M. (2003) 'New Labour and the Turn to Community Regeneration', in R. Imrie and M. Raco (eds) *Urban Renaissance? New Labour, Community and Urban Policy*. Bristol: Policy Press.

Johnstone, Charlie and Mooney, G. (2005) 'Locales of "Disorder" and "Disorganisation"? Exploring New Labour's Approach to Council Estates, Paper presented to the Securing the Urban Renaissance: Policing, Community and Disorder Conference, Glasgow, June.

Johnstone, Craig (2004) 'Crime, Disorder and the Urban Renaissance', in C. Johnstone and M. Whitehead (eds) *New Horizons in British Urban Policy*. Aldershot: Ashgate.

Jones, P. and Wilks-Heeg, S. (2004) 'Capitalising Culture: Liverpool 2008', *Local Economy* 19(4): 341–60.

Lees, L. (2003) 'Visions of "Urban Renaissance": the Urban Task Force Report and the Urban White Paper', in R. Imrie and M. Raco (eds) *Urban Renaissance? New Labour, Community and Urban Policy*. Bristol: Policy Press.

Liverpool City Council (2005) *Licensing Policy Statement*. Liverpool: Liverpool City Council.

Matthews, R. (1992) 'Replacing Broken Windows: Crime, Incivilities and Urban Change' in R. Matthews and J. Young (eds) *Issues in Realist Criminology*. London: Sage.

Matthews, R. (2003) 'Enforcing Respect and Reducing Responsibility: a Response to the White Paper on Anti-Social Behaviour', *Community Safety Journal*, 2(4): 5–8.

Mersey Partnership (2005) *Merseyside Economic Review 2005*. Summary, http://merseyside.org.uk/

Mooney, G. (2004) 'Cultural Policy and Urban Transformation? Critical Reflections on Glasgow, European City of Culture 1990' *Local Economy,* 19(4): 327–40.

Morrison, Z. (2003) 'Cultural Justice and Addressing "Social Exclusion": a Case Study of a Single Regeneration Budget project in Blackbird Leys, Oxford', in R. Imrie and M. Raco (Eds) *Urban Renaissance? New Labour, Community and Urban Policy*. Bristol: Policy Press.

Munck, R. (ed.) (2003) *Reinventing the City? Liverpool in Comparative Perspective*. Liverpool: Liverpool University Press.

Raco, M. (2003) 'Remaking Place and Securitising Space: Urban Regeneration and the Strategies, Tactics and Practices of Policing in the UK', *Urban Studies,* 40(9): 1869–87.

Renewal.net (no date) Case Study 'Young Voices in Regeneration', http://renewal.net/

Rice, J., Bather, H., Slack, A., McHarron, S. and Slack, C. (2005) 'Section 30 Scandal Exposed', *Nerve* Issue 6. http://catalystmedia.org.uk/issues/nerve6/section30.htm

Social Exclusion Unit (SEU) (2001) *A New Commitment to Neighbourhood Renewal: A National Strategy Action Plan*. http://www.cabinet-office.gov.uk?seu/2001/Action%20Plan/contents.htm

Stephen, D. E. and Squires, P. (2003) *Community Safety, Enforcement and Anti-Social Behaviour Contracts: An Evaluation of the Work of the Community Safety Team in the East Brighton 'New Deal for Communities' Area*. Brighton: University of Brighton, Health and Social Policy Research Centre.

Wilson, J. Q. and Kelling, G. L. (1982) 'Broken Windows: The Police and Neighborhood Safety', *Atlantic Monthly* 249(3): 29–38.

Wood, M. (2004) *Perceptions and Experience of Anti-Social Behaviour: Findings from the 2003/2004 British Crime Survey*. London: Home Office.

Worpole, K. (2003) *No Particular Place to Go? Children, Young People and Public Space*. http://www.groundwork.org.uk/what/publications/youth.htm

Young, J. (1999) *The Exclusive Society*. London: Sage.

Young, J. (2001) 'Identity, Community and Social Exclusion', in R. Matthews and J. Pitts (eds) *Crime, Disorder and Community Safety: A New Agenda*. London: Routledge.

Work and Social Order: The 'New Deal' for the Young Unemployed

Phil Mizen

Introduction

It is certainly the case that successive New Labour governments have set about the problems of youth with considerable vigour. An unusually candid acceptance of the severity of the divisions that have opened up between young and old, and between different social categories of young people, combined with the acknowledgement that (previous) government policy served to entrench many of the problems now facing the young, has sometimes been matched by genuinely innovative ways of thinking. Whether manifest in problems of independent living, family disintegration, sexual health, drug use, school drop-out or rough sleeping, New Labour has seemingly taken the unprecedented step of moving outside of the government's conventional concern with the problem *of* youth, to think the 'unthinkable' and respond to the problems experienced *by* young people through rational, 'joined-up solutions' (Coles, 2000).

A key example of this has been the New Deal for Young People (NDYP). Promoted as a radical innovation for addressing long-term youth unemployment, the programme is an exemplar of New Labour's fundamental thinking on how best to respond to many of the problems of youth. The underpinning claim is that modern techniques of government are capable of reconciling the contradictions between a market-led strategy aimed at delivering continuing economic growth and wider considerations of social justice for unemployed young workers. By significantly increasing the resources prioritised for education and training, New Labour is convinced that returns to the economy can be maximised as employers respond positively to an increase in the supply of knowledgeable, skilful and productive young workers. At the same time, the government is equally convinced that public investment in education and training can further deliver concrete benefits to both young workers and their communities. By encouraging – compelling even – participation in programmes like NDYP, not only is New Labour confident that it can overcome the root causes of young people's 'social exclusion' by effecting their swift integration back into work; it is equally adamant that the same will serve to combat anti-social behaviour, disorder and crime. First and foremost a 'welfare to work' measure, NDYP is nevertheless also actively promoted as being capable of removing one of the key contemporary 'threats' to social cohesion; the presence of large numbers of working-class young people with no money and little to do.

Whether the claim that the NDYP will be able to to provide young people with sustained and meaningful alternatives to the destructiveness of long-term unemployment is justified or not, is the central concern of this chapter. In the next section, fuller attention is given to NDYP's detail, structure and operation and this is then followed by a more systematic examination of the underlying principles informing both NDYP and its supporting architecture. Particular emphasis is given to the idea of the 'social investment state' and its belief in a publicly-funded programme of investment in education and training as capable of delivering the government's twin objectives of economic growth and high levels of youth employment. Drawing upon the considerable amount of data already available on the programme, this is then followed by a critical evaluation of the performance of NDYP to date. The argument developed here is that the practical value of NDYP is significantly less positive than is often claimed and that, when stripped down to its essential details, NDYP's impact on the employment prospects of the young unemployed is both limited and contingent upon encouraging low-skilled, low-wage and insecure forms of work. This theme of NDYP's costs is further brought to the fore in the chapter's final sections. Here it is argued that the real significance of NDYP and its supporting structures lies not in the practical improvements it extends to the young unemployed, but in its role in eroding the rights and resources that Labour governments have traditionally extended to marginal and unemployed young workers.

Another New Deal for the young unemployed

It is easy to forget the significance of NDYP. Taking centre-stage in the programme for 'national renewal' upon which New Labour fought and won the 1997 General Election, NDYP was situated alongside four other key election pledges by committing a Labour government to: 'get 250,000 young unemployed off benefit and into work' (Labour Party, 1997: 5). A 'flagship' policy of the first New Labour government that rapidly became its biggest labour market programme, NDYP has provided the core of a more extensive programme of 'welfare to work' which subsequently generated eight other 'new deal' sister programmes. Funded initially by a £2.8 billion 'windfall' tax on the profits of the privatised utilities, NDYP apparently comprised a measure of redistributive justice, by redirecting relatively substantial capital towards some of the most disadvantaged groups of working-class youth.

Additional resources are not the only thing 'new' about the programme. Aimed at young workers unemployed for six months or longer, NDYP provides participants with enhanced job search and preparation skills, combined with opportunities for work experience and/or education. Often referred to in terms of an 'active labour market policy', a key aim of the programme is to keep young people attached to the labour market in order to prevent them from drifting into periods of sustained economic inactivity and 'benefits dependency' (Treasury, 2002).

Initially planned to run for four years, NDYP has since emerged as a longer-term feature of New Labour's plans for the young working class. It begins with a 'Gateway' period lasting for up to four months, in which participants are given intensive counselling and support through 'personal advisors' who assess 'job readiness' and assist with the search for work. In reality, much of this initial activity is directed towards matching unemployed young workers to existing job vacancies in the open labour market, since the government's conviction is that much youth unemployment stems from the failure of young people to take up existing work opportunities. For those failing to get jobs during the 'Gateway' phase, or who are not deemed 'job ready', the next move is to one of four 'New Deal Options' lasting in most cases for up to six months: a subsidised job with a private or public sector employer for which the employer receives a £60 per week subsidy; a place on the newly-created Environmental Task Force (ETF) or with a participating voluntary sector organisation, for which the trainee is paid their benefit plus a small additional weekly payment; or study on an education or training course leading to a qualification up to NVQ Level 2 (Perkins-Cohen, 2002). As the government has repeatedly reiterated, there is no 'fifth option' of remaining unemployed. For young people out of work and claiming benefits for six months or more, NDYP is *de facto* a compulsory programme.

New Deal squares the circle?

For all its claims of 'newness' and innovation, NDYP is actually located within a well-established Labour tradition stressing the importance of education, training and employment to the young working class. Whether expressed in terms of economic regeneration and jobs, or tackling inequality and promoting opportunity, NDYP is part of a long heritage in which successive Labour governments have pledged reform of education and training as one of the principal means of meeting working-class young people's need for work. The pledge to use education and training measures like NDYP in this way is thus, at one level, a restatement of familiar intentions. New Labour's commitment to combine 'a skilled and educated workforce with investment in the latest technological innovations, as the route to higher wages and employment' (Labour Party, 1997: 11), for instance, echoes the sentiments of Harold Wilson's Labour governments of the 1960s whereby 'new schools and universities open to all would produce the white-coated technicians capable of fusing the white heat of scientific revolution with rapid social advance' (Ainley, 1988: 66).

NDYP does not represent a simple restatement of past positions, however. In fact, the difference between New Labour's approach to the problems confronting the young working class, and those of previous Labour governments is, in many respects, marked. For all the familiar emphasis on education and training as a basis for social justice, NDYP actually represents a fundamental shift in how the government seeks to deal with the young working class. Gone is the commitment to education and training as an explicit strategy to counter class-based inequalities and the unequal and exploitative consequences of free market forces. Instead New Labour's primary approach to the young working class has been redefined within the much narrower, pragmatic and instrumental imperatives of the 'Third Way' 'social investment state' (Giddens, 1998: 117).

Described elsewhere as a strategy of 'progressive competitiveness' (Coates, 2000), New Labour governments have sought to use increased public investment in education and training as a complement to the free market. Direct economic intervention to stimulate demand for youth labour, or regulate the types of work being created by the free market, is now explicitly rejected (Martell and Driver, 1998). Instead, investment in the supply qualities of (young) labour is conceptualised as one of the keys to economic success, because '[g]rowth is centrally driven by the accumulation or stock of human capital, which also, through the embodiment of technical knowledge, provides the basis for innovation' (Treasury, 2002: 2). By investing in youth labour, therefore, the belief is that governments can foster the development of 'human capital' necessary to sustain economic growth and full employment. In a supposedly globalised economy, the quality of a nation's 'human capital' is not only seen as crucial to its ability to succeed in securing additional inward capital flows necessary for new businesses and jobs but, as one of the few resources still nationally anchored, the quality of the skills and qualifications possessed by the labour force remains amenable to a degree of direct government control. By using a substantial injection of public funds to directly enhance the quality of youth labour entering the labour market – the skills, qualifications, attitudes and motivations possessed by young workers – New Labour is convinced that the 'social investment state' can provide the economy with a much-needed critical edge in an increasingly competitive world: 'we are talking about investing in human capital in an age of knowledge ... we will have to unlock the potential of every young person' (DfEE, 1997: 3).

Furthermore, described by Crouch (1997) as the latest 'philosopher's stone', education and training are also seen to be capable of squaring the circle of market-led growth combined with greater social justice: 'knowledge and skills are seen as presenting opportunities: individuals who acquire advanced levels of education are more likely to secure prosperous futures ...' (ibid.: 367). The role of education and training thus goes beyond economic imperatives and becomes the principal means of reducing the risk of the young working class from being exposed to what New Labour terms 'social exclusion'; that web of seemingly inter-connected problems such as unemployment, poverty, drug use, *anti-social behaviour, disorder* and *crime* (Levitas, 1998). On the one hand, participation in education and training programmes is held to bring tangible benefits to unemployed young workers through more skills and qualifications, the potential for stable or higher earnings and, ultimately, enhanced life-time security of employment. On the other hand, Ministers are equally clear that measures like NDYP bring 'rewards' via their implicit social control and anti-youth crime functions (Coles, 2000). Not only do they bring the potential for a reduction in the costs of policing communities stressed by disintegrating social cohesion, but by placing more and more young people into education or training programmes for longer and longer periods of time, the potential threat of crime and social disorder can be ameliorated and possibly removed. Ministers have repeatedly claimed: 'the best way of cutting crime is to give people jobs' (Jack Straw, quoted in Levitas, 1998: 123); or as Tony Blair might say, programmes like NDYP are a central plank of New Labour's determination to get 'tough on the causes of crime'.

Thus, with the 'social investment' state of the Third Way comes New Labour's belief that the pursuit of economic growth and market competitiveness can be reconciled with community renewal, social justice *and* crime and disorder reduction strategies. On the one hand, giving over significant amounts of additional public expenditure to education and training can aid competitiveness and economic growth as employers eagerly take advantage of the increasingly well-educated, productive and committed young workers entering the labour market. On the other hand, 'communities' can benefit from a much-lessened risk of young people experiencing 'social exclusion' and the damaging consequences that invariably follow. To put it another way, newly qualified and skilled young people are not only better placed to take advantage of the more limited opportunities for work consequent upon a leaner and more 'efficient' free market economy, but communities are also relieved of some of the threats to social order brought about by large numbers of working-class youths with too much time on their hands and too little to do.

Assessing the New Deal

Assessing the capacity of NDYP to live up to these claims is certainly helped by the considerable amounts of data on the programme's performance. One of the ways in which New Labour neutralised the considerable scepticism and critique that had developed in respect of government programmes for the young unemployed during the 1980s and 1990s, was to ensure that: 'monitoring and evaluation were built into the design of New Deal programmes ... based on a comprehensive programme of qualitative and quantitative research, a New Deal Evaluation Service Database and internal Employment Service analysis of management data' (Hasluck, 2001: 231). Much of this is readily available through regular statistical bulletins, updates and research reports placed on the

Department for Work and Pension's website (2004; 2005). Statistics can also be found in summary on the website of the Trades Unions Congress (2005).

What this data tells us is that by December 2004, approximately 1.25 million young people had started on the programme, of whom approximately three quarters were young men (Department for Work and Pensions, 2004). At December 2004, just over 70,000 young people were actually on NDYP, of which approximately two-thirds were in the 'Gateway' phase, one-fifth were participating in an 'Option' and the remainder were subject to the programme's 'Follow-Through' phase of support for programme leavers. From the same data, it seems that NDYP has replicated wider divisions within the labour market, as young women have found themselves concentrated in the voluntary sector option and ethnic minority young people are significantly under-represented on the employment option. Young unemployed black males, in particular, are much less likely to come into contact with employers through the New Deal, in effect significantly reducing their employment chances and increasing their likelihood of dropping-out. This was certainly the experience of previous government programmes for unemployed young people and in this respect, NDYP would seem to have failed to break the cycle of discrimination and neglect experienced by black young people participating on government work experience and training programmes since the late 1970s (Mizen, 2003b).

Data relating to the experiences of participating young people on the programme conveys additional interesting messages. Not dissimilar to earlier training and employment initiatives, generally high levels of satisfaction among participants relate primarily to the otherwise unavailable direct access that their programmes give them to employers. Trainees on the now-defunct Youth Training Scheme (YTS), for instance, demonstrated a similarly instrumental orientation (Mizen, 1995). Participants in NDYP also show little willingness to opt-in to the programme's ethos of work-focused preparation and training, and many also remain sceptical of its capacity to deliver its pledge to create opportunities for high quality training. These sentiments are perhaps to be expected given that early programme evaluations noted that poor training was widespread (McIlroy, 2000). In 2002 the Adult Learning Inspectorate, the organisation that oversees all publicly-funded work-based training for people aged over 16 in England, further reported that the majority of NDYP's on-the-job-training opportunities were inadequate (Adult Learning Inspectorate, 2002) and subsequent reports point only to modest improvements.

The same Adult Learning Inspectorate report also pointed to endemic early leaving on NDYP's work-based training programmes; another sign of the programme's continuing failure. Other performance data confirms that one in ten participants opt to leave before their first interview with an advisor, and one in seven drop-out before completing their New Deal Option (Ritchie, 2000). Participant's reasons for early leaving show that NDYP continues to be equated with the remedial functions associated with previous government programmes and that a deeply-entrenched culture of hostility and mistrust towards such measures endures. Many NDYP participants continue to display the same mixture of indifference, suspicion and resistance that was evident within earlier programmes (Mizen, 1995). Some enrolment on NDYP is more readily conceptualised as having instrumental (to defend benefit entitlements) rather than intrinsic value. The high rates of early leaving NDYP are all the more significant given the considerable sanctions that can be applied to those failing to complete New Deal without good cause (see below). In the first quarter of 2002, for instance, 3,000 young people on a NDYP 'Option' were sanctioned for non-attendance (including early leaving) approximately one in eight of the total (Kemp, 2005).

NDYP has proved similarly inadequate in leading the young unemployed into jobs. As early as 1999, major inroads had already been made into cutting the number of young people unemployed for 12 months or longer, and the number of 18–24-year-olds experiencing unemployment for over six months had been halved (Riley and Young, 1999). The government's general election target of getting 250,000 long-term unemployed young people off benefits and into work was met by 2001 and, by December 2004, around 450,000 young people had left New Deal to take up an unsubsidised job (Department for Work and Pensions, 2004). However, such 'headline grabbing' has to be interpreted alongside the fact that only 38 per cent of NDYP leavers enter work; and this is in the context of sustained and substantial reductions to general unemployment. At its peak, during the 'Lawson boom' of the late 1980s, for example, two-thirds of young people left the much-maligned YTS to enter work (Mizen, 1995). While many young people joining NDYP are dealing with especially problematic circumstances, Peck (2001: 13) nevertheless reminds us that the programme has, 'join[ed] a long list of moderately effective programme yielding modest outcomes'.

The quality of the jobs entered by leavers also tends to cluster around the expanding low-skilled and insecure sections of the labour market (Blundell et al., 2003). Consequently, of those finding work among the first 700,000 young people to go through NDYP, only three-quarters were still in employment three months later; the benchmark against which New Deal's capacity to lead to 'sustained' employment is measured (Trade Union Congress, 2002a). Far from providing a 'gateway' into the types of jobs necessary if young people are to secure stable and sustainable futures, for many, NDYP has created what amounts to a 'revolving door' of insecure and temporary employment, followed by a further period of unemployment before returning to another spell on a programme.

One of the great paradoxes of government programmes for the young unemployed is that they can exacerbate the very problems they are supposed to solve (Mizen, 2003b). By providing employers with a source of heavily subsidised labour, government programmes can set up perverse incentives by encouraging employers to cease employing unsubsidised labour, sack existing workers in favour of subsidised workers, or use subsidised labour when that young person would have been employed in any respect. For these reasons, considerable effort has been put into estimating how many of the total number leaving NDYP for employment would have failed to find jobs without participation on the programme; in effect, how many *additional* jobs the programme has created. The conclusions are not especially flattering. Evaluation of its first two years estimated that the 550,000 young people who had been through NDYP had brought about a net reduction in unemployment of only 30,000 (Riley and Young, 1999). A report from the government's financial watchdog, the National Audit Office, also concluded that the net job creation effects of the programme during the first two years of existence was somewhere between 8,000 to 20,000 new jobs (National Audit Office, 2002). And a more recent estimation suggested that only 17,000 new jobs were created among the 375,000 leaving the programme for work up to 2002 (Blundell et al., 2003).

Behind the New Deal

With such an inauspicious record, it is worth asking why NDYP continues to enjoy so much prominence. Certainly there are progressive elements: a redistribution (at least to begin with) of resources from the shareholders of privatised utilities to an identifiable group of young people often experiencing acute difficulties; real and important increases in funding; the generation of some genuinely creative measures; a more nuanced way of responding to the needs of the young unemployed; and, from the perspectives of young unemployed, some acknowledgement that NDYP offers them something to do within a context of limited (legitimate) alternatives. But such factors do not themselves account for the programme's primary significance. Indeed, there are good reasons to believe that the key contribution of NDYP derives not from its practical value in finding sustainable and decent forms of employment for the young unemployed; nor, by implication, in its worth as a means of crime and disorder reduction. On the contrary, the importance of NDYP is to be found in its embodiment of New Labour's extensive and systematic *withdrawal* of sources of public support for the young working class. It is to the very origins of the worklessness, insecurity and marginalisation that blight the lives of many working-class young people, the free market, that NDYP turns, in its quest for 'solutions' to the problems of long-term unemployment (Mizen, 2003b).

As Coates (2000) has argued, New Labour's strategy of 'progressive competitiveness' actually involves the steady erosion of working-class people's rights to and claims over previously available sources of public support. This process of disengagement predated NDYP by some time and, well before New Labour's first general election victory in 1997, the Party had retreated from more substantive commitments to supporting the welfare of the young working class. Sound reasons for opposing compulsion in government programmes for the unemployed were rejected in favour of support for the Conservative's punitive regime (Mizen, 2003a), despite consistent evidence that working-class young people need little encouragement to participate in programmes of obvious quality

(Wolfe, 2003). A similarly well-reasoned policy of reinstating the unemployment benefits for school leavers removed by Conservative administrations in the 1980s was also abandoned, again despite strong evidence of the effectiveness of these benefits in getting resources to those young people most in need (Andrews and Jacobs, 1990). More significantly perhaps, Labour's key industrial policy of developing skills training provision through a compulsory training levy on employers was dropped in favour of the Conservative's voluntaristic approach. This was again despite the fact that previous attempts to let the free market 'decide' in this way had actually accelerated the decline of Britain's skills training infrastructure (Peck, 1991). Possibly most significant of all, Labour's historic commitment to direct government intervention in the economy to generate full employment comprising decent jobs for all school leavers, was also rejected in favour of the pursuit of 'full employability'.

This quest for 'employability' – of which NDYP is clearly a key part – is revealing since it indicates the extent of New Labour's withdrawal from direct support for the needs of the young. Through replacing the commitment to full employment with 'full employability', the historic link between Labour governments and the direct management of market forces in order to guarantee full employment has been jettisoned. In its place, New Labour has effectively accepted that young people's aspirations for work must be confined within what the free market has to offer, so that 'insecurity has ceased to be presented as a structural feature of the labour market. Rather job security had become something that individuals achieve ... a question of individual deficiency' (Levitas, 1998: 120). In doing so, the idea of 'employability' promotes young people's individual adaptations as the solution to structural insecurity and the austerity of market forces. Furthermore, in resorting to 'employability', schemes like NDYP continue to reduce more general questions of working-class young people's lack of jobs to the same neo-liberal orthodoxy to emerge during the late 1970s. Clearly apparent under Margaret Thatcher's governments, the young unemployed were redefined as 'deficient' workers and roundly blamed for their own plight. Rather than seeing mass youth unemployment as a consequence of industrial decline, structural adjustment, lack of investment and the primacy of profits over jobs, what was generated was a taken-for-granted philosophy in which the young, '... by their very nature, [are] lacking in appropriate skills, qualities, habits and attitudes' (Davies, 1986: 54) necessary for a successful working life.

NDYP also endorses a further aspect of neo-liberal orthodoxy that stresses 'solutions' to youth unemployment through low wages. While New Labour has publicly set its face against low pay, the logic of NDYP and its supporting architecture is very different. By using the programme to time-limit claims for unemployment benefit to six months, and by requiring work experience or training in exchange for benefits, not only does New Labour coerce the young unemployed to do (in the words of one of NDYP's principal architects) 'something rather than nothing', it also compels their restoration to the 'universe of employable people' (Layard, 1997: 336). This is predicated upon a pathological construction that 'unemployment benefits are a subsidy to idleness, and it should not be surprising that they lead to an increase in idleness ... [and because] unemployed people often adjust to unemployment as a different lifestyle' (ibid.: 334–5). By compulsorily reintegrating the young back into work, not only are the long-term unemployed held to reacquire the work habits that they have (self?) evidently lost, but the stock of people available in the labour market is increased, thus intensifying competition for jobs.

> Employers will [thus] find there are more employable people in the labour market and that they can more easily fill their vacancies. This increases downwards pressure on wages, making possible a higher level of employment at the same level of inflationary pressure. (Layard, 1997: 337)

NDYP's role in institutionalising low-paid work is, however, effaced within the political discourse accompanying the programme. This reduces the problem of young people's 'social exclusion' to issues of direct entry into paid employment, so that questions of the character of that work – low pay, exploitation, discrimination, or the suitability of employment to an individual's needs – are effectively sidelined (Levitas, 1998). Consequently, NDYP's function in actually accelerating the erosion of working-class young people's purchase on the labour market is generally ignored. Employers have little incentive, for instance, to create secure, well-paid and decent jobs when they can benefit from New Deal's subsidies equivalent to 40–50 per cent of a participant's wage cost (Blundell et al., 2003); or when they can use the programme to obtain up to six months free labour without any obligation to provide subsequent permanent employment. Using public subsidies to encourage the take-up of low-paid jobs clearly helps New Labour to restate a work ethic among the young working class, much dented by over two decades of mass unemployment. It may also further divert otherwise unoccupied young people from anti-social behaviour, disorder and crime. But in the final analysis, such practices serve to actively reconstitute the young unemployed into a source of cheap and flexible labour, while simultaneously deepening structural divisions and widening social and economic polarisation (Byrne, 1999).

Of course, Ministers tend to rebut such critique by pointing to the National Minimum Wage (NMW) as one of their principal responses against low pay. In its first three years, the NMW did benefit around 105,000 18–21-year-olds (Low Pay Commission, 2001), but such figures reveal the depth of the problem facing young people searching for decent work. In any case, it is doubtful whether the NMW is adequate to the task at hand. The lower rates of minimum pay for 18–21-year-olds (£4.25 per hour, from October 2005) and, five years after its introduction, for school leavers (£3 per hour), are significantly below the adult rate (£5.05 per hour); itself calculated mainly according to the needs of employers (Edwards, 1998). Such low minimum rates are of little practical value in reversing the severely depressed rates of pay that working-class young people now all too often encounter in their search for work. Pay levels for under-18s fell from 42 to 25 per cent of the adult rate between 1979 and 1994, and for 18–20-years-olds the corresponding fall was from 61 to 49 per cent. As Novak (1998: 19) has noted: 'the relative fortunes of young workers on low wages have deteriorated markedly since the late 1970s, from being almost 70 per cent of the overall median earnings to just over half ... The relative pay of this group deteriorated faster than low-paid workers overall.'

That NDYP now offers the *only* way to secure a legitimate income for young people unemployed for six months or longer is testament to the scale of New Labour's disengagement from the young working class through the creation of the toughest unemployment benefits regime the UK has ever seen. A young unemployed person's non-compliance with a direction from the benefit authorities to join NDYP can, in some cases, lead to the denial of benefits for up to six months (Mizen, 2003b). This is despite the Employment Service's own research revealing that benefit sanctions fall disproportionately on those young people whose only misdemeanour is genuine doubts over NDYP's suitability to their specific needs, ignorance or a simple failure of communication (Britton, 2002; Trade Union Congress, 2002b). It is thus something of a vicious irony that those working-class young people experiencing the most acute forms of 'social exclusion' – drug and alcohol users, the homeless, those in poor health or with a criminal record – are most likely to experience benefit penalties for non-compliance.

Conclusion

Without the willingness of government to exercise direct regulation over employers and the labour market, the prospects of NDYP getting young people off the dole and into work – and, by doing, offering reasonable prospects for reducing youth crime – will most likely remain doubtful. At best, NDYP will continue to provide young people with an alternative to unemployment by leading them into low quality training and work experience placements, prior to their ultimate entry into those sections of the labour market in which low-skilled, poorly-paid work and short-term working have become endemic. At worst, NDYP may actually serve to consolidate the problems experienced by many young people, by deepening the already considerable scepticism surrounding government employment and training programmes, while further blaming the young unemployed for their own 'deficiencies'. In either case, the prospects for the foreseeable future are that NDYP and its supporting framework will further lock many working-class young people into increasingly informal and precarious modes of existence.

Beyond this, NDYP symbolises a more fundamental transformation in the relationship between government, state agencies and working-class young people. Rather than securing employment for young people through active regulation of market forces, NDYP now 'guarantees' an unemployed young person a place on a work experience or training programme that they are effectively coerced into accepting. Instead of committing government to distributing the benefits of economic growth to advantage all young people, New Labour – through NDYP – has substituted traditional (Labour) commitments to full employment for young people with the concept of 'full employability'. In other words, through NDYP and its supporting architecture, New Labour has disengaged from the provision of public investment that is essential if lasting and mean-ingful benefits for the young working class are to be realised and sustained. Indeed, it is in its relationship to this process of disengagement that the broader significance of New Labour's commitment to the 'social investment state', and to the reform of education and training for working-class young people, resides. By holding out the offer of more 'relevant' education and/or training and work experience delivering increasingly 'vocational' outcomes, New Labour seeks a degree of political protection from the consequences of the market-led policies that it has self-consciously set in motion, including the risk of anti-social behaviour, disorder and crime. It is through the education and/or training programmes of the 'social investment state', that government seeks both to secure social order and extend a modicum of relief to working-class young people and their parents growing increasingly anxious about what the future has to hold.

References

Adult Learning Inspectorate (2002) *Annual Report of the Chief Inspector 2001–02*. Coventry: Adult Learning Inspectorate.

Ainley, Pat (1988) *From School to YTS*. Milton Keynes: Open University Press.

Andrews, K. and Jacobs, J. (1990) *Punishing the Poor*. London: Macmillan.

Blundell, R., Reed, H., Van Reenan, J. and Shephard, A. (2003) 'The Impact of the New Deal for Young People on the Labour Market: A Four Year Assessment', in R. Dickens, P. Gregg and J. Wadsworth (eds) *The Labour Market Under New Labour: The State of Working Britain*. Basingstoke: Palgrave.

Britton, L. (2002) 'Sanctions and the Hard to Help', *Working Brief*, 130, London: Centre for Economic and Social Inclusion.

Byrne, David (1999) *Social Exclusion*. Milton Keynes: Open University Press.

Coates, David (2000) *Models of Capitalism: Growth and Stagnation in the Modern Era*. Cambridge: Polity Press.

Coles, Bob (2000) *Joined-up Youth Research, Policy and Practice*. Leicester: Youth Work Press.

Crouch, Colin (1997) 'Skills-Based Full Employment: the Latest Philosopher's Stone', *British Journal of Industrial Relations*, 35(3): 367–91.

Davies, Bernard (1986) *Threatening Youth: Towards a National Youth Policy*. Milton Keynes: Open University Press.

Department for Work and Pensions (2004) *New Deal for Young People and Long-Term Unemployed People aged 25+: Statistics to December 2004*. London: Department for Work and Pensions, www.dss.gov.uk/asd/ndyp.asp – accessed June 2005.

Department for Work and Pensions (2005) *New Deal for Young People and Long-Term Unemployed People 25+: Statistics to March 2005*. London: Department for Work and Pension, www.dss.gov.uk/asd/ndyp.asp – accessed June 2005.

(DfEE) Department for Education and Employment (1997) *Excellence in Schools.* Cm 3681. London: Stationery Office.

Edwards, Paul (1998) 'Minimum Pay', *European Industrial Relations Observatory On-line,* eiroline, www.eiro.eurofound.ie/1998/07/Feature/UK9807135F.html

Furlong, Andy and Cartmel, Fred (1997) *Young People and Social Change: individualisation and risk in late modernity*. Buckingham: Open University Press.

Giddens, Anthony (1998) *The Third Way*. Cambridge: Polity Press.

Hasluck, Chris (2001) 'Lessons from the New Deal: Finding Work, Promoting Employability', *New Economy*, 8(4): 230–4.

Kemp, Peter (2005) 'Young People and Unemployment: From Welfare to Workfare?', in M. Barry (ed.) *Youth Policy and Social Inclusion: Critical Debates with Young People*. London: Routledge.

Labour Party (1997) *New Britain: Because Britain Deserves Better*. London: Labour Party.

Layard, Richard (1997) 'Preventing Long-Term Unemployment: An Economic Analysis', in D. Snower and G. de la Dehesa (eds) *Unemployment Policy: Government Options for the Labour Market.* Cambridge: Cambridge University Press.

Levitas, Ruth (1998) *The Inclusive Society? Social Exclusion and New Labour*. Basingstoke: Macmillan.

Low Pay Commission (2001) *The National Minimum Wage: Making a Difference*. Third Report of the Low Pay Commission, Cm 5075. London: Stationery Office.

Martell, Stephen and Driver, Luke (1998) *New Labour: Politics After Thatcherism*. Cambridge: Polity Press.

McIlroy, Richard (2000) 'How is the New Deal for Young People Working?', *European Industrial Relations Observatory On-line*, eiroline, www.eiro.eurofound.i.e./print/2000/02/feature/UK0002155F.html

Mizen, Phil (1995) *Young People, Training and the State: In and Against the Training State*. London: Cassell.

Mizen, Phil (2003a) 'The Best Days of Your Life? Youth, Policy and Blair's New Labour', *Critical Social Policy*, 23(4): 453–76.

Mizen, Phil (2003b) *The Changing State of Youth*. Basingstoke: Palgrave.

National Audit Office (2002) *A New Deal for Young People*. London: The Stationery Office.

Novak, Tony (1998) 'Young People, Class and Poverty', in H. Jones (ed.) *Towards a Classless Society?* London: Routledge.

Peck, Jamie (1991) 'Letting the Market Decide (with public money): Training and Enterprise Councils and the Future of Labour Market Programmes', *Critical Social Policy*, 11(1): 37–54.

Peck, Jamie (2001) 'Job Alert! Spins and Statistics in Welfare to Work Policy', *Benefits*, Jan/Feb, 30: 11–15.

Perkins-Cohen, Jacquie (2002) 'Extending New Deal to all Young People', *Working Brief*, 136, London: Centre for Social and Economic Inclusion.

Riley, R. and Young, G. (1999) *The Macroeconomic Impact of the New Deal for Young People*. London: National Institute for Economic Research, Discussion Paper No. 184.

Ritchie, J. (2000) 'New Deal for Young People: Participant's Perspectives', *Policy Studies*, 24. pp. 301–12.

Trades Union Congress (2002a) *New Deal 18 to 24: Latest Results*. London: Trades Union Congress, Briefing Document, 19 February.

Trades Union Congress (2002b) *New Deal Sanctions*. London: Trades Union Congress.

Trades Union Congress (2005) *New Deal: An Occasional Briefing*. London: Trades Union Congress, No. 92, June, http://www.tuc.org.uk/welfare – accessed June 2005.

Treasury (2002) *The Changing Welfare State: Employment Opportunity for All*. London: H.M. Treasury and Department for Work and Pensions.

Wolfe, Alison (2003) *Does Education Matter?*. London: Penguin.

PART THREE

Future Directions

Critical Anatomy: Towards a Principled Youth Justice

14

Barry Goldson and John Muncie

Introduction

In this final part and concluding chapter, we aim to both distil and develop some of the core themes that run through the book. We reflect upon the contested and dynamic nature of youth justice and argue that, in the final analysis, youth justice systems are relative constructs subject to the varying impulses of policymakers and the means by which the power to 'define' is exercised and applied. By focusing most specifically upon England and Wales, we examine the complexities, contradictions and controversies that characterise contemporary youth justice policy. In keeping with many of the preceding chapters, we argue that the processes of policy formation have tended to negate evidence within a political context in which 'toughness' imperatives eclipse rationality and responsibility. There is little coherence within the broader corpus of policy with regard to children and young people, and there is an uneasy relation, if not distinct fracture, between the correctionalist priorities that typify youth justice policy and the more inclusive and benign rationales that are said to characterise other core dimensions of state policy. From critical reflection we conclude with a prospective vision; by mapping the contours of a principled youth justice informed by international human rights instruments, progressive policy and practice from elsewhere and some of the key messages embedded within research evidence and practice experience.

Youth justice: Thematics, contestation and change

The antecedents of contemporary youth justice in the UK can be traced back to the 'invention' of 'juvenile delinquency' in the early nineteenth century, and the subsequent inception of a specific corpus of legislation, court structures, policies, procedures and practices for the processing of 'young offenders' at the beginning of the twentieth (Hendrick, see Chapter 1 of this volume; Magarey, 1978; Muncie, 2004: 49–82). Throughout this period – from the early nineteenth century to the present – policy reform and practice development have not followed an even linear trajectory. Harris and Webb (1987: 79), for example, have noted that youth justice 'is riddled with paradox, irony, even contradiction ... [it] exists as a function of the child care and criminal justice systems on either side of it, a meeting place of two otherwise separate worlds'. Similarly, Muncie and Hughes (2002: 1) have reflected that: 'youth justice is a history of conflict, contradictions, ambiguity and compromise ... [it] tends to act on an amalgam of rationales, oscillating around and beyond the caring ethos of social services and the neo-liberal legalistic ethos of responsibility and punishment'. The means by which 'two otherwise separate worlds' are reconciled or, to put it another way, the balance that is struck between the 'caring ethos' and the 'ethos of responsibility and punishment', is subject to the vagaries of political imperative and policy contingency. In short, youth justice systems are dynamic and ever-changing sites of contestation and change, the settlements of competing and/or intersecting thematic concepts including: 'welfare'; 'justice'; 'informalism'; 'rights'; 'responsibilities' and 'retribution/punishment' (Goldson, 2004a).

The principle that children and young people should be protected from the full weight of 'adult' criminal justice systems underpins the concept of *welfare* in youth justice. Welfare is a long-established feature of youth justice in many jurisdictions (Muncie, 2002; 2005; Muncie and Goldson, 2006a). In England and Wales, for example, section 44 of the Children and Young Persons Act 1933 provides that: '*every court* in dealing with a child or young person who is brought before it either as an offender or otherwise shall *have regard to* the *welfare* of the child or young person'. Similarly, section 1(1) of the Children Act 1989 states that: 'when a court determines *any question* with respect to [a child] ... the child's *welfare* shall be the court's *paramount consideration'*. Welfare and welfarism, however, have also attracted critique from a variety of sources. Conservative critics have traditionally argued that the primary function of the youth justice system should be to *control* young offenders rather than to *care* for them and, for this reason, welfare-based systems are conceptualised as being too lenient and 'soft on crime'. Conversely, many academic commentators and radical youth justice practitioners have tended to question the legitimacy of imposing wide-ranging criminal justice interventions on children and their families on the basis of 'need', and have challenged individualised notions of 'rehabilitation' and 'treatment'. The same academics and radical practitioners, together with children's human rights advocates and legal professionals, have also argued that wide-ranging discretionary judgements in respect of 'welfare' can serve to undermine the child's *right* to 'justice'.

In contrast to the free-ranging and 'needs'-oriented interventions legitimised by reference to welfare, the concept of procedural *justice* provides that the intensity of formal intervention should be proportionate to the severity/gravity of the offence, rather than the level of perceived 'need'. First, it is claimed that the legal rights of children and young people must be secured and safeguarded through *due legal process*. Second, formal intervention is conceived in terms of 'restrictions of liberty' that must be limited to the minimum necessary, in accordance with principles of *proportionality*.

Moving beyond both welfare and justice-based rationales, *informalism* is underpinned by a range of theoretical perspectives, practical propositions and 'destructuring impulses' (Cohen, 1985) that combine to challenge the legitimacy of formal youth justice intervention *per se*. Informalism shifts the conceptual emphasis by problematising the formal legal and disciplinary apparatus of youth justice, as distinct from individual 'young offenders' (Goldson, 2004b).

Specified *rights* in respect of children and young people within youth justice systems are not only provided, in many jurisdictions, by domestic statute; there are a range of international conventions, standards, treaties and rules that also inform youth justice law, policy and practice (Lansdown and Newell, 1994: 199–225; Monaghan, 2005; Scraton and Haydon, 2002; Unicef, 1998). Particularly notable in this respect are: the 'United Nations Standard Minimum Rules for the Administration of Juvenile Justice' (the Beijing Rules, 1985); the 'United Nations Guidelines for the Prevention of Juvenile Delinquency' (the Riyadh Guidelines, 1990); and the 'United Nations Rules for the Protection of Juveniles Deprived of their Liberty' (the JDL Rules, 1990). Perhaps most important of all is the 'United Nations Convention on the Rights of the Child' (UNCRC, 1989), which sets out principles and detailed standards for the rights of children, for the care of children, for laws, policies and practices which impact on children, and for both formal and informal relationships with children. Just as welfare is tempered by justice, and vice versa, so rights are mitigated by *responsibilities*. The concept of responsibility is most clearly expressed in youth justice with regard to the age of criminal minority, otherwise known as the age of criminal responsibility (Bandalli, 2000). This relates to the age at which a child is held to be fully accountable in criminal law: the point when a child's act of transgression can be formally processed as a 'crime'. The complex question of responsibility is complicated further in many 'modern' youth justice systems, by the fact that parents can also be held to be formally responsible for their children's behaviour (Goldson and Jamieson, 2002; Henricson and Bainham, 2005).

Finally, in terms of underpinning thematics, throughout the history of youth justice *retribution* has remained ever present and the state has always reserved the 'power to punish' (Garland and Young, 1983). Ultimately, retribution and *punishment* are expressed through the practices of institutional containment and child imprisonment (Goldson, see Chapter 10 of this volume).

Youth justice systems then, are complex formations and it is difficult, if at all possible, to conceptualise them with reference to any totalising rationale or even to compartmentalise them into discrete self-standing 'models'. Rather their core components are drawn from a variety of otherwise competing and contradictory thematic sources. In this sense 'welfare' and 'justice', 'rights' and 'responsibilities', 'informalism' and 'punitivism' *co-exist*, however uneasily. Clearly, there are times and places when certain thematic priorities are more ascendant than others. For example, the 1960s and 1970s in England and Wales when 'welfare' was emphasised, and the 1980s and early 1990s when 'justice' imperatives reached a level of primacy. In the final analysis, however, youth justice systems are dynamic, ever-changing, hybridised forms that are temporally and spatially contingent (Goldson, 2004a; Muncie and Hughes, 2002). Policy responses and practice formations within any given system not only change over time (the temporal dimension) and place (the specificities and peculiarities of localism within the same jurisdiction), but youth justice systems also vary from one country or jurisdiction to another (the spatial factor) (Muncie and Goldson, 2006a).

Christie has observed that: 'acts are not, they *become*. So also with crime. Crime does not exist. Crime is created. First there are acts. Then follows a long process of giving meaning to those acts' (cited in Scraton, 2002: 25). By adopting similar reasoning, youth justice might be conceived as a *relative* construct; its particular meaning and specific form being derived from the power of 'definers' at any given time. In this way, governments, formal administrations, judicial bodies and correctional agencies *choose* to give particular 'meanings' to specified 'acts'; to govern identifiable groups of children (White and Cunneen, see Chapter 2; Webster, see Chapter 3, and Gelsthorpe and Sharpe, see Chapter 4 of this volume) and to manage youth justice systems, in accordance with widely divergent ideological imperatives, political calculations, cultural priorities, judicial conceptualisations and operational strategies. Ultimately, similar acts can elicit quite different responses and, as a consequence, children's experiences of 'justice' are differentiated, diverse and disparate across time and space.

Contemporary policy analysis: Complexities, contradictions and controversies

Youth justice policy analysis is a challenging enterprise. As noted, the thematics and rationales that underpin laws, policies, practices and system configurations are contested and subject to constant movement and change. Throughout history, such flux has been heavily influenced, if not determined by, political exigencies and specific sectoral interests (Hendrick, see Chapter 1 of this volume). Indeed, as each of the preceding chapters has revealed, any reading of youth justice policy in the modern period (particularly in England and Wales) has to engage with the complex, contradictory and controversial phenomena that impact upon it, in order to understand its rationalities *and* its irrationalities. In this sense, the tensions within *and* between notions of 'evidenced-based policy' on the one hand, and a consolidating politics of 'toughness' on the other, fracture and distort the broader corpus of policy in relation to children and young people. It follows that the conceptual and institutionalised contours that might otherwise be expected to differentiate policies and practices that 'work' from those that fail, have become decidedly blurred. Inclusionary (welfare) *and* exclusionary (punitive) rationales drift in and out of policy and practice, making paradoxical formations that undermine any notion of coherence and 'joined-up' strategy.

Evidenced-based policy vs. the politics of 'toughness'

New Labour claims that 'modernisation' is being applied across all policy domains. The principal contention is that 'modernised' government (and governance) provide for greater coherence; operationalised and delivered through 'joined-up' approaches under an overarching commitment to 'evidence-based' policy formation. As Smith observes (see Chapter 6 of this volume), the 1999 *Modernising Government* White Paper argued that policy formation must be informed by evidence and routinely subjected to evaluative scrutiny and audit (Cabinet Office, 1999a). It follows, ostensibly at least, that the government has committed itself to 'professional' policy formation whereby 'policy making must be soundly based on evidence of what works' (Cabinet Office, 1999b). This is presented as a progressive and rational shift from 'opinion-based' to 'evidence-based' policy (Davies, cited in Smith – Chapter 6 of this volume); from ideological conviction and/or pure speculation to 'scientific realism' and the 'pragmatic solution' (Muncie, 2002).

The *rhetoric* of 'evidenced-based' policy and 'what works' rationales has claimed significant purchase within criminal justice discourses in general, and youth justice more particularly. On one level it is difficult to quarrel with any tendency that claims to apply evidence – drawn from research and evaluation findings and/or reflexive praxis – to the processes of policy formation and practice development. This presupposes an uncomplicated relational process within which problems (or 'promising approaches') are readily identified and questions are raised, research and evaluation seek understanding and provide 'solutions', the very same 'solutions' are then applied to policy and practice, and progress ensues. At its simplest, it is a mechanistic formulation whereby youth justice policy is no longer 'hampered' by any adherence to competing philosophical principles. Policy-makers are liberated from having to wrestle with thematic complexities – welfare, justice, human rights, responsibility, informalism, retribution and punitivism – rather, they simply need to translate 'hard evidence' into policy by means of technical scientific transfer.

The *reality*, however, is that both the social world and the processes of youth justice policy formation are far more complex. In the final analysis, the positivist assumption that quasi-scientific laws and rational prediction are not only possible and desirable, but also essential, for modernising youth governance is flawed (Newman, 2001; Smith, 2002 and Chapter 6 of this volume). 'Programme evaluation' is never a pure science. Most commissioners of evaluation research might want the 'facts' but facts do not speak for themselves. Moreover, the supposition that intervention 'programmes', in and of themselves, might produce certain readily measurable results or 'outcomes' or, to put it another way, that such results and outcomes can be directly attributed, in the short term, to particular forms of intervention is, at best, tenuous. Indeed, this is a 'way of seeing' more akin to public sector managerialism than it is to serious criminological research. Within the managerialist project, rationalised inputs and outputs are conceptualised in scientific and technical terms and evaluations are 'dominated by notions of productivity, task remits and quantifiable outcomes ... [whereby] evaluation comes to rest solely on indicators of internal system performance' (Muncie, 1999a: 287–9). The unpredictability, variability and intrinsic complexity of the social and the political, however, militate against such crude generality and supposed uniformity. The search for the consistently efficient (and cost-effective) practice tends to mean that the dynamics of local contingencies are often overlooked. 'What works' in some contexts (spatial and temporal) may not 'work' in others. In this regard, Braithwaite has observed that it is 'contextualised usefulness that counts, not decontextualised statistical power' (cited in Smith, 2000: 4), and Smith himself, in respect of his youth justice research in Scotland notes that:

> one of the strongest lessons has been that context matters, that it makes little sense to try and understand a special project without reference to the local environment which sustains it (or fails to do so). (Smith, 2000: 6)

The lives of children and young people involved in youth justice processes are complex and reliance on a single theory of 'reasoning and rehabilitation' or a discrete form of cognitive intervention is unlikely to produce the desired effect in terms of crime prevention (McNeill, see Chapter 9 this volume). Whilst it is possible to view some modes of intervention with a guarded optimism, it is unlikely that any can be readily transferred from one jurisdiction to another, or indeed from one locality to the next in a way that might deliver the same 'results' (Muncie, 2002; Newburn and Sparks, 2004).

There are multiple problems and controversies associated with 'evidenced-based' policy and 'what works' rationales as they are currently formulated within contemporary youth justice. Although some of these problems are signalled above, it is not our intention to engage with the detail here (for a fuller discussion see Bateman – Chapter 5 of this volume; Bottoms, 2005; Pitts, 2001; Smith – Chapter 6 of this volume; Wilcox, 2003). Particularly noteworthy, however, are the processes of selective filtering whereby some 'evidence' is privileged and emphasised, whilst other 'evidence' is 'forgotten' and 'buried'. Such subjective and conditional (as distinct from objective and scientific) processes are seemingly contingent upon the extent to which 'evidence' is politically convenient, rather than methodologically rigorous and/or criminologically significant (Goldson, 2001). There is then – as many of the chapters in this volume reveal – a conspicuous discordance between key messages from research and practice experience (the evidence) on the one hand, and core aspects of 'modern' youth justice policy on the other.

Beyond the specific limitations of 'evidenced-based policy' and 'what works' discourses, the principal, and by far the most controversial, contradiction in respect of 'modern' youth justice policy formation rests at the juncture where rationality collides with political imperative. In this way, Garland detects:

> a new relationship between politicians, the public and penal experts ... in which politicians are more directive, penal experts are less influential, and public opinion becomes a key reference point for evaluating options. Criminal justice is now more vulnerable to shifts of public mood and political reaction ... The populist current in contemporary crime policy is, to some extent, a political posture or tactic, adopted for short term electoral advantage ... Almost inevitably the demand is for more effective penal control ... What this amounts to is a kind of retaliatory law-making, acting out the punitive urges and controlling anxieties of expressive justice. Its chief aims are to assuage popular outrage, reassure the public, and restore 'credibility' of the system, all of which are *political* rather than *penological* concerns. (Garland, 2001: 172–73, emphases added)

Indeed, the 'new relationship' and 'populist current' that have served to re-politicise contemporary youth justice policy in the UK generally, and in England and Wales more particularly, can be traced back to the early 1990s. At this time, and for a variety of reasons that are explored in greater detail elsewhere (see for example, Davis and Bourhill, 1997; Goldson, 1997 and Chapter 10 of this volume; Hay, 1995; Haydon and Scraton, 2000; Muncie, 2004), political, professional and public attention turned to the question of youth crime. Within a context of 'moral panic' (Cohen, 1972), 'respectable fears' (Pearson, 1983) were mobilised, child offenders were systematically 'demonised' and a punitive authoritarian politics began to congeal around youth justice. Furthermore, such processes – originally activated by the Conservative Party in 1993 – have not only endured over time, but have also eclipsed the traditional ideological differences that conventionally distinguished Conservative and Labour youth justice policies. The two main political parties have converged around a 'new correctionalism' (Muncie and Goldson, 2006b) that has been driven by three successive New Labour governments since 1997. Moreover, the politicisation of youth crime and justice has been accompanied by extraordinarily energetic, and consistently 'tough' reform, within which any genuine notion of rational 'evidenced-based' policy formation has been all but subverted by political priorities and 'electoral anxieties' (Pitts, 2000).

The politics of 'toughness' is a prime example of the burgeoning influence of American policy formation in England and Wales. Indeed, in 1998, Jack Straw, Home Secretary at the time, referred to a 'special relationship' and explained that: 'the two governments are learning more from one another all the time, there is now a deep ideological relationship' (cited in Pitts, 2000: 3). Pursuing and popularising 'tough' responses to crime in general, and youth crime in particular, through processes of 'policy transfer', seemingly is but one manifestation of that 'deep ideological relationship' (Jones and Newburn, 2004; Muncie, 2002). Not unlike the US, therefore, actuarialism and intensive modes of early intervention at one end (Smith, see Chapter 7 of this volume), and an increasing reliance on penal custody at the other (Goldson, see Chapter 10 of this volume), mark the polar points of a new correctional continuum in youth justice. Such 'tough' approaches are being pursued in the explicit knowledge that they not only fail to deliver – in terms of crime prevention and community safety – but that they are also inclined to impose substantial costs in terms of social harm:

> Many of the most notorious American innovations, including some that England has embraced ... have been conspicuously unsuccessful and at devastating social and economic cost ... They have ... produced unjustly severe punishments, ballooned the prison population, and, once enacted, proven remarkably hard to repeal ... The current Labour government has knowingly adopted policies known to be ineffective ... because of an arguable belief that its own continuation in office justifies the unnecessary human suffering and waste of public resources that its policies produce ... Until the early 1990s only America developed an hyperbolic law-and-order politics and cruel, simplistic policies that were based more on ideology and politicians' perceived self-interest than on evidence ... And then in the early 1990s, England broke ranks with other Western countries and began to emulate American politics and policies. (Tonry, 2004: vii–ix)

Within this context 'evidence' counts for little.

It doesn't seem to matter that numerous self-report and other studies indicate that offending is a relatively 'normal' part of growing-up for most young people, the majority of whom 'grow out of crime' (Rutherford, 1992). Nor does it count that children and young people are responsible for a relatively small minority of recorded and detected crimes or, perhaps more significantly, that the incidence of youth crime appears to be in decline when measured over the last decade or so. Equally irrelevant, it would seem, is the fact that most offences committed by children and young people are directed against property not people, and that those offences generally regarded as the least serious comprise almost half of all offences for which children and young people are responsible (Bateman, see Chapter 5 of this volume). Within the contemporary politics of youth justice policy, all of this becomes secondary to appeasing public concern and securing electoral gain. Here too, research evidence reveals that contradictions abound:

The public is not as concerned about youth crime as some commentators have suggested ... Nor do people favour locking up young offenders as much as one might infer ... the more detail that respondents had about the person they were 'sentencing', the less likely they were to favour the imposition of a term of custody ... When public opinion is complex and multilayered in this way, there can be no justification for privileging people's unconsidered desire for tougher punishment and ignoring other dimensions to their views. (Hough and Roberts, 2004: x–xi)

The tendency for 'ordinary people' to be less punitive once they are given detail about the 'offender', is particularly salient given all that is known about the adverse social circumstances and multiple disadvantages that afflict the most 'problematic' child offenders (Gelsthorpe and Sharpe – Chapter 4 – Goldson; Chapter 10; Hancock – Chapter 12; Haines and O'Mahony – Chapter 8; McNeill – Chapter 9; White and Cunneen – Chapter 2; Webster – Chapter 3 – all this volume). In other words, if the government placed more emphasis on *informing* public opinion – by explaining the complex problems that many 'young offenders' experience – rather than simply *reacting* to its illiberal impulses, it might provide the basis for a more rational and responsible – not to mention compassionate – youth justice policy. Furthermore, this would allow the government to impose a greater sense of coherence to the broader corpus of policy with regard to children and young people, by closing the schism that currently fractures it (Goldson, 2002).

'Every Child Matters' vs. 'No More Excuses'

On coming to power in 1997, the first New Labour government placed considerable emphasis on the significance of securing social justice for children in general, and on 'tackling' child poverty in particular. This presented, and continues to present, a formidable challenge. In 1979, 10 per cent (1.4 million) of all children in the UK were living in poverty (defined as below 50 per cent of mean income after housing costs), but by 1999/2000 the corresponding figures had risen to 34 per cent or 4.3 million children (Department of Social Security, 2001). The Commission on Social Justice observed that: 'Britain is not a good place in which to be a child' (cited in Piachaud, 2001: 446); and it is well established that the corrosive effects of poverty on children's lives are far-reaching (Goldson et al., 2002; HM Treasury, 2004; Preston, 2005). Accordingly, shortly after being elected, the New Labour government announced its 'historic aim' (Blair, 1999) to reduce child poverty by a quarter by 2004/05, halve it by 2010 and eradicate it completely by 2020. Piachaud has noted that:

The period since 1997 – effectively since 1999 – has seen more rapid government action against child poverty than at any other previous time. New benefits and tax credits have been introduced, existing benefits have been increased and many other measures have been taken to tackle poverty ... Whether the target of reducing child poverty by one-quarter by 2004/05 will be met remains in doubt ... What has, however, been clearly demonstrated is that child poverty is not inevitable or inexorable ... More sobering, the level of child poverty in 2004/05 remains twice what it was in 1979. There is a very long way to go to get back to the 1979 level, let alone abolish child poverty. (2005: 14–15)

In addressing the challenges presented by the 'anti-child poverty' strategy and the wider 'social inclusion' agenda with regard to children and in addition to increasing child benefits and enhancing tax credits, an extraordinarily wide-ranging sequence of cross-government initiatives, policy developments and 'modernising' service re-configurations have been introduced. Such reforms cover the full-range of health, social care, education, training and employment services, alongside regeneration and 'neighbourhood renewal' programmes.

By way of example, during its first term in government, New Labour introduced: Health Action Zones (HAZs) (multi-agency partnerships embracing the National Health Service (NHS), local authorities, the voluntary sector, the business sector and local communities) to tackle inequalities in health; the National Healthy School Standard – a national programme to support schools to develop a healthy school ethos; the Children's Taskforce to implement the programme of NHS and social care reform; and the Children's National Service Framework to draw together health and social services. Turning to social care: 'Quality Protects' was launched by the Department of Health in order to deliver the objectives set out in the *Modernising Social Services* White Paper 1999; the 'Sure Start' programme was implemented as an integral part of a wider initiative to raise the standard of services for children that also includes the 'National Childcare Strategy' and 'Early Years Development and Childcare Partnerships'. With regard to education, training and employment, Education Action Zones (EAZs) were established as part of the 'Excellence in Cities' initiative; the 'Connexions' service was launched and the New Deal for Young People was implemented (Mizen, see Chapter 13 of this volume). Finally, initiatives including the New Deal for Communities; the Neighbourhood Renewal Fund and the Single Regeneration Budget have been targetted at some of the poorest and most disadvantaged communities (Hancock, see Chapter 12 of this volume).

More recently, *Every Child Matters – Change for Children* – the government's programme 'of local and national action through which the whole system transformation of children's services' is being executed – encapsulates an extraordinarily wide-ranging and energetic strategy (HM Government, 2005). The government's stated aim is:

for *every child*, whatever their *background* or their *circumstances*, to have the support they need to:

- Be healthy
- Stay safe

- Enjoy and achieve
- Make a positive contribution
- Achieve economic well-being

... Over the next few years, every local authority will be working with its partners, through children's trusts, to find out *what works best for children and
young people* in its area and act on it ... In March 2005, the first Children's
Commissioner for England was appointed, to give children and young people a
voice in government and in public life. The Commissioner will pay particular
attention to gathering and putting forward the views of the *most vulnerable*
children and young people in society, and will promote their involvement ...
(Department for Education and Skills, 2005: 1, emphases added)

The 'well-being' of children, based upon the five 'Every Child Matters' outcomes,
is defined statutorily by the Children Act 2004 and the government youth expects it be
operationalised by effective 'joined-up' practices in 'safeguarding and promoting
the welfare of children' across the full range of appropriate agencies (HM
Government, 2005: 3). 'Standards' for such practices have been determined (see
for example, Department for Education and Skills and Department of Health,
2004) and their rationales and statutory authority have been expressed through,
and provided by, a multitude of 'Command Papers', 'Policy Statements', volumes
of official 'Guidance', 'Departmental' and 'Select Committee Reports', and Acts of
Parliament (see for example, HM Government, 2005: 140–6).

Such an approach is not beyond critique. George (2002: 104) has observed
that despite substantial financial investment, and the multitude of new
initiatives, 'their coverage is by no means comprehensive' (see also Land, 2002).
Others have argued that many government 'anti-poverty', child 'welfare' and/or
community regeneration initiatives are – at least partly – formulated on the
basis of correcting individual 'deficits', as distinct from addressing profound forms
of social and economic polarisation and inequality by way of redistributive strategies
(Goldson and Jamieson, 2002; Hancock – Chapter 12 of this volume; Piachaud, 2005;
Sutherland et al., 2003; Webster – Chapter 3 of this volume; White and Cunneen –
Chapter 2 of this volume). Mizen (Chapter 13 of this volume) contends that many of
the same initiatives, framed within the context of 'the social investment state',
are conditional and ultimately require (lone) parents (women), and young people
themselves, to enter the labour market taking up insecure and poorly rewarded
jobs. Indeed, 'helping people to help themselves', 'pathways into work' and 'lib-
eration from dependency' are concepts that are deeply embedded within New
Labour's welfare reform ideology.

It is not our purpose here to critically evaluate the underpinning rationales, or
the efficacy, of the government's 'anti-child poverty' and 'Every Child Matters'
programmes, however. Rather to observe that some children appear to 'matter'
more than others, and within the contemporary politics of youth justice, 'child
offenders' are distanced symbolically and institutionally from the inclusionary
thrust. Despite the rhetoric of 'inclusivity', 'well-being', 'safeguarding welfare',

taking particular account of the 'most vulnerable' children and promoting their involvement, the more benign and progressive elements of policy are selectively (as distinct from comprehensively) applied. This raises further complexities, contradictions and controversies and the varying rationales that cut across policy recall the 'victim'–'threat' and the 'deserving'–'undeserving' binaries that are historically embedded within policy responses to (working-class) children and young people in England and Wales (Goldson, 2004c; Hendrick, 1994; 2003; and Chapter 1 of this volume). Indeed, when the constructionist gaze shifts from the child as 'victim' to the child as 'threat', inclusionary welfarism is starkly displaced by exclusionary punitivism:

> We need a new approach to catch, convict, punish and rehabilitate more of them [child offenders] … persistent offending should lead to increased punishment … firmer measures will be taken … our proposals are based on a simple principle: stay straight or you will stay supervised or go inside. (Labour Party, 2001: 33)

Such crude dichotomies are located within a context whereby major strategic policy documents comprise platforms upon which the most senior government, ministers distinguish between 'decent law abiding citizens' and 'offenders' (Blair, 2004a: 5), whilst others pledge that government will 'protect the innocent' and 'pursue the guilty' (Blunkett et al., 2004: 7). The mission 'across the country', it is claimed, is to support 'decent families and communities' in their 'struggle against thugs and vandals who make their lives a misery' (Blair, 2004b: 5).

The 'child in need' construct, which is so evident in respect of the 'Every Child Matters' agenda, is substituted within youth justice discourse by a 'responsibilised' and 'adulterised' 'young offender'. The more benign expressions of welfarism which inform notions of social justice are displaced by the punitive correctionalism integral to New Labour's youth justice (Muncie and Goldson, 2006b). Notions of family support and relief are reframed as questions of parental (ir)responsibility and family failure (Drakeford and McCarthy, 2000; Goldson and Jamieson, 2002). The very fact that troubled and troublesome children are invariably one of the same is disregarded. The wealth of research evidence and practice experience confirming that child 'offenders' are almost exclusively drawn from the most disadvantaged, neglected and damaged families, neighbourhoods and communities is dismissed as an 'excusing' distraction within a context in which there can be 'no more excuses' (Home Office, 1997). New Labour's political calculations are such that being 'tough on crime', and hard on the children who commit it, is crucial, despite all the manifest contradictions. The same calculations, and the actions that flow from them, amount to more than sound-bite posturing and symbolic representation: they have exercised significant material purchase and have given rise to a 'blizzard of initiatives, crackdowns and targets' (Neather, 2004: 11), a 'toughening up [of] every aspect of the criminal justice system' (Blair, 2004b: 6), introduced via innumerable policy statements and ultimately implemented through statute.

Taken together, developments in law and policy following the election of the first New Labour government in 1997, have formulated the most radical overhaul of the youth justice system in England and Wales since the inception of the first juvenile courts in 1908. The pace of legislative development and policy reform has been extraordinary. The Crime and Disorder Act 1998, the Youth Justice and Criminal Evidence Act 1999, the Criminal Justice and Court Services Act 2000, the Powers of the Criminal Courts (Sentencing) Act 2000, the Criminal Justice and Police Act 2001, the Police Reform Act 2002, the Anti-Social Behaviour Act 2003, the Criminal Justice Act 2003, the Cleaner Neighbourhood and Environment Act 2005 and the Serious Organised Crime and Police Act 2005 have each impacted, to a greater or lesser extent, on the youth justice system. Three pieces of legislation are particularly significant.

First, the Crime and Disorder Act 1998 served to completely restructure the youth justice system in England and Wales by establishing a new national and local infrastructure. The establishment of multi-agency 'Youth Offending Teams' signalled a fundamental shift in youth justice policy and practice away from statutory child-welfare structures at both the local and the national level. Locally, the Youth Offending Teams have been organisationally separated from social care and child welfare services and are managed instead under the umbrella of multi-agency 'steering groups' and Chief Executives Departments, where they are tied into corporate 'crime and disorder reduction' and 'community safety' strategies (Hughes and Follett, see Chapter 11 of this volume). Nationally, youth justice services no longer fall within the Department of Health's portfolio – or more latterly within the remit of the Department for Education and Skills which is coordinating the 'Every Child Matters' agenda – rather the Youth Offending Teams are accountable to, and ultimately managed by, the Home Office. In other words, youth justice services in England and Wales have been systematically and institutionally distanced (locally and nationally) from mainstream child welfare services. The Crime and Disorder Act 1998 also introduced a range of new interventionist powers and sentencing disposals including: Anti-Social Behaviour Orders (s.1); Parenting Orders (s.8); Local child curfew schemes (s.14); Reprimands and warnings (ss.65 and 66); Reparation Orders (s.67); Action Plan Orders (s.69); and the Detention and Training Order (s.73). The Act further abolished the long-established principle of *doli incapax* that provided legal safeguards in respect of children aged 10–13 years (Bandalli, 2000).

Second, the Youth Justice and Criminal Evidence Act 1999 introduced a new interventionist sentence, the Referral Order (s.1) for almost all children and young people appearing in court on first conviction, effectively making it a mandatory sentence (Haines, 2000; Haines and O'Mahony – Chapter 8 of this volume; Wonnacott, 1999). This effectively signalled the abandonment of diversionary strategies and the consolidation of early – often quite intensive – modes of (criminalising) intervention (Goldson, 2000).

Third, the Anti-Social Behaviour Act 2003 was implemented following the publication in March 2003 of a White Paper entitled *Respect and Responsibility: Taking a Stand Against Anti-Social Behaviour*. The White Paper (Home Office, 2003: 1–2) set out a starkly authoritarian vision of a 'something for something society' where rights are reserved for the 'responsible [...] decent law abiding majority', whilst the so-called 'out of control minority' face a raft of new punishments and sanctions. Children and young people are especially targeted by the provisions of the legislation (Hughes and Follett – Chapter 11 of this volume; Walsh, 2003). Furthermore, the Anti-Social Behavior Act also made the parents of children regarded as being 'disorderly', 'anti-social' or 'criminally inclined', eligible targets for formal statutory orders (Nacro, 2004).

Inevitably, the consequences of such wide-ranging developments in youth justice law and policy are far-reaching and multi-faceted and it is not practical to engage a comprehensive analysis here. Moreover, we have argued elsewhere that it is difficult to identify any consistent rationale and/or philosophical core that coheres contemporary youth justice in England and Wales (Muncie and Goldson, 2006b). That said, four issues are particularly noteworthy. First, the radical organisational restructuring of youth justice has served to institutionalise its separation from the 'Every Child Matters' framework. Second, the conflation of crime, disorder and anti-social behaviour (Hughes and Follett, see Chapter 11 of this volume) and the concomitant emphasis on 'risk' and pre-emptive or pre-offence intervention (Smith, see Chapter 7 of this volume) have served to 'define deviance up' and legitimise the ever-extending reach of the youth justice system. Third, the intensification of intensive post-offence intervention, increasingly operationalised through electronic monitoring and surveillance technologies (McNeill, see Chapter 9 of this volume; Nellis, 2004) has consolidated correctional ideology and practice. Fourth, the expansion and diversification of custodial sanctions has rendered England and Wales the carceral capital of Europe (Goldson, see Chapter 10 of this volume). All of this is at loggerheads with 'evidence', it is contrary to the principles and rationales of 'Every Child Matters' and it is ultimately rooted in a cynical politics of 'toughness'.

Towards a principled youth justice

If contemporary youth justice in England and Wales privileges the more repressive and regressive conceptual thematics that we considered at the beginning of this chapter; if 'evidence' has been overshadowed by political calculations; and if the broad corpus of policy has been fractured in the way that we have argued, it begs the question: what might a progressive youth justice system comprise? We conclude, therefore, by mapping the broad contours of a principled youth justice informed by the international human rights framework, lessons that might be drawn from comparative analysis and some of the key messages from research and practice experience.

The international human rights framework

As noted earlier in this chapter, specified *rights* in respect of children and young people within youth justice systems are provided by a range of international conventions, standards, treaties and rules which, taken together, provide a strong foundation for a principled youth justice.

The *United Nations Standard Minimum Rules for the Administration of Juvenile Justice* (the Beijing Rules) were adopted by the United Nations in 1985 and provide guidance for the protection of children's rights in the development of *separate* and *specialist* juvenile/youth justice systems. They were a direct response to a call made by the Sixth United Nations Congress on the Prevention of Crime and the Treatment of Offenders which convened in 1980. The Rules operate within a framework of two other sets of international juvenile/youth justice standards, both of which were adopted in 1990: the *United Nations Guidelines for the Prevention of Juvenile Delinquency* (the Riyadh Guidelines), and the *United Nations Rules for the Protection of Juveniles Deprived of their Liberty* (the JDL Rules). Also in 1990, the World Summit on Children assembled in New York, constituting the largest gathering of state leaders in history. They declared that the 'well being of children requires political action at the highest level', and they pledged: 'we are determined to take that action. We ourselves make a solemn commitment to give high priority to the rights of children' (cited in Lansdown and Newell, 1994: xi). The *United Nations Convention on the Rights of the Child* (UNCRC) was seen to embody such commitment and it set out comprehensive minimum standards for the treatment of *all* children. The UNCRC has subsequently been ratified by 192 countries, making it the most widely adopted of all international conventions (Office of the United Nations High Commissioner for Human Rights, 2006). Although it does not relate exclusively to youth justice, many of its provisions ('Articles') are directly focused upon children in conflict with the law.

It is not practical here to engage with the comprehensive detail of international conventions, standards, treaties and rules but some of their provisions are particularly noteworthy. Article 2 of the UNCRC provides for non-discrimination, consistent with the Beijing Rules that state, at Rule 2.1, that: 'the following Standard Minimum Rules shall be applied to juvenile offenders impartially, without distinction of any kind, for example as to race, colour, sex, language, religion'. Furthermore, Article 3 of the UNCRC provides that the best interests of the child should be a primary consideration in all actions, courts and law and this too echoes other international human rights instruments. Although such instruments fall short of establishing a minimum age of criminal responsibility – or to give any explicit guidance as to what might constitute an internationally acceptable age limit below which prosecution should be impossible – Article 4.1 of the Beijing Rules states that the age of criminal minority should 'not be fixed at too low an age level, bearing in mind the facts of emotional, mental and intellectual maturity'. More generally, the international instruments provide clear guidance in two crucially important respects.

First, with regard to generic principles of youth justice intervention. Rule 5.1 of the Beijing Rules states that: 'the juvenile justice system ... shall ensure that any reaction to juvenile offenders shall always be in proportion to the circumstances of both the offenders and the offence'. Similarly, Rules 17.1(b) and 17.1(d) provide that: 'restrictions on the personal liberty of the juvenile shall ... be limited to the possible minimum', and 'the well-being of the juvenile shall be the guiding factor in her or his case' (this is reiterated in Article 40.4 of the UNCRC). Indeed, the international instruments enshrine the concept of proportionality to offset the likelihood of over-zealous intervention and concomitant forms of injustice. In essence, this important principle requires no more and no less than a fair and proportional reaction in any case where a child is convicted of a criminal offence.

Second, in respect of custodial detention. Rule 19.1 of the Beijing Rules provides that: 'the placement of a juvenile in an institution shall always be a disposition of last resort and for the minimum necessary period', and Article 37 of the UNCRC states: 'imprisonment of a child shall be ... used only as a measure of last resort and for the shortest appropriate period of time ... every child deprived of liberty shall be treated with humanity and respect for the inherent dignity of the human person'.

Lessons from comparative analysis

Whilst we have argued here, and elsewhere (Muncie and Goldson, 2006c), that it is simply not possible to directly transfer youth justice systems, even particular modes of intervention, from one location to another, there are certainly positive lessons that can be drawn from comparative analysis, particularly in observing elements of more progressive policy and practice.

In general terms the most constructive youth justice systems appear to be situated in jurisdictions/countries where there is a political willingness to sustain welfare protectionism or to subsume youth justice within alternative forms of conflict resolution. A cultural and political sensibility that imprisoning young people is not only harmful but also self-defeating is also crucial. Some of the key drivers of the more diversionary, decriminalising and decarcerative youth justice systems are derived from restatements of a 'children first' philosophy; a commitment to pardon and to protect, but above all a preparedness to depoliticise youth crime and justice. In policy terms this involves the objective of removing all children from *prison service* custody and a greater commitment to suspending sentences and employing inclusionary and participative community-based interventions as direct alternatives to incarceration. Compliance both with the spirit and the content of the international human rights framework is also pivotal.

In more specific terms, whereas UK jurisdictions hold children to be criminally responsible at conspicuously young ages (8 in Scotland, 10 in England and

Wales and Northern Ireland), other countries delay the formal criminalisation of the young: from aged 12 in Canada, the Netherlands and Turkey; 13 in France; 14 in Germany, Italy, Japan, New Zealand and Spain; 15 in Denmark, Finland, Norway and Sweden; and 18 in Belgium and Luxembourg (Muncie and Goldson, 2006a). Whilst the age of criminal responsibility cannot be regarded as the exclusive determining characteristic of progressive or repressive youth justice systems, it is certainly significant. So, although Scotland, for example, sets its age of criminal minority at 8, the juvenile court was abolished in 1968 being replaced by a welfare tribunal for the majority of under-16-year-old offenders (McAra, 2006; McNeill, see Chapter 9 of this volume). As a result it has long been maintained that the Children's Hearing system ensures that child welfare considerations hold a pivotal position for younger offenders and provide a credible alternative to the punitive nature of youth justice pursued in many other jurisdictions (Bottoms, 2002; Bottoms and Dignan, 2004). That said, Belgium with an age of criminal responsibility set at 18, arguably comprises the youth justice system that is the 'most deliberately welfare-oriented of all' (Put and Walgrave, 2006). The Youth Protection Act 1965 established principles of social protection and judicial protection to apply to all those under the age of 21. With a few exceptions, no punishments are available to the under-18s in Belgium. Any judicial intervention for children and young people is conceptualised as educative and protective, as distinct from punitive and responsibilising. In principle it is the needs of the child or young person that determine the nature of the intervention. In Finland, children's needs are conceptualised and met with reference to structural or systems-based analyses and juvenile/youth justice policy is informed by an awareness of socio-economic conditions rather than a reliance on responsibilisation and individual pathology. As a result there remains, even in the wake of the recent politicisation of youth crime, a remarkable political consensus that investing in health and social services is more likely to deliver positive outcomes than developing penal institutions (Lappi-Seppälä, 2006).

In the same way that some youth justice jurisdictions manage to resist (or delay) processes of child criminalisation, retain a progressive welfare ethic and locate youth crime and justice within forms of social–structural analysis and response, others sustain decarcerative priorities. Most jurisdictions in Australia, for example, have witnessed substantial falls in child imprisonment since the 1980s, seemingly as a result of extending diversionary options including the use of youth conferencing (Cunneen and White, 2006). Recent evidence from Canada also suggests a growing decarcerative movement (Smandych, 2006). A number of European countries, such as Italy (Nelken, 2006) and Finland (Lappi-Seppälä, 2006), have been able to report significant *decreases* in their daily count of youth (under 21) incarceration between 1992 and 2002. According to the UN data, such countries as Japan, Norway and Sweden similarly stand out as having been able to keep youth imprisonment to an absolute minimum and as maintaining such toleration throughout the 1990s (Muncie and Goldson, 2006a). Whether politically, pragmatically or economically inspired, a case establishing the damaging effects of custody on children (and the wider community) has repeatedly been made and acknowledged. Finland's experience, for example, seems to show that high incarceration rates and tough penal regimes do not control crime. They are unnecessary. Decarceration can be pursued without sacrificing public safety (Lappi-Seppälä, 2006). Indeed a progressive consensus appears to exist in Nordic countries (Iceland, Norway, Sweden, Finland, Denmark) that 'forward-looking' social and educational measures together with mediation take precedence over prosecution and punishment.

Similarly, Italy currently appears at the vanguard of youth penal reductionism in Europe (Nelken, 2006). New penal laws in the late 1980s explicitly stressed leniency for children and young people in order that their educational progress and personal development were not interrupted. Diversion takes precedence over formal early intervention. In particular, avoidance of conviction and refusal of punishment is facilitated through the mechanisms of *irrilevanza* (insufficient seriousness), *perdono* (judicial pardon) and *messa alla prova* (pre-trial probation for all offences). As a result, young people tend to be imprisoned only for very few serious violent offences and only when the conditions of *messa alla prova* have not been met. As Nelken (2006) observes, this means that many serious offences do not even end up with a conviction, let alone a prison sentence. Child 'offenders' are primarily regarded as being in need of support and guidance rather than requiring retribution, denunciation or punitive intervention.

It would be unwise to idealise international youth justice systems and/or to assume that they are free of the complexities, tensions and even contradictions that we have discussed with regard to the UK, and England and Wales in particular. That said, there are clearly lessons to be drawn from comparative analysis that can inform the construction of a more progressive, coherent, rights compliant and ultimately effective youth justice system.

A principled youth justice

As stated, contemporary youth justice reforms in England and Wales essentially derive from, and are legitimised by, a new politics of 'toughness' on the one hand, and a range of pragmatic orientations and 'what works' discourses on the other. The former is myopic and crudely instrumentalist. The latter privileges individualisation and responsibilisation whilst essentially disregarding social-structural analyses and the primary significance of material contexts. In this way the contradictions and consequences of structural injustice and the aetiological complexities of youth crime are reformulated in the guise of individual failings. Indeed, as we have argued, youth justice policies are increasingly located within a wider ideological context within which social, economic and political problems are redefined as issues to be *managed* rather than *resolved*.

The combined effect of this, as discussed throughout this volume, has been to: tighten procedures; impose homogeneous 'standards' and 'targets'; emphasise the 'management' and 'correction' of 'young offenders'; intensify criminalising modes of intervention; downplay social welfare traditions and profile the overtly controlling functions of the youth justice apparatus. This characterises a broader and deeper movement in criminal justice in England and Wales, away from rehabilitative and transformative optimism towards greater surveillance, regulation and, ultimately, punishment.

Such policy reform is fundamentally inconsistent with the provisions encapsulated within the international human rights framework including: child-specific justice systems; anti-discriminatory priorities; 'best interest' principles; proportionality and minimum necessary intervention/criminalisation; holistic community-based services and the avoidance of institutionalisation and penal custody. Equally, youth justice in England and Wales is conspicuously out of step with policies and practices in some of the more progressive international jurisdictions where welfare protectionism and non-criminalising, inclusionary and participative community resolutions to social harm are emphasised. Moreover, as each of the preceding chapters has illustrated, modern youth justice in England and Wales is, in many important respects, paradoxically incompatible with youth crime prevention and community safety objectives.

In broad terms, highly interventionist youth justice systems that responsibilise children at an early age and rely upon correctional techniques to 'treat' or 'fix' them, contain seriously problematic tendencies. To begin, the processes of identifying 'risk' and/or attributing criminogenic 'labels', mediated as they inevitably are through the structural relations of class, 'race' and gender (see Part 1 of this volume), are invariably unevenly applied and the most structurally disadvantaged children and young people are especially susceptible to criminalisation. Furthermore, research findings and practice experiences continue to affirm, as they have for very many years, that 'labelling' invariably invokes antagonistic 'social reaction' which, in turn, tends to produce enduring and spiralling negative consequences (Becker, 1963). Drawing an ever-expanding population of children and young people into the shallow end of the youth justice system and, in the final analysis, exposing increasing numbers to custodial detention at the deep end of the same system, are both damaging and counterproductive. In this way Edwin Lemert (1967) noted that 'social control leads to deviance' and David Matza (1969: 80) illuminated the contradiction that 'the very effort to prevent, intervene, arrest and "cure" ... [can] precipitate or seriously aggravate the tendency society wishes to guard against'.

The critical contextualisation that runs through this volume is consistent with the international human rights framework and is reflected in the more progressive youth justice systems within the international community. Moreover, its supporting foundations cohere with a wealth of research evidence and practice experience that, taken together, validate destructuring impulses and the efficacy and integrity of diversionary, decriminalising and decarcerative responses. It follows that ethically legitimate, rights-compliant and effective approaches to youth crime and justice must be located within a broad corpus of *social and economic policy* rather than the narrower confines of *youth/criminal justice policy*. In other words, it is imperative that principled approaches to youth justice must focus at the macro level upon the complex and intrinsically harmful socio-economic structural conditions that give rise to youth crime *and* youth criminalisation, as distinct from an exclusive correctional emphasis at the microcosmic level of individual children and families. Such an approach, formulated around six core principles, necessitates a conceptual and organisational reframing of youth crime and justice and, paradoxically, a substantially reduced role for the conventional youth justice apparatus itself.

First, is the principle that policy should *comprehensively* address the *social* and *economic* conditions that are known to give rise to conflict, harm, social distress, crime and criminalisation, particularly *poverty* and *inequality*. It is no coincidence that youth justice systems characteristically serve to process (and punish) the children of the poor. This is not to suggest that all poor children commit crime, or that only poor children offend, but the corollaries between child poverty, social and economic inequality, youth crime and criminalisation are undeniable. It follows that the children who are most heavily exposed to correctional intervention, surveillance and punishment within the youth justice system in England and Wales, are routinely drawn from some of the most disadvantaged families, neighbourhoods and communities. Young people for whom the fabric of life invariably stretches across poverty; family discord; public care; drug and alcohol misuse; mental distress; ill-health; emotional, physical and sexual abuse; self-harm; homelessness; isolation; loneliness; circumscribed educational and employment opportunities; 'hollowed-out' communities and the most pressing sense of distress and alienation, are the very children targetted by the youth justice apparatus. Notwithstanding New Labour's proclaimed 'historic aim' to end child poverty, children without a parent in paid employment continue to face a 74 per cent risk of poverty (Preston, 2005) and the proportion of children in such households in the UK is the highest in Europe (Palmer et al., 2005). Moreover, despite all of the anti-child poverty rhetoric, it remains the case that 28 per cent of British children (3.5 million) are condemned to poverty in one of the world's richest nations (Flaherty et al., 2004). The corrosive impact of poverty and structural inequality on children, families and communities is profound (Goldson et al., 2002) and is key to understanding the problems both experienced and perpetuated by identifiable sections of the young (White and Cunneen, see Chapter 2; Webster, see Chapter 3; Hughes and Follett, see Chapter 11; Hancock, see Chapter 12; Mizen, see Chapter 13 of this volume).

Second, and closely related to the first point, are the principles of *universality*, *comprehensiveness* and *re-engaging* the *'social'*. This requires dispensing with forms of conditionality that bolster the 'deserving–undeserving schism' (Goldson, 2002) and instead providing holistic services that meet the needs and safeguard and promote the well-being of *all* children and young people. It necessitates closing the contradictory and antagonistic fractures that have opened between 'every child matters' priorities and the 'no more excuses' imperatives characteristic of the 'new correctionalism' (Muncie and Goldson, 2006b). It amounts to transgressing hollow rhetorical constructions and actually implementing comprehensively redistributionist and genuinely inclusionary strategies that explicitly address the practical realities and complexities of children's lived experiences. In essence this requires the conceptual and institutional decriminalisation of social need. 'Normal' social institutions – including families (however they are configured), 'communities', youth services, leisure and recreational services, health provision, schools, training and employment initiatives – need to be adequately resourced and supported. The industrial-scale expansion of the youth justice system should be curtailed and resources redirected to generic 'children first' services. If for no other reason, this is necessary because as Bateman and Pitts (2005: 257) have observed: 'those factors which appear to be most closely associated with persistent and serious youth crime ... are those which are least amenable to intervention by agents of the youth justice system'. Conversely, normalising and decriminalising approaches – intrinsic to the principles of universality, comprehensiveness and re-engaging the 'social' – are substantiated by robust research evidence. One of the most ambitious and comprehensive research analyses of youth crime prevention programmes in the world, for example, demonstrated that, even for 'serious, violent and chronic juvenile offenders', some of the most effective responses emanate from initiatives that are located *outside* of the formal criminal justice system (decriminalisation), build upon children's and young people's strengths as distinct from emphasising their 'deficits' (normalisation) and adopt a social-structural approach rather than drawing on individualised, criminogenic and/or medico-psychological perspectives (contextualisation) (Howell et al., 1995).

Third, is the principle of *diversion*. Children and young people should be routinely diverted away from formal youth justice interventions. This follows from the first two principles and, in many respects, it is the antithesis of the interventionist and net-widening tendencies that characterise contemporary youth justice policy in England and Wales. Diversion is not only consistent with the human rights framework and the more progressive international youth justice systems, but it has also been shown to be an effective strategy in terms of youth crime prevention (Bell et al., 1999; Goldson, 2000; Kemp et al., 2002; Pragnell, 2005). Of course, the most effective diversionary strategy is literally to remove children and young people from the reach of the youth justice system altogether, by significantly raising the age of criminal responsibility. There are strong grounds to support this proposition, not least evidence from jurisdictions where the age of criminal responsibility is substantially higher than it is in England and Wales and where 'it can be shown that there are no negative consequences to be seen in terms of crime rates' (Dunkel, 1996: 38).

Fourth, is the principle of *child-appropriate justice*. In the minority of cases where formal youth justice intervention is deemed unavoidable, it should be provided within a child-appropriate context. The intensity and duration of intervention should be proportionate to the severity of the offence and limited to the minimum that is absolutely necessary and its rationale should be explicit, evidenced-based and likely to provide positive outcomes for the 'young offender' and, where relevant, to any injured party (Haines and O'Mahony, see Chapter 8 of this volume). The contemporary youth justice system in England and Wales essentially mirrors the adult system. As stated, children are fully responsibilised and, in effect, adulterised at the age of 10. Furthermore, the specific targeting and criminalisation of children by way of Anti-social Behaviour Orders (Hughes and Follett, see Chapter 11 of this volume; Squires and Stephen, 2005), together with modes of intervention and attendant practices that are routinely applied to children within the youth justice system itself, including: court orders with rigorous requirements and conditions; electronic monitoring and surveillance technologies; the increasing propensity to publicly 'name and shame' and, ulti-mately, penal custody, are more akin to punitive adult 'justice'. International human rights agencies are consistent in their critique of the adulterised youth justice system in England and Wales (United Nations Committee on the Rights of the Child, 1995 and 2002; Office for the Commissioner for Human Rights, 2005). It is imperative that such critique is constructively applied to inform a more child-appropriate youth justice system.

Fifth, is the principle of *abolitionism*. A principled youth justice is, almost by definition, rational. Interventions that are ineffective or, more problematically, that violate international human rights obligations, are known to be damaging and harmful and/or aggravate the very issues that they seek to resolve, are pro-foundly irrational and should be abolished. This applies, in varying degrees to: specious expressions of actuarialism and over-zealous modes of early inter-vention (Goldson, 2000; Smith, see Chapter 7 of this volume); the net-widening effect of 'anti-social behaviour' initiatives (Hughes and Follett, see Chapter 11 of this volume); and most spectacularly of all, the practices of imprisonment (Goldson, 2005 and Chapter 10 of this volume; Sim, 2004). This is not to imply that nothing should be done with regard to youth crime, or that troubled and troublesome children and young people should simply be left to fend for them-selves without the care, guidance, support and supervision that they may well need. The central argument, however, is that the youth justice system is singu-larly unfit for purpose. Rather – in keeping with the four principles outlined above and much of the analysis developed throughout this volume – the aboli-tionist principle fixes the analytical gaze upon the complex social and economic conditions that give rise to social harm and emphasises the imperatives of universality, diversionary strategies and child-appropriate justice. It challenges fundamentally moribund and iatrogenic modes of criminalising intervention in such a way that its realisation necessitates the radical transformation and sub-stantial diminution of the entire correctional apparatus. Furthermore, this prin-ciple extends beyond destructuring the depth and reach of the youth justice system itself; it also requires a critical rethinking of the conceptual origins, significances and meanings attributed to terms such as 'youth disorder', 'anti-social behaviour', 'youth crime' and 'young offender'. It offers an invitation to 'start from a different place'; to focus upon 'the social origins of harms ... [and engage with] a view of the world that sees human agency as defined by structures' (Hillyard et al., 2005: 61). This connects back to the central importance of critical contextualisation, the structural relations of class, 'race' and gender and the material realities of poverty and inequality.

Sixth, are the related principles of *depoliticisation* and *tolerance*. The politicisation of youth crime and justice, particularly in England and Wales, has been both implicitly signalled and explicitly analysed throughout this volume. It has served to demonise identifiable constituencies of the young (Scraton, 1997), to legitimise 'ill-considered but attention grabbing tough-on-crime proposals' (Tonry, 2004: 2) and to 'institutionalise intolerance' (Muncie, 1999b). Moreover, as we have seen, 'zero tolerance', 'tough on crime' and 'no more excuses' sentiments have claimed significant material purchase with regard to policy formation, system expansion and practical intervention. Senior politicians repeatedly refer to an increasingly anxious, risk-averse and fearful public and selective constructions of 'public opinion' are mobilised and presented as primary legitimising rationales for the 'tough on crime' agenda. Such reactive politicisation not only negates evidence and distorts policy formation, however, it is also underpinned by a skewed reading of public opinion itself. Indeed, as discussed earlier, findings from the first survey to systematically explore public opinion and public attitudes to youth crime and justice in England and Wales revealed complex, multilayered and even contradictory conceptualisations. Whilst the survey found that the public tend to have a more pessimistic view of youth crime than is justified by the official crime statistics – hardly surprising given the sensationalist and amplificatory nature of media representations (Jewkes, 2004) – people are also significantly less recriminatory and punitive than is often supposed (Hough and Roberts, 2004: ix). Furthermore:

> When the nature of public attitudes is explored in depth using sophisticated research methods, quite different results emerge compared to the often-cited rudimentary surveys ... [T]here is little evidence to support the view that harsh penal and criminal policies are favoured as a means of addressing offending behaviour (Hancock, 2004: 63).

and:

> Close analysis would suggest that there is something of a 'comedy of errors' in which policy and practice [are] not based on a proper understanding of public opinion (Allen, 2002: 6).

A genuinely evidenced-based approach to youth crime and justice requires politicians and policy makers to remain cognisant of the complexities of public opinion. Moreover, senior politicians have a responsibility to *inform* public opinion as distinct from simply reacting to over-simplified and fundamentally erroneous interpretations of it. A principled youth justice, therefore, must transgress crude politicisation and the perpetuation of 'populist punitiveness' (Bottoms, 1995) and engage instead with more sophisticated, measured and dignified approaches. Ultimately this demands the depoliticisation of youth crime and justice and the development of more progressively tolerant, human rights compliant, non-criminalising, inclusionary and participative strategies.

Conclusion

The historical and theoretical foundations of youth justice policy formation comprise a complex of competing, if not contradictory, conceptual thematics: welfare; justice; informalism; rights; responsibilities; retribution and punishment. Youth justice systems are not only temporally and spatially contingent but, at any specific place and time, they take hybridised and multi-faceted forms. Within this context, we have attempted to present both a critical anatomy of contemporary policy and a vision of a principled youth justice. Building upon a critical analysis of 'what works' and 'evidenced-based' paradigms, we have argued that opportunistic political calculations have displaced integrity and rationality in the formulation of youth justice policy in England and Wales. This has imposed serious inconsistencies and fractures within the broader corpus of child/youth policy. Furthermore, it has negated evidence, it has distanced youth justice policy from the provisions of international human rights standards, treaties conventions and rules and it has defined England and Wales as one of the most punitive jurisdictions in the industrialised democratic world. The chapter in particular, and the volume more generally, have aimed to intervene critically. By synthesising the human rights framework, progressive elements from international youth justice and evidence drawn from research and practice, we have identified a set of principles that might inform future thinking. In this sense we hope that the end of the book marks the beginning of a more ambitious civilising project.

References

Allen, R. (2002) 'There Must be Some Way of Dealing with Kids': Young Offenders, Public Attitudes and Policy Change', *Youth Justice* 2(1): 3–13.

Bandalli, S. (2000) 'Children, Responsibility and the New Youth Justice', in B. Goldson (ed.) *The New Youth Justice*. Lyme Regis: Russell House Publishing.

Bateman, T. and Pitts, J. (2005) 'Conclusion: What the Evidence Tells Us', in T. Bateman and J. Pitts (eds) *The RHP Companion to Youth Justice*. Lyme Regis: Russell House Publishing.

Becker, H. (1963) *Outsiders*. New York: Free Press.

Bell, A., Hodgson, M. and Pragnell, S. (1999) 'Diverting Children and Young People from Crime and the Criminal Justice System', in B. Goldson (ed.) *Youth Justice: Contemporary Policy and Practice*. Aldershot: Ashgate.

Blair, T. (1999) 'Beveridge Revisited: a Welfare State for the 21st Century', Lecture by the Prime Minister delivered at Toynbee Hall, 18 March.

Blair, T. (2004a) 'Foreword', in *Cutting Crime, Delivering Justice: A Strategic Plan for Criminal Justice*. London: The Stationery Office.

Blair, T. (2004b) 'Foreword', in *Confident Communities in a Secure Britain: The Home Office Strategic Plan 2004–08*. London: The Stationery Office.

Blunkett, D., Falconer, C. and Goldsmith, P. (2004) 'Preface', in *Cutting Crime, Delivering Justice: A Strategic Plan for Criminal Justice*. London: The Stationery Office.

Bottoms, A. (1995) 'The Philosophy and Politics of Punishment and Sentencing', in C. Clarkson and R. Morgan (eds) *The Politics of Sentencing Reform*. Oxford: Clarendon Press.

Bottoms, A. (2002) 'The Divergent Development of Juvenile Justice Policy and Practice in England and Scotland', in M. Rosenheim et al. (eds) *A Century of Juvenile Justice*. Chicago: University of Chicago Press.

Bottoms, A. (2005) 'Methodology matters', *Safer Society*, 25: 10–12.

Bottoms, A. and Dignan, J. (2004) 'Youth Justice in Britain', *Crime and Justice: A Review of Research*, 31: 21–183.

Cabinet Office (1999a) *Modernising Government*. London: The Stationery Office.

Cabinet Office (1999b) *Professional Policy Making for the Twenty-First Century*. London: Cabinet Office.

Cohen, S. (1972) *Folk Devils and Moral Panics: The Creation of the Mods and Rockers*. London: MacGibbon and Kee.

Cohen, S. (1985) *Visions of Social Control*. Cambridge: Polity Press.

Cunneen, C. and White, R. (2006) 'Australia: Control, Containment or Empowerment', in J. Muncie and B. Goldson (eds) *Comparative Youth Justice: Critical Issues*. London: Sage.

Davis, H. and Bourhill, M. (1997) '"Crisis": The Demonization of Children and Young People', in P. Scraton (ed.) *'Childhood' in 'Crisis'?* London: UCL Press.

Department for Education and Skills (2005) *Every Child Matters – Change for Children: Aims and Outcomes*, http://everychildmatters.gov.uk.aims/

Department for Education and Skills and Department of Health (2004) *National Service Framework for Children, Young People and Maternity Services: Executive Summary*. London: Department of Health.

Department of Social Security (2001) *Households Below Average Income*. London: Department of Social Security.

Drakeford, M. and McCarthy, K. (2000) 'Parents, Responsibility and the New Youth Justice', in B. Goldson (ed.) *The New Youth Justice*. Lyme Regis: Russell House Publishing.

Dunkel, F. (1996) 'Current Directions in Criminal Policy', in W. McCarney, (ed.) *Juvenile Delinquents and Young People in Danger in an Open Environment*. Winchester: Waterside Books.

Flaherty, J., Veit-Wilson, J. and Dornan, P. (2004) *Poverty: the Facts*, 5th Edition. London: Child Poverty Action Group.

Garland, D. (2001) *The Culture of Control*. Oxford: Oxford University Press.

Garland, D. and Young, P. (eds) (1983) *The Power to Punish: Contemporary Penality and Social Analysis*. London: Heinemann.

George, M. (2002) 'Poor planning', *Guardian Society*, 20 February: 104.

Goldson, B. (1997) 'Children in Trouble: State Responses to Juvenile Crime', in P. Scraton (ed.) *'Childhood' in 'Crisis'?* London: UCL Press.

Goldson, B. (2000) 'Wither Diversion? Interventionism and the New Youth Justice', in B. Goldson (ed.) *The New Youth Justice*. Lyme Regis: Russell House Publishing.

Goldson, B. (2001) 'A Rational Youth Justice? Some Critical Reflections on the Research, Policy and Practice Relation', *Probation Journal*, 48(2): 76–85.

Goldson, B. (2002) 'New Labour, Social Justice and Children: Political Calculation and the Deserving–undeserving Schism', *British Journal of Social Work*, 32(6): 683–95.

Goldson, B. (2004a) 'Youth Crime and Youth Justice', in J. Muncie and D. Wilson (eds) *Student Handbook of Criminal Justice and Criminology*. London: Cavendish Publishing.

Goldson, B. (2004b) 'Beyond Formalism: Towards "Informal" Approaches to Youth Crime and Youth Justice', in T. Bateman and J. Pitts (eds) *The RHP Companion to Youth Justice*. Lyme Regis: Russell House Publishing.

Goldson, B. (2004c) 'Victims or Threats? Children Care and Control', in J. Fink (ed.) *Care: Personal Lives and Social Policy*. Bristol: The Policy Press in association with The Open University.

Goldson, B. and Jamieson, J. (2002) 'Youth Crime, the "Parenting Deficit" and State Intervention: a Contextual Critique', *Youth Justice*, 2(2): 82–99.

Goldson, B. (2005) 'Child Imprisonment: a Case for Abolition', *Youth Justice* 5(2): 77–90.

Goldson, B., Lavalette, M. and McKechnie, J. (eds) (2002) *Children, Welfare and the State*. London: Sage.

Haines, K. (2000) 'Referral Orders and Youth Offender Panels: Restorative Approaches and the New Youth Justice', in B. Goldson (ed.) *The New Youth Justice*. Lyme Regis: Russell House Publishing.

Harris, R. and Webb, D. (1987) *Welfare, Power and Juvenile Justice*. London: Tavistock.

Hancock, L. (2004) 'Criminal Justice, Public Opinion, Fear and Popular Politics', in J. Muncie and D. Wilson (eds) *Student Handbook of Criminal Justice and Criminology*. London: Cavendish Publishing.

Hay, C. (1995) 'Mobilisation through interpellation: James Bulger, juvenile crime and the construction of a moral panic', *Social and Legal Studies,* 4(2): 197–223.

Haydon, D. and Scraton, P. (2000) "Condemn a Little More, Understand a Little Less": the Political Context and Rights' Implications of the Domestic and European Rulings in the Venables-Thompson Case', *Journal of Law and Society,* 27(3): 416–48.

Hendrick, H. (1994) *Child Welfare: England 1872–1989*. London: Routledge.

Hendrick, H. (2003) *Child Welfare: Historical Dimensions, Contemporary Debate*. Bristol: The Policy Press.

Henricson, C. and Bainham, A. (2005) *The Child and Family Policy Divide*. York: Joseph Rowntree Foundation.

Hillyard, P., Pantazis, C., Tombs, S. and Gordon, D. (2005) '"Social Harm"' and its Limits', in P. Hillyard, C. Pantazis, S. Tombs, D. Gordon and D. Dorling (eds) *Criminal Obsessions: Why Harm Matters More than Crime*. London: Crime and Society Foundation.

HM Government (2005) *An Overview of Cross-Government Guidance: Every Child Matters Change for Children*. London: Department for Education and Skills.

HM Treasury (2004) *Child Poverty Review*. London: The Stationery Office.

Home Office (1997) *No More Excuses – A New Approach to Tackling Youth Crime in England and Wales.* London: Home Office.

Home Office (2003) *Respect and Responsibility – Taking a Stand Against Anti-Social Behaviour*. London: The Stationery Office.

Hough, M. and Roberts, J. (2004) *Youth Crime and Youth Justice: Public Opinion in England and Wales*. Bristol: The Policy Press.

Howell, J. C., Krisberg, B., Hawkins, J. D. and Wilson, J. J. (eds) (1995) *Serious, Violent and Chronic Juvenile Offenders: A Sourcebook*. London: Sage.

Jones, T. and Newburn, T. (2004) 'The Convergence of US and UK Crime Control Policy: Exploring Substance and Process', in T. Newburn and R. Sparks (eds) *Criminal Justice and Political Cultures: National and International Dimensions of Crime Control*. Cullompton: Willan, pp. 123–51.

Jewkes, Y. (2004) 'Media Representations of Criminal Justice', in J. Muncie and D. Wilson (eds) *Student Handbook of Criminal Justice and Criminology*. London: Cavendish Publishing.

Kemp, V., Sorsby, A., Liddle, M. and Merrington, S. (2002) *Assessing Responses to Youth Offending in Northamptonshire*. Research Briefing 2. London: Nacro.

Labour Party (2001) *Ambitions for Britain: Labour's Manifesto 2001*. London: Labour Party.

Land, H. (2002) *Meeting the Child Poverty Challenge*. London: The Daycare Trust.

Lansdown, G. and Newell, P. (eds) (1994) *UK Agenda for Children*. London: Children's Rights Development Unit.

Lappi-Seppälä, T. (2006) 'Finland: A Model of Tolerance', in J. Muncie and B. Goldson (eds) *Comparative Youth Justice: Critical Issues*. London: Sage.

Lemert, E. (1967) *Human Deviance, Social Problems and Social Control*. Englewood Cliffs New Jersey: Prentice Hall.

Magarey, S. (1978) 'The Invention of Juvenile Delinquency in Early Nineteenth-Century England', *Labour History*, 34: 11–25.

Matza, D. (1969) *Becoming Deviant*. Englewood Cliffs New Jersey: Prentice Hall.

McAra, L. (2006) 'Welfare in Crisis? Key Developments in Scottish Youth Justice', in J. Muncie and B. Goldson (eds) *Comparative Youth Justice: Critical Issues*. London: Sage.

Monaghan, G. (2005) 'Children's Human Rights and Youth Justice', in T. Bateman and J. Pitts (eds) *The RHP Companion to Youth Justice*. Lyme Regis: Russell House Publishing.

Muncie, J. (1999a) *Youth and Crime: A Critical Introduction*. London: Sage.

Muncie, J. (1999b) 'Institutionalised Intolerance: Youth Justice and the 1998 Crime and Disorder Act', *Critical Social Policy*, 19(22): 147–75.

Muncie, J. (2002) 'Policy Transfers and What Works: Some Reflections on Comparative Youth Justice', *Youth Justice*, 1(3): 27–35.

Muncie, J. (2004) *Youth and Crime*. (2nd edn) London: Sage.

Muncie, J. (2005) 'The Globalization of Crime Control – the Case of Youth and Juvenile Justice: Neo-Liberalism, Policy Convergence and International Conventions', *Theoretical Criminology*, 9(1): 35–64.

Muncie, J. and Goldson, B. (eds) (2006a) *Comparative Youth Justice: Critical Issues*. London: Sage.

Muncie, J. and Goldson, B. (2006b) 'England and Wales: The New Correctionalism', in J. Muncie and B. Goldson (eds) *Comparative Youth Justice: Critical Issues*. London: Sage.

Muncie, J. and Goldson, B. (2006c) 'States of Transition: Convergence and Diversity in International Youth Justice', in J. Muncie and B. Goldson (eds) *Comparative Youth Justice: Critical Issues*. London: Sage.

Muncie, J. and Hughes, G. (2002) 'Modes of Youth Governance: Political Rationalities, Criminalisation and Resistance', in J. Muncie, G. Hughes and E. McLaughlin (eds) *Youth Justice: Critical Readings*. London: Sage.

Nacro (2004) *Parenting Provision in a Youth Justice Context*, Youth Crime Briefing, June. London: Nacro.

Neather, A. (2004) 'Fears Haunting New Labour', *Evening Standard*, 5 April.

Nelken, D. (2006) 'Italy: A Lesson in Tolerance?', in J. Muncie and B. Goldson (eds) *Comparative Youth Justice: Critical Issues*. London: Sage.

Nellis, M. (2004) 'The "Tracking" Controversy: The Roots of Mentoring and Electronic Monitoring', *Youth Justice*, 4(2): 77–99.

Newburn, T. and Sparks, R. (2004) *Criminal Justice and Political Cultures: National and International dimensions of crime control*. Cullompton: Willan.

Newman, J. (2001) *Modernising Governance*. London: Sage.

Office for the Commissioner for Human Rights (2005) *Report by Mr Alvaro Gil-Robles, Commissioner for Human Rights, on His Visit to the United Kingdom 4-12 November 2004*. Strasbourg: Council of Europe.

Office of the United Nations High Commissioner for Human Rights (2006) *Convention on the Rights of the Child*. http://www.ohchr.org/english/countries/ratification/11.htm, accessed 22.01.06.

Palmer, G., Carr, J. and Kenway, P. (2005) *Monitoring Poverty and Social Exclusion in the UK 2005*. York: Joseph Rowntree Foundation

Pearson, G. (1983) *Hooligan: A History of Respectable Fears*. London: Macmillan.

Piachaud, D. (2001) 'Child Poverty, Opportunities and Quality of Life', *The Political Quarterly*, 72(4): 446–53.

Piachaud, D. (2005) 'Child Poverty: an Overview', in G. Preston (ed.) *At Greatest Risk: The Children Most Likely to be Poor*. London: Child Poverty Action Group.

Pitts, J. (2000) 'The New Youth Justice and the Politics of Electoral Anxiety', in B. Goldson (ed.) *The New Youth Justice*. Lyme Regis: Russell House Publishing.

Pitts, J. (2001) *The New Politics of Youth Crime: Discipline or Solidarity?*. Basingstoke: Palgrave.

Pragnell, S. (2005) 'Reprimands and Final Warnings', in T. Bateman and J. Pitts (eds) *The RHP Companion to Youth Justice*. Lyme Regis: Russell House Publishing.

Preston, G. (ed.) (2005) *At Greatest Risk: The Children Most Likely to Be Poor*. London: Child Poverty Action Group.

Put, J. and Walgrave, L. (2006) 'Belgium: from Protection Towards Accountability', in J. Muncie and B. Goldson (eds) *Comparative Youth Justice: Critical Issues*. London: Sage.

Rutherford, A. (1992) *Growing Out of Crime: The New Era*. Winchester: Waterside Books.

Scraton, P. (ed) (1997) *'Childhood' in 'Crisis'?* London: UCL Press.

Scraton, P. (2002) 'Defining "Power" and Challenging "Knowledge": Critical Analysis as Resistance in the UK', in K. Carrington and R. Hogg (eds) *Critical Criminology: Issues, Debates, Challenges*. Cullompton: Willan.

Scraton, P. and Haydon, D. (2002) 'Challenging the Criminalisation of Children and Young People: Securing a Rights-Based Agenda', in J. Muncie, G. Hughes and E. McLaughlin (eds) *Youth Justice: Critical Readings*. London: Sage.

Sim, J. (2004) 'Thinking About Imprisonment', in J. Muncie and D.Wilson (eds) *Student Handbook of Criminal Justice and Criminology*. London: Cavendish Publishing.

Smandych, R. (2006) 'Canada: Repenalisation and Young Offenders' Rights', in J. Muncie and B. Goldson (eds) *Comparative Youth Justice: Critical Issues*. London: Sage.

Smith, D. (2000) 'The Limits of Positivism Revisited', paper presented at the ESRC-funded seminar series *Theorising Social Work Research*. http://www.nisw.org.uk/tswr/smith.html

Smith, D. (2002) 'The Limits of Positivism Revisited', *Social Work and Social Sciences Review*, 10(1): 27–37.

Squires, P. and Stephen, D. (2005) *Rougher Justice: Anti-social Behaviour and Young People*. Cullompton: Willan.

Sutherland, H., Sefton, D. and Piachaud, D. (2003) *Poverty in Britain: The Impact of Government policy since 1997*. York: Joseph Rowntree Foundation.

Tonry, M. (2004) *Punishment and Politics: Evidence and Emulation in the Making of English Crime Control Policy*. Cullompton: Willan.

UNICEF (1998) *Innocenti Digest: Juvenile Justice*. Florence: International Child Development Centre.

United Nations Committee on the Rights of the Child (1995) *Eighth Session. Consideration of Reports Submitted by States Parties Under Article 44 of the Convention*. Geneva: Office of the United Nations High Commissioner for Human Rights.

United Nations Committee on the Rights of the Child (2002) *Concluding Observations of the Committee on the Rights of the Child: United Kingdom of Great Britain and Northern Ireland*. Geneva: United Nations.

Walsh, C. (2003) 'Dispersal of Rights: a Critical Comment on Specified Provisions of the Anti-Social Behaviour Bill', *Youth Justice*, 3(2): 104–11.

Wilcox, A. (2003) 'Evidenced-Based Youth Justice? Some Valuable Lessons from an Evaluation for the Youth Justice Board', *Youth Justice,* 3(1): 19–33.

Wonnacott, C. (1999) 'New Legislation. The Counterfeit Contract – Reform, Pretence and Muddled Principles in the New Referral Order', *Child and Family Law Quarterly*, 11(3): 271–87.

Index

Entries in *italics* denote reports and Latin terms.

see also penal custody/institutions
Integrated Support Plans (ISPs) 98
intensive supervision and surveillance
        programmes (ISSPs) 126–7
inter-war years 9
international human rights framework
        217–18, 221
interventions see state interventions
intolerance 140, 143–6, 225
    see also tolerance
IRT see Identification, Referral and Tracking
ISPs see Integrated Support Plans
ISSPs see intensive supervision and
        surveillance programmes
Italy 220

job creation 194
    see also employment
'joined-up' government 78, 79
Jones, Denis 71
juvenile delinquency 3–15,
        48–50, 53, 139

Kelling, G. 161–2, 175, 176

labelling youth 181, 221
labour market 187–98
    see also employment
Labour Party see New Labour
legislation
    historical contexts 5–7
    see also individual legislation;
        state intervention
leisure facilities 174
Liberal Reforms 7–9
Liberalism 11–12
    see also neo-liberalism
Lipsey, M.W. 129
local authorities 164–8
Local Government Acts
        (1999/2000) 165
localism 206
low-paid work 195–7

McCold, P. 111–12
McGuire, J. 128–9
McNeill, Fergus 125–38
Mair, G. 84
Major, John 141–2
male offending see boys' offending
managerialism 93, 96, 98,
        129–30, 208, 220–1
marginalisation of youth 19–20
market-led approaches 173, 180,
        187, 190, 194–5
Maruna, S. 132
Matthews, R. 168

maturation thesis 72–3, 131
mechanical control 93
medicine (evidence-based) 81
men see boys' offending
meta-analysis 82
Mika, H. 111
minimum wage rates 196–7
minority ethnic youth 30–46
    see also race
misleading evidence 66–8
misrecognition 180, 183
Misspent Youth report (Audit
        Commission) 68, 70, 72
mixed-parentage youth 37–8
Mizen, Phil 187–200
modernisation movement 78–9,
        93, 103, 207
monetary costs, imprisonment 150–1
moral categorisation of youth 21
moral failings, actuarialism 102–4
moral panics 55–6, 58, 161, 209
Morgan Report (1991) 161
Morrison, Z. 180
Muncie, John 93, 203–31

National Minimum Wage (NMW) 196–7
NDYP see New Deal for
        Young People
'needs'-oriented interventions 204–5
NEET (not in education, employment or
        training) population 40
neighbourhood renewal strategy
        172–3, 175–6, 179
    see also urban regeneration
neo-liberalism 12–13, 183
net-widening effects
    ASBOs 167
    evidence-based policy 80
    girls' behaviour regulation 50
    referral orders 113
    restorative cautioning 115
New Deal for Communities 173
New Deal for Young People (NDYP)
        xiii, 187–200
New Labour
    anti-social behaviour 157–60, 162–4
    maturation thesis 72
    New Deal for Young People 187–200
    penal custody 142–3
    policy analysis 207, 209, 211–16
    reforms ix, 68, 70
    research/evaluation/evidence 78–80
    urban regeneration 173–4
'new punitiveness' 140, 146, 152
Newburn, T. 113
nineteenth century 4–5, 204
    see also Victorian years

NMW *see* National Minimum Wage
No More Excuses (New Labour) ix, 72, 79,
    143, 211–16
normalisation principle 223
Northern Ireland ix–x, 115–16
nostalgia 3
not in education, employment
    or training *see* NEET
'nuisance' test 144

offence categories 51, 66–7
O'Mahony, David 110–24
On Track programme 94
ONSET form 97, 98
order *see* social order
over-representation, youth in justice
    system 33–4, 37, 71

parental participation 112
Parental Responsibility
    Contracts 101
parenting orders 128
partnerships, community safety
    158–60, 163–9
party politics 4, 11–12, 140–3, 152
    see also individual political parties
Pathfinder evaluations 86–7, 88
Pawson, R. 82
pay levels 195, 196–7
penal custody/institutions 139–56
    child numbers 139–40, 145
    comparative analysis 218–20
    intolerance 140, 143–6
    irrationality/indifference 146–51
    politics 140–3
    population figures 144–5
    statistical evidence 75
    Victorian years 6–7
    see also custodial sentences;
        institutionalisation
persistent offending 126–8,
    132–3, 144
    see also re-conviction/-offending rates
Phillips, C. 33–9
Police Reform Act (2002) 160
policing youth 30–6, 71, 114–15, 167–8
policy analysis 206–16
policy rationales
    actuarialism 92–109
    anti-social behaviour 157–71
    community supervision 125–38
    penal custody 139–56
    research/evaluation 78–91
    restorative approaches 110–24
    urban regeneration 172–86
    work/social order 187–200
    see also evidence-based policy

politics/politicisation
    anti-social behaviour 161
    critical analysis 225–6
    penal custody 140–3, 152
    policy analysis 209
    reforms 68
    'toughness' 207–11, 214–15, 220
    see also party politics
positivism 83
poverty
    children 146–7, 211–16, 222
    coercion 22
    crime/criminalisation 18
    nineteenth century 4–5
    social ecology 20–1
    urban regeneration 182
Powers of the Criminal Courts (Sentencing)
    Act (2000) 144
practitioner's roles 81–2, 134–5
pre-court disposals 99–100
predictive tools 95, 101–2
preventative work
    actuarial practice 97–9
    child imprisonment failure 149–50
    community safety 160
    community supervision 125, 136
    principles 94
    'real' policy/practice 104–6
    statistical analysis 68
Priestley, P. 128–9
primary desistance 132
principled youth justice model 203–31
prisons *see* penal custody/institutions
private spaces 53
pro-social modelling 120–1
probation service 83–6, 133
'problem' of youth 158–60, 176
programme fetishism 84
progressive competitiveness 190, 194
property crime 72–3, 115, 210
psychological explanations of
    offending 53, 54
public investment, education/training 187–8,
    190–1, 198
public opinion 177–8, 210–11, 225–6
public spaces 23–4, 26, 35–6,
    53, 56, 179
punitive justice *see* retributive/
    punitive justice

race/racialisation 25–6, 30–46, 52, 192
racism 19, 34–6, 145–6
randomised controlled trials
    (RCTs) 85–7, 88
re-conviction/-offending rates
    102, 126–7, 150
realist synthesis 82